INTERNAL ORGANISATION, EFFICIENCY AND PROFIT

Edited by
Steve Thompson & Mike Wright

Philip Allan
OXFORD AND NEW JERSEY

First published 1988 by

PHILIP ALLAN PUBLISHERS LIMITED
MARKET PLACE
DEDDINGTON
OXFORD OX5 4SE (UK)
and
171 FIRST AVENUE
ATLANTIC HIGHLANDS, NJ 07716 (USA)

British Library Cataloguing in Publication Data

Internal organisation, efficiency and
  profit.
  1.   Business firms. Organisation
  I.   Thompson, R.S.   II.   Wright, Mike
  658.1'1

  ISBN 0–86003–080–6
  ISBN 0–86003–183–7 Pbk

Library of Congress Cataloging in Publication Data

Internal organisation, efficiency, and profit / edited by R.S.
  Thompson and Mike Wright.
      p.   cm.
   ISBN 0–86003–080–6.   ISBN 0–86003–183–7 (pbk.)
    1. Organizational effectiveness.   2. Efficiency, Industrial.
  3. Industrial organization.   4. Profit.   I. Thompson, R.S.
  II. Wright, Mike, 1952–
  HD58.9.I57   1988
  338'.06—dc19   88–24103
                        CIP

Typeset in 10/12 Times by Columns of Reading.
Printed and bound in Great Britain by The Alden Press, Oxford.

To Anne and Maryse

Contents

Preface

For a long time, industrial organisation specialists had regarded the industry as the key element of analysis and had considered the firm to be a 'black box'. However, as Oliver Williamson observed in 1972:

> If one of the most remarkable attributes of American capitalism is its adaptive capacity to invent efficient and viable forms of response to changing technological, market, and organisational conditions, to characterise the system in conventional industry terms, to the neglect of internal organisation, easily misses much of what accounts for its most significant accomplishments (Williamson 1972).

The last decade and a half, of course, has seen considerable attention being paid to the inner workings of the firm, particularly as a result of the work of Oliver Williamson and the earlier insights provided by Ronald Coase. Similarly, further advances have been made by researchers in the areas of business policy, organisation theory, management accounting and agency theory. Unfortunately, many of these developments have been taking place along parallel lines. It seemed to us that useful insights for further research could be gained by drawing together these strands in one volume. Each chapter has been contributed by an internationally respected specialist who was asked to write a freestanding review of developments in their particular area. Given the rich diversity of the chapters here it would be futile to attempt to present a unified view of the issues involved, but the last three chapters provide a synthesis of some of the themes from the earlier part of the book. We intend that the book as a whole will provide a stimulus to teachers, students and researchers across the broad spectrum of what is understood by the internal organisation of the firm.

Our first duty is to thank the authors of the chapters for the quality of their contributions. It is hoped that readers of the book will learn as much as we have from their reviews of the various parts of the literature. Several authors have made acknowledgements in their individual chapters. We would also like to thank the following people. In particular, Trevor Buck read most of the chapters and made very useful suggestions which helped to shape the book. Other colleagues who offered comments and encouragement are Brian Chiplin, John Coyne, Christine Ennew, Paul Hallwood, Leonard Wrigley, Ian Davidson, Ken Robbie and Denis O'Brien. Martin Walker who read the whole manuscript also provided very helpful comments.

We acknowledge Spicer and Oppenheim and Barclays Development Capital Ltd for financial support for the work on which the management buy-out material in Chapter 10 is based, and University College Cork who provided a Staff Development Grant to enable the two editors to meet from time to time.

Secretaries Vivienne Murray, Rosemary Reid and Jill Elkington performed miracles in preparing the typescript and Pat Kenny, who drew the short straw, deserves our eternal thanks for collating the vast number of references.

Thanks also to Kathy Wilson, from Philip Allan Publishers, for her forbearance!

Steve Thompson
Mike Wright

Contributors

Steve Thompson is currently Senior Lecturer in Business Economics at UMIST and Visiting Associate Professor at Bentley College, Waltham, Massachusetts. He previously taught at University College, Cork, Ireland. Dr Thompson has published over thirty articles in industrial and financial economics in publications, which include the *Journal of Industrial Economics*, *International Journal of Industrial Organisation*, *Journal of Monetary Economics*, *The Manchester School* and the *Oxford Bulletin of Economics and Statistics*.

Mike Wright is Reader in Financial Studies and Director of the Centre for Management Buy-out Research at the University of Nottingham. Dr Wright has published numerous papers on buy-outs, divestment, competition policy, financial services, state enterprises and control systems in journals, which include the *Antitrust Bulletin*, *Accounting and Business Research*, *Journal of Business Finance and Accounting*, *European Journal of Operational Research*, *Energy Policy*, *Fiscal Studies* and *Public Administration*. His books include, *Competition Policy, Profitability and Growth* (1979), *Management Buy-Outs* (1985), *Manage Information Technology* (1985), *Divestment and Strategic Change* (1986), *The Future of the Building Societies* (1986), *Spicer and Pegler's Management Buy-Outs* (1987), and *The Logic of Mergers* (1987).

John Cable is Senior Lecturer and former Chairman of the Department of Economics, University of Warwick. Dr Cable has held previous positions at the University of Manchester and The International Institute of Management, Berlin. His principal publications cover internal labour markets, advertising, mergers, employee participation, and intra-firm organisation and corporate finance in Britain, Germany and Japan. He is currently writing books on profit sharing, participation, and enterprise performance (with Nicholas Wilson) and the economics of the firm.

Dennis C. Mueller is Professor of Economics at the University of Maryland. He is past President of both the Public Choice Society and the Southern Economic Association. His books include *Profits in the Long Run* (1986), *Public Choice* (1979), and *Public Choice II* (1988), all with Cambridge University Press.

David Otley is Professor of Management Control in the Department of Accounting and Finance at the University of Lancaster, where his research is concerned with developing a better understanding of the processes of control in large organisations. He is Chairman of the Management Control Association, author of numerous articles and books, and an editorial board member of *Accounting and Business Research, Accounting Organisations and Society*, and *Accounting, Auditing and Accountability*.

Trevor Buck is Senior Lecturer in the Department of Industrial Economics at the University of Nottingham. His publications include *Comparative Industrial Systems* (1982), *Modern Soviet Economic Performance* (1987) and journal articles on the internal organisation of firms under different economic systems. He is currently researching into executive share option schemes.

Peter J. Buckley is Professor of Managerial Economics at the University of Bradford Management Centre and a Visiting Professor of Economics at the University of Reading. He has published nine books in English and one in German and written many articles on the theory and strategy of multinational in British, American, European and Japanese journals. He is Chairman of the UK Region of the Academy of International Business, and in 1985 was elected a Fellow of the Academy of International Business. His current research interests include an ESRC-funded study of the foreign market servicing policies and competitiveness of British firms, the theory of international joint ventures and European direct investment in Japan.

Paul Marginson is Senior Research Fellow at the Industrial Relations Research Unit at the University of Warwick. He is co-author of *Beyond the Workplace: Managing Industrial Relations in the Multi-Establishment Enterprise* and has written articles on corporate structure and labour relations.

Frank Stephen is Reader in Economics at the University of Strathclyde and author of a number of books including *An Economic Analysis of Producer Cooperatives* (1984), *The Economics of the Law* (1988) and *Firms, Organisation and Labour* (1984). Dr Stephen, who also edits the *Journal of Economic Studies*, is currently carrying out research on economic aspects of the supply of legal services in the UK. He has published in a number of leading journals including the *American Economic Review, Economic Journal* and the *Canadian Journal of Economics*.

1

Introduction

STEVE THOMPSON AND MIKE WRIGHT

1.1 Internal Organisation, Economics and Related Disciplines

This book is concerned with the organisation of activities within and between modern firms. The primary focus is an economic one, in the sense that the chapters which follow examine the efficiency of different structural arrangements: economics, is, after all, the discipline which seeks to identify efficient resource allocations. Nevertheless, any examination of real-world institutions must draw upon the resources of other disciplines besides economics and several contributions here owe an obvious debt to organisation theory and law—especially the study of property rights.

However, perhaps the business-related disciplines most relevant to any study of internal organisation—and hence to this volume—are those of *business policy* and *management accounting*. Students of the former, especially those following in the Harvard tradition of Chandler (1962) have emphasised the importance of *strategy* and *structure*—both individually and interactively—as variables in the analysis of firm behaviour. Here, as elsewhere, business policy writers stress the importance of the firm's historic circumstances in determining its current opportunities. (This contrasts with the ahistoric models of economic theory.) The primary focus of management accounting, on the other hand, is on information systems and control problems within the firm. The practical skills of past accountants have enabled large, complex corporate forms to evolve. The academic skills of some contemporary management accountants are helping to formulate general hypotheses of organisational control—as shown by Otley in Chapter 5 below.

By contrast, the widespread interest of economists, even industrial economists, in internal organisation issues is of quite recent origin. The 'black box' view of the firm—i.e. that its essentials can be described by a single objective function reflecting the decision maker's desire to maximise profits or perhaps utility—has been dominant in the literature.

1

This inevitably reflects the discipline's predominant interest in markets, in general, and in the characteristics and existence of market equilibria in particular. This concern with the properties of market outcomes—including their efficiency characteristics—has tended to obscure the importance of intra-organisational decisions in resource allocation.

It was not merely that economists tended to view organisational characteristics as irrelevant details, although this was frequently the case, but also that a simplified, even emaciated, model of the firm facilitated more general theorising. For example, as Marris and Mueller (1980) point out, the *classical* economists' implicit assumption of constant returns yields cost-determined prices, and the firm becomes a largely empty construct. In the *neoclassical* theory of the firm the assumptions were widened to allow increasing returns and product differentiation (Robinson 1933, Chamberlin 1933).[1] This process both reflected and encouraged the interest of some economists in aspects of real firm operation, particularly in the shape of the average cost curve and in pricing. However, the typical firm of neoclassical theory remains a single-product entity described entirely by its revenue and cost functions.

In the 1950s and early 1960s the academic division of labour among students of the firm was almost complete. Economists concerned themselves with the firm's *external* relations—particularly how firms interacted with one another through markets. The *internal* workings of the firm were the responsibility of the students of management (including industrial relations) and business policy. This dichotomy occurred despite the rise of '*industrial organisation*' (IO) as a major empirical field, particularly in the USA. This was because most IO work occurred within the *structure-conduct-performance* framework of Bain (1956) and Mason (1939). Here the focus of interest tended to be on the role of market characteristics—mainly concentration and barriers to entry—in raising *industry* profitability. The implicit underlying theory thus remained that of perfect competition: supra-normal profits were to be explained by imperfections in market structure.

From the early 1960s the writings of the behavioural and managerialist theorists (Cyert and March 1963, Baumol 1959, Marris 1964 and Williamson 1964) re-focused attention on decision taking within the firm. Around the same time there occurred a renewal of interest in Coase's (1937) explanation for the existence of firms (see below) and examinations of the economics of bureaucracy (Tullock 1965, Monsen and Downs 1965). In a related development, Leibenstein (1966) examined the inefficiencies resulting from the apparent departure of agents from optimising behaviour. These and other contributions encouraged economists to look inside the 'black box'. In consequence, the past two decades have witnessed considerable theoretical and empirical efforts by economists to determine the properties of alternative organisational forms—internal as well as market-oriented.

The problem has been that whilst the theologians of the subject have acknowledged the importance of firm organisation for resource allocation, the undergraduate 'faithful' tend to be offered the undiluted neoclassical 'gospel'. This is particularly true at the level of intermediate micro-economics. (And many undergraduates on business courses do not take this subject any further.) Here, much of the apparatus still taught under the 'Theory of The Firm' heading offers little assistance in understanding the behaviour of large modern corporations. For example, the items which merit any mention of large firms on the business pages of the national press are such things as: mergers and divestments, major investments, changes in financial structure, decisions to extend or contract the product range or to 'go multinational'. Furthermore, these appear to be the 'strategic' policy matters which concern senior executives (Weston 1970). By contrast, the decision variables in our intermediate models—especially price/quantity and, perhaps, advertising—are actually *lower level* decisions: they are the responsibility of middle management and not the boardroom.

Of course, the 'irrelevance' of the traditional theory of the firm can be overstated. Any firm's success depends ultimately upon satisfactory outcomes in its product markets. Furthermore, many more complex models of firm behaviour—including, for example, investment to deter entry, cross-subsidisation to facilitate predation and vertical integration to end successive stage monopolies (Waterson 1984)—do involve top level (i.e. strategic) decision takers. Nevertheless, there remains some substantial force to the criticism that mainstream economics has been slow to address the problems of contemporary business.

1.2 The Role of Internal Organisation

At anything above its simplest level, i.e. sole proprietorships or perhaps domestic production, the firm is a form of social organisation: that is, it involves separate agents working together in some purposeful way. This gives rise to the need for an internal structure—first, to determine *how* the agents are to co-operate to further the organisation's formal goals; and second, to provide a mechanism which ensures that these agents' subsequent performance in this regard falls within tolerable limits. These functions of co-ordination and supervision provide the economic rationale for the firm's internal structural apparatus.

Coase's classic paper on the 'Nature of the Firm' (1937) emphasised its role as co-ordinator of factor inputs. Coase argued that firms reduce transactions costs in two important respects: first they economise on the informational costs of using markets, self supply avoiding expensive search effort; second, factors are hired on incomplete contracts, which allows subsequent direction to their most valuable uses, as circumstances change. The extent to which this co-ordination function constitutes an authority relation is open to debate. However, the firm will exercise some degree of control over the deployment of its factor inputs whenever their owners face significant re-contracting costs with third parties.

It is important not to equate the function of co-ordination with the apparatus of hierarchy. Firms with non-hierarchical internal structures such as labour co-operatives can and do survive in capitalist economies, even if they are relatively scarce. Nevertheless, most firms appear to possess a recognisable hierarchical 'pyramid', with the peak co-ordinator instructing subordinates who, in turn, instruct their subordinates, etc. This pattern is generally attributed to the limited 'span of control' of any individual manager (Arrow 1974, Williamson 1975) which implies that continuing firm growth will involve the addition of new hierarchical layers. However, since information is likely to be lost or distorted as it is transmitted across each layer, increasing the height of the pyramid may reduce the efficiency of the firm. After Simon (1955), a number of economists— including Williamson (1967) and Marris and Mueller (1980)—have analysed the implications of this 'control loss' problem for the optimal size of the firm.[2]

The need for monitoring arises predominantly from a recognition that an individual's self-interest is not entirely suppressed when he or she enters an economic relationship. This was recognised at a very early stage in the development of economics by Adam Smith, who drew attention to the behavioural differences between owner–managers and salaried agents a full century and a half before Berle and Means (1932).[3] Subsequent work by the managerial theorists have investigated the implications of managerial freedom to pursue alternative maximands, such as sales revenue (Baumol 1959), growth (Marris 1964) or multi-element utility functions (Williamson 1964).

The managers' functions of interpreting objectives and formulating plans may give them particular scope for indulging their self interests within the firm. The discretion of those occupying subordinate layers may be limited to 'shirking'—i.e. substituting on-the-job leisure for effort. (Leibenstein 1966). In either case, however, monitoring the contributions of those supplying labour services to the firm may be useful in ensuring that efforts are directed in support of organisational goals.

Alchian and Demsetz (1972) suggest that monitoring by hierarchical superiors is necessary where 'team production' (i.e. inseparable marginal factor productivities) makes it impossible to meter individual output contributions. They contrast the 'classical' (i.e. owner-managed) firm with the modern corporation and its dispersed shareholdings. They suggest that in the former the manager's residual claimant status motivates him to police shirking. In the latter case, they argue that the unrestricted saleability of claims to the residual (i.e. shares) threatens the job tenure of under-performing managers and so encourages them to monitor their subordinates. (1972, p. 788)

Subsequent work in a related literature has viewed shirking as a typical example of the costs associated with a *principal–agent* relationship, in which one party has some discretion in choosing how to act in the interest of the other (see Chapter 4). Jensen and Meckling (1976) and subsequent authors have emphasised the role of monitoring and bonding expenditures in reducing the agent's deviation from the principal's desired objectives and so lowering the *agency costs* of the relationship. The optimal design of an organisational structure for any set of activities is one that minimises the sum of production and agency costs.[4]

1.3 Structure and Strategy

Alfred Chandler (1962), in his pioneering study of the evolution of the American corporation, demonstrated a clear historical connection between the firm's internal structure and the scope of its activities. Chandler identified three separate stages of product market development: local involvement in a single market; sales to several geographically distinct but otherwise similar markets; and involvement in different product markets. He showed that for each stage of market development there appeared to be an appropriate basic structure. The localised single product firm used a departmental or functional structure. As the number of local markets was increased, so local versions of this structure were replicated and a central head office added. Finally, the multi-product firm used a divisionalised structure in which routine decision-making was delegated to profit-accountable divisional management groups, whilst overall planning remained the responsibility of head office.

Wrigley (1970) extended Chandler's insights by a more systematic examination of the characteristics of 100 of the leading 500 US manufacturing corporations. He found that the extent of firm diversification was not random, but was related to the company's 'core skills', i.e. its basic product technology or market knowledge. Wrigley also refined Chandler's categorisation by distinguishing *single product* firms (more than 95% sales from one product), *dominant product* firms (70–95% from one output), *related product* (more than 30% sales from outside basic business) and *unrelated product* firms. this amended classification strongly reinforced Chandler's observation of a link between strategy and structure, as shown in Table 1.1.

Table 1.1   Wrigley's Strategies and Structures

Stage	Strategy	% of Firms	Structure	
			Functional	*Multidivisional*
I	Single product	6	6	0
II	Dominant product	14	5	9
III	Related product	60	3	57
IV	Unrelated product	20	0	20
		100%	14%	86%

Sources: Wrigley (1970), tabulated in this form by Leontiades (1980), p. 32.

Subsequent work by Rumelt (1974) and others has employed more refined strategic categories to examine this process of diversification. Channon (1973, 1978) used a similar methodology to examine UK manufacturing and service companies, and Dyas and Thanheiser (1976) applied it to those in France and Germany. This work has revealed some national variations but has tended to confirm the strategy–structure association of Chandler and Wrigley.

1.4   Synthesis: The Role of Oliver Williamson

It is clear that by the late 1960s internal organisational issues were being discussed in several different ways in the economics and business literatures. The major figure in synthesising these ideas and in subsequently developing a unified theory of organisations has been Oliver Williamson. His continuing contributions have had a major impact in shaping the efforts of other researchers and the rest of this volume owes an obvious debt to him.

Williamson's (1970) initial interest in the internal structure of the firm seems to have followed his concern with managerial discretion (1964) and with the difficulties of control loss in corporate hierarchies (1967). He interpreted the decentralisation of decision making in multi-divisional (M-form) firms as both a means of curbing sub-goal pursuit and a way of reducing the height of the 'control pyramid'. However, in subsequent contributions he extended the Coasian notion of the firm as a device to reduce transactions costs. In Williamson (1971b) he showed that the cost savings from vertical integration could best be viewed as contractual rather than technological in nature. In *Markets and Hierarchies* (1975), Williamson took external trading and internal organisation as competing modes of handling transactions. He set out to identify key factors which influenced the transactions costs and so determined which mode was

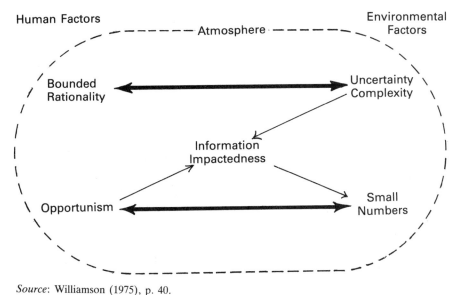

Source: Williamson (1975), p. 40.

Figure 1.1 Williamson's Organisational Failures Approach

chosen. He also argued that in a suitably structured firm the internal allocation of labour and capital would be less costly than reliance on traditional factor markets. Putting the decentralisation and internal factor market arguments together led Williamson to conjecture that diversified firms possessing an M-form structure should, *ceteris paribus*, enjoy a superior profit performance to those multi-product firms which retained functional, holding company or undeveloped divisional structures. This 'M-form hypothesis' is examined in detail by John Cable in Chapter 2.

Williamson's analysis of transactions costs—his 'organisational failures' approach—is shown in Figure 1.1. He assumes individual *opportunism* and *bounded rationality* (i.e. limitations on individuals' information processing capacities.) He also assumes that the typical economic environment will be either truly *uncertain* or at least so *complex* as to deny complete analysis by individuals with bounded rationality. The conjunction of uncertainty and opportunism is likely to lead to the exploitation of informational asymmetries (*information impactedness*) with attendant problems for market transactions. In turn, the asymmetric distribution of information and skills among opportunistic traders can lead to *small numbers* of potential buyers or sellers with the consequent costs of bilateral monopoly. Finally, Williamson acknowledges that attitudinal or non-economic factors (*atmosphere*) influence our willingness to transact—consider, for example, an employee's preference for a convivial work environment.

In subsequent work Williamson (1979) has elaborated on the *information impactedness/ oportunism/small numbers* interactions. He has suggested that asset specificity and the frequency of transacting determine the broad characteristics of contracting arrangements ('governance structures'). This is because idiosyncratic investments in physical or human capital and infrequent trading raise the hazards of becoming involved in an exchange relationship. Williamson developed a typology of 'governance structures' associated with the different combinations of frequency and investment characteristics, as shown in Figure 1.2.

Market governance—spot contracting—is efficient where investments are non-specific and where there are large numbers of potential suppliers. Where recurrent transacting and specific investments are present, the parties may have a continuing relationship. Williamson suggests that the choice here is between *unified governance* (integration under common control) and *bilateral governance* if a recognition of mutual dependence is sufficient to curb opportunism.[5] *Trilateral governance* involves an agreement to use third party arbitration in the event of a dispute: it is associated with transactions which are infrequent but which involve specific investments by one or both participants. Williamson shows that contract law has evolved to facilitate his *bilateral* and *trilateral* governance

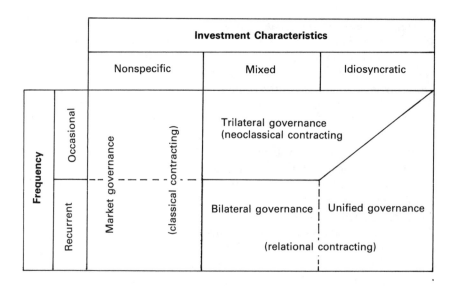

Source: Williamson (1979), reprinted in Williamson, O.E. (1985)
The Economic Institutions of Capitalism, The Free Press.

Figure 1.2   Efficient Governance

forms as well as the completely impersonal exchange of classical contracting. The notion of governance structures significantly develops the theory of organisational choice beyond a simple markets-versus-hierarchies dichotomy to encompass intermediate forms.

Williamson's approach to the internal organisation of the firm is developed further throughout the book. His work has attracted a great deal of attention from students of the organisation of the firm, who have sought to develop his theoretical framework and to subject his propositions to empirical testing. Additionally, recent developments have taken place which view the organisation of the firm from other perspectives.

1.5 The Purpose and Plan of the Book

The function of this book is to present an up-to-date review of the literature on the internal organisation of the firm. Each chapter is intended to be both a freestanding contribution and a complement to the others. Each author has reviewed recent theoretical ideas and empirical results according to a particular perspective on the firm or in the context of an aspect of the firm's operations. In so far as the work of Oliver Williamson forms a key element of many of the chapters presented here, our intention is to provide a critical appraisal of his contribution in the light of empirical tests and of other perspectives on the organisation of the firm. In this way it is hoped that a synthesis of ideas and pointers for further research will emerge.

It would be heroic to claim that a unified view of the internal organisation of the firm has been achieved. Within the subject there are divergent opinions. In particular, two opposing positions can be detected among economists: one tends to see intra-organisational conflict as inherently inefficient—exemplified in those managerialist models where 'slack' and staff perquisites are pursued. A second view—typified by the agency cost approach—sees an enduring organisational form as evidence of successful adaptation to the problems of opportunism. Any reader of this book will recognise such differences in evaluation in the following chapters. However, it is possible to argue that a framework of organisational choice is becoming clearer. Most of the contributions are explicitly or implicitly concerned with the economic properties of the multi-divisional form of organisation. This reflects the apparent dominance of this kind of structure among large corporations in the western economies (see Chapter 2) and the empirical effort which has gone into the study of this form since the publication of *Markets and Hierarchies*. But the appropriate organisational form is not static, nor is change adequately portrayed as involving a unidirectional move from markets to hierarchies or from functional to divisional forms. Rather, very much wider perspectives, which allow frequent adaptation of both the scope of activities and their internal configuration, need to be adopted.

In Chapter 2, John Cable develops and assesses the *M-form hypothesis*. He then reviews the empirical evidence on the spread of the M-form and considers these structures' impact on firm performance.

Chapters 3, 4 and 5 examine different perspectives on the organisation of the firm's activities. In Chapter 3, Dennis Mueller develops a *life cycle model* of firm growth. He shows that the external growth phase of the firm is typically associated with maturity in its original product markets. He examines the empirical evidence on the consequences of diversification for the firm and its shareholders. Steve Thompson reviews the *agency cost* literature, in Chapter 4, and examines the owner–manager conflict and the ways in which monitoring and bonding expenditures may reduce this. The argument is then extended to intra-firm agency problems within divisionalisation organisations. In Chapter 5, David Otley outlines the contribution of *contingency theory*. In particular, he draws on the insights of management accounting in identifying the environmental, technological and cultural features which influence the design of internal control systems.

Chapters 6 and 7 examine organisational structure and control in an international context. In Chapter 6, Trevor Buck compares control devices in *economic systems* based on *markets*, *planning* and *clan* organisation. He then examines the extent to which planned and market systems are converging towards decentralised forms of decision taking and resource allocation. Peter Buckley, in Chapter 7, considers the organisation of the *multinational enterprise*. He develops an argument for multinationals based upon internalising transactions costs and then examines its economic implications for the global organisation of these enterprises.

Chapters 8 and 9 address aspects of the internal factor markets for labour and capital. In Chapter 8, Paul Marginson suggests that the M-form may have both *efficiency* and *control advantages* in deploying labour. He presents evidence to support the view that in the UK the M-form was adopted to reduce labour costs and strengthen the employers' bargaining positions. He also considers the extent of counter-veiling reorganisation on the labour side. Frank Stephen and Steve Thompson examine the M-form as an *internal capital market* in Chapter 9. They contrast external and internal investment decisions. However, they suggest that the process of internal decision making is more complex than that implied by a simple separation of divisional and headquarters responsibilities. Stephen and Thompson review evidence which indicates that many divisionalised firms fail to achieve an M-form's internal market for funds.

In Chapter 10, Mike Wright seeks to pull together much of the preceding discussion of internal and external activities by an explicit consideration of the *boundaries* of the *firm*. Wright examines the role of some intermediate contractual forms, including franchising and joint ventures, in avoiding the control problems of internal ownership. He then considers the range of externalisation devices (buyouts, spin-offs, etc.) which are used to divest unwanted parts of modern multiproduct firms and which—as Williamson (1987, pp. 51–53) has also recently suggested— appear to be a response to organisational failure.

In Chapter 11, the editors examine some of the implications of the preceding discussion for the design of public policy, particularly with respect to antitrust issues and to the privatisation of publicly-owned productive assets. Finally in Chapter 12 the authors summarise the issues covered throughout the book.

Notes

1. These points are discussed in detail by O'Brien (1984) pp. 34–6.
2. Williamson (1975, pp. 122–3) recognised that in addition to 'natural' control loss there could be a distortion or selective transmission of information by opportunistic individuals within any hierarchy.
3. Smith wrote:
   > The directors of such (joint stock) companies, however, being the managers of other people's money than of their own, it cannot well be expected, that they should look after it with the same anxious vigilance with which the partners in a private copartnery frequently watch over their own. *Wealth of Nations* Book V, Chapter 1, reprinted in Putterman (1986) pp. 40–1.

   The impact of Berle and Means is discussed in Chapter 4.
4. The agency costs include both any monitoring and bonding expenditures incurred and the residual loss of the agency relationship, including the benefit of transactions not undertaken because of agency problems—these are described more fully in Chapter 4.
5. The problems of *bilateral governance* (Williamson 1985, pp. 75–7) arise from the prisoner's dilemma-type game in which the participants find themselves: they have an incentive to co-operate and maintain a long term association; however, each may benefit by opportunistic behaviour at the expense of the other.

2

Organisational Form and Economic Performance

JOHN R. CABLE

2.1 Introduction

The range of alternative forms in which economic activity can be organised is very wide. This chapter considers alternative internal structures within large, incorporated, private-sector firms. The central focus is on what has been described as 'the most significant organisational innovation of the twentieth century' (Williamson 1985, p. 279), namely the multi-divisional (MD) or M-form corporation. This is now the most common form of organisation amongst large, diversified firms in America, Europe and elsewhere. The complexity and size of the activities which can be embraced by such companies are striking: one of the pioneers of M-form, General Motors, employs approximately the same number of people as did the whole of manufacturing industry in The Netherlands (Radner 1986). More generally, M-form companies tend to be concentrated in the top 100 companies in most countries of the developed world. The economic implications of this form of organisation, in particular with respect to efficiency and resource allocation, are consequently of considerable significance for overall economic performance.

Development of the underlying economic theory of M-form is due to Williamson (1970,1975), following Chandler's (1962) pioneering work on the history of the multi-divisonal innovation. The main objective of this chapter is to set out succinctly the economics of M-form, and to review the empirical evidence on its performance effects now available from a substantial number of studies. Attempts to model the M-form diffusion process are also evaluated. But we begin by considering what exactly M-form organisation is.

2.2   M-Form Organisation and its Effects

In the M-form firm, production activities are broken down into a number of quasi-autonomous operating divisions (typically profit centres based on products, brands or geographical areas). The activities are coordinated via a general office, assisted by an elite staff, which undertakes strategic planning and resource allocation among the divisions, and exercises a characteristic form of monitoring and control over them. The M-form may be distinguished both from the traditional, functionally decentralised, unitary (U-form) firm, and from the holding company (H-form) firm which, though divisionalised, lacks the requisite general office functions (see Figure 2.1). The advantages of M-form that are predicted in given, fairly general, circumstances can best be seen by contrast with these organisational alternatives.

U-form firms are functionally specialised, hierarchically arranged organisations, with pyramidal internal structures of the type illustrated in Figure 2.1(a). Thus there is a single peak coordinator (a person or board of directors), to whom are responsible the heads of specialist departments dealing with production, marketing, purchasing, finance, etc. Within each functional area there may be several further horizontal layers of responsibility, and vertical demarcations of more finely specialised tasks. This structure can be optimal below some level of firm size and complexity of operations, not least because of its exploitation of the time-honoured principle of the division of labour. As the firm grows in size and complexity of operations, however, the U-form becomes increasingly dysfunctional.[1] Firstly, the benefits of specialisation in central, functionally arranged departments erode as the diversity of products, brands and local market conditions increases. Secondly, for given spans of control (i.e. holding managerial technology constant), expansion at the base (production) level of a pyramidal structure like the U-form requires the addition of extra hierarchical levels in the organisation (see Figure 2.1(b)). Thus, in the stylised situation sketched in Figure 2.2(a), a doubling of capacity at the basic work process level has vertical as well as horizontal implications as long as control span (which is 2 in both cases) is held constant; in case (b) a fourth hierarchical level is needed.

Two types of problem arise as the firm expands in this way. Firstly, there will be a cumulative loss in overall control. Even when there is no intention to distort or misunderstand communications and instructions between hierarchical levels, only a fraction of what is intended will register or be implemented at each stage.[2] Suppose that, in a chain of command with n levels, only a fraction (p) of what is intended is actually carried out: control loss at each stage is then $(1 - p)$. Assuming that no systematic correction takes place, the degree of overall control (C) now

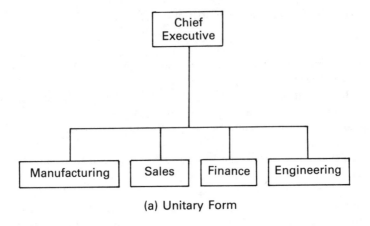

(a) Unitary Form

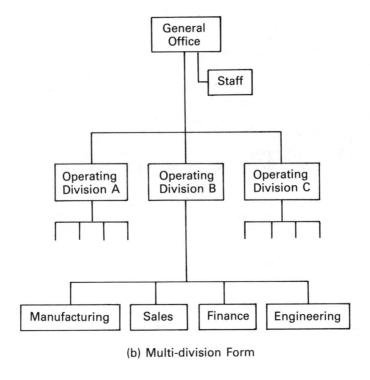

(b) Multi-division Form

Source: Williamson (1970), p. 116.

Figure 2.1 U- and M-Form Organisational Structures

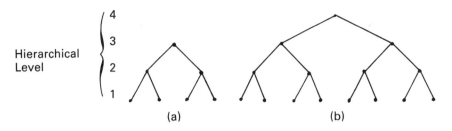

Figure 2.2   Spans of Control

declines with the number of hierarchical levels (n) according to the relation $C = p^{n-1}$. Thus, even if p is as high as 0.9, there is a cumulative control loss of nearly 20 per cent in a three-level hierarchy, 27 per cent in a four-level hierarchy, and so on. The effective limit to the height of an organisational hierarchy is evidently quite low.

Secondly, radial expansion of a U-form structure results in a progressive communications overload at the top, 'peak coordinator' level. This is simply because there is more information flowing in the larger system and, if reporting and command systems continue to require the same amount of information at each stage, more must end up at the top level. Economising on the breadth or depth of information at any level will tend to exacerbate the previous control-loss problem. The alternative remedy, which firms seem to prefer in practice, is to augment peak-level capacity. Typically, this entails promoting the heads of functional departments to board level. But this has the drawback that personnel with executive responsibilities for different operational areas are involved in matters of overall strategy. Scope now exists for 'partisan' influences from operating areas to impinge on strategic choices, and for sub-unit goals—in particular the pursuit of non-profit, managerial objectives as modelled by managerial theorists (Baumol 1959; Marris 1964; Williamson 1964)—to intrude on overall organisational goals. As a result, the organisation tends to depart from least-cost, profit-oriented behaviour.

In short, as U-form firms grow and diversify, they encounter problems associated with key elements in the more general 'markets and hierarchies' framework within which Williamson (1975) sets his analysis of organisational form: in particular, the complexity and uncertainty which characterises the business environment; the behavioural concept of 'bounded rationality' arising from the limited information-processing and decision-making capacity of human agents (Simon 1955); and 'opportunism'—the tendency of individuals to pursue self-interested behaviour within whatever constraints are in force.

The M-form alternative solves or alleviates these problems in the following way. To split activities into separate divisions allows production to continue in U-form sub-units which are sufficiently small and specialised to fall below the threshold at which U-form ceases to be efficient. The divisions are quasi-autonomous, with complete discretion over operating decisions, and with only profit and loss responsibility to the central general office. In this way the M-form structure circumvents the U-form's problems of cumulative control loss and communications overload (the qualitative shift to financial reporting, from divisional level to general office, offering a substantial economy of information). The separation of strategic and operating decision making is also institution-alised. The general office does not interfere with the day-to-day running of the divisions, and so remains free of partisan allegiances; divisional personnel do not participate in strategic decision making, which is reserved as a general office function.

Thus far, however, the M-form would be indistinguishable from the H-form holding company. This also consists of a financial grouping of 'divisions' or subsidiary companies, linked to a parent company. But the H-form is nothing more than a financial grouping, perhaps little more than a portfolio operation with minimal central functions. The M-form, by contrast, has crucial additional characteristics concerning centralised strategy formation and divisional control. A key difference lies in the treatment of financial surpluses (profits) earned at divisional level. In the H-form, these tend to be retained for reinvestment at the discretion of divisional management. Capital investment under this system, therefore, tends to go with past success. In the M-form, however, divisional surpluses are pooled and reallocated among divisions by the general office on the basis of expected future yield, after evaluation of competing divisional bids.

Thus the M-form may be seen as a miniaturised capital market, in which the general office proxies the role of shareholders in the external capital market *vis-à-vis* independent companies. Williamson argues, however, that competition for capital funds will be much more intense in the internal capital market of the M-form firm than in the external capital market at large. This is due to the superior inference and intervention capabilities of the general office, assisted by its elite specialist staff, compared with those of ordinary shareholders. The general office has access to internal divisional information; has constitutional authority to carry out internal audits; and can intervene selectively and at a relatively early stage to correct departures from acceptable policies and performance (for example, by manipulation of the managerial incentive and appoint-ment machinery). External shareholders, by contrast, are asymmetrically less well-informed than the directors, especially with respect to future investment opportunities; can generally initiate investigations of the company only where there is evidence of malfeasance or fraud; and can typically intervene only by taking drastic action, for example removing the directors *en bloc* (and hence the whole of top management), in response to 'egregious departures' from shareholder welfare maximising behaviour. The difference, in Williamson's words, is like that of 'the scalpel versus the ax', (1970, p. 140). The result, in Williamson's view, is that capital-market constraints on managerial behaviour will be more severe in the M-form than elsewhere.

More generally, and taking all aspects of the M-form and its alternatives into account, Williamson predicts that:

> The organisation and operation of the large enterprise along the lines of the M-form favours goal pursuit and least-cost behaviour more nearly associated with the neoclassical profit maximization hypothesis than does the U-form [functional] alternative. (1970, p. 134).

Under certain conditions any gains from adopting M-form will be observable in the accounting and stock market results of companies, and this opens up the possibility of testing for what may be termed the *firm level* effects of M-form on performance.

According to Williamson there are also external, or 'systemic' benefits of M-form, i.e. favourable repercussions of its adoption on the operation of the economic system as a whole, outside of the adopting firms. Such effects are predicted in both product and capital markets, and in what Manne (1965) and others have called the 'market for corporate control', i.e. the takeover market.

In the case of the product market, the argument is that firms which have not adopted the M-form will be forced to cut slack and improve efficiency in order to compete with those that have. Systemic benefits in the allocation of capital are expected in the sense that an economy with a two-tiered system of capital transfer (with the external capital market distributing capital among M-form firms, and their general offices metering funds among divisions) should outperform an economy which relies entirely on the external capital market, and thus does not exploit the informational and interventional advantages which, as we have seen, are expected to accrue in the internal capital markets within M-form firms. Thus, capital transfer from declining to growth areas of profitable investment should come about sooner, and with greater certainty, in the former system.

In the market for corporate control, Williamson argues that the conglomerate variant of the M-form firm provides a more effective takeover instrument than the traditional firm. This is primarily a result of lower transactions costs in absorbing new divisions, as opposed to integrating an acquired firm's activities into each of the U-form's functional departments, though Williamson also refers to the 'superior inference capability' of the general office in identifying takeover candidates, gained from its experience in monitoring and evaluating divisions.[3] Either way, the presence of M-form firms increases takeover risk, and hence provides further, system-wide pressure on firms to attend to profit-related goals and maintain valuation ratios (ratios of stock market to asset value). In general, the systemic effects of M-form are seen as an all-round sharpening of the competitive process.

Qualifications and Counter-Arguments

The foregoing sketch of the M-form organisation appears to depict an institution whose effects are unambiguously benign. There are, however, a number of qualifications and counter-arguments which may be put.

(1)   M-form is not necessarily optimal in all circumstances. Williamson himself allows that U-form may dominate below some (unspecified) threshold of size and diversification. Chandler (1962) found inter-industry differences in the uptake of M-form: least in copper and nickel, steel, aluminium, and materials; most in electrical and elec-tronic engineering, power machines and automobiles, and chemicals. Caves (1980) summarises the factors discouraging M-form as 'customers and products that are few in number . . . [backward] vertically related production processes that require intricate temporal coordination and hence a heavy volume of top-level tactical decisions . . . large absolute scales of efficient production and high capital requirements . . . ' and finally notes that 'the output of a production process can be heterogeneous without mandating MD organisation as long as the process itself remains fully integrated'. Steer (1973) likewise argues that M-form may not be optimal in process industries, where technology does not allow divisionalisation of production except at great cost, and also in highly unstable environments, e.g. in research-intensive industries, or industries where there is very rapid introduction of new products. Thus, M-form is not a universal solution to the problem of internal organisation in large companies.

(2)   Where M-form *is* privately effective for a company as a way of postponing the onset of managerial diseconomies of scale due to control loss etc., this will yield economic gains for society at large *only* as long as there are unexploited technical economies of scale or scope to be reaped: that is, as long as managerial diseconomies are the effective constraint on optimum scale of production. Otherwise, society could be just as well off with a larger number of smaller firms, producing a given output vector at no greater total resource

cost.[4] On the other hand, in an industry where managerial constraints do bind before technical constraints, but can be relaxed by the adoption of M-form, this can have anti-competitive effects, raising optimum firm size and hence the degree of seller concentration for a given total market. In the limit, where managerial factors are the only source of scale diseconomies (i.e. long-run average production costs decline continuously over the relevant range, but average total costs rise at some point because of managerial diseconomies), organisational innovations like M-form may serve to bring about the cost conditions for natural monopoly.

(3) Other implications of M-form for competition are mixed. Williamson presents the claimed advantages of M-form, e.g. in the transfer of capital, as part of an 'affirmative case' for conglomerates, which might otherwise be lacking. But conglomeracy can have adverse antitrust implications, too, concerning reciprocity and the possible suppression of potential competition,[5] and in so far as the advantages of M-form result in there being more conglomerate firms (with greater diversity of activities) than would otherwise exist, an increase in these socially unwelcome effects may also occur. As we have seen, Williamson also credits M-form with an intensification of competition on the takeover market, raising the probability of takeover for poor stock market performers. But from a social viewpoint, there may be an interior optimum level of such a takeover threat. Exceeding this could for example encourage companies to be unduly short term in their outlook, and risk-averse in their behaviour.[6] If so, it would depend on which side of this optimum a particular economy lay, as to whether the introduction of M-form would raise or lower welfare. Finally, Schwarz and Thompson (1986) have recently shown that the ability of incumbent firms to divisionalise in an oligopolistic industry enables them to pre-empt all rational, non-innovative entry.[7]

(4) With respect to the intensity of capital market competition, there is one sense in which it is the external capital market which is relatively advantaged in exerting continuous, rather than discrete, corrective pressure. Thus the exit of *marginal* shareholders can provide an early and, if necessary, progressive sanction on a company's performance, via its valuation ratio whereas, in this case, it is the general office for whom exit is a drastic, 'all or nothing' sanction.

(5) Where the development of internal capital markets involves the disappearance of autonomous companies (to become M-form divisions) their independent financial reporting is lost to the external market. The investment scope of the market is reduced, and the

number of observations on which inter-company evaluations can be made is also lessened. It could even happen that public reporting on the performance of an entire industry may vanish. In this respect, the relationship between the internal and external markets is not wholly symbiotic, as Williamson maintains.

(6) Relatively close attention to least-cost, profit-oriented behaviour in M-form firms than elsewhere will come about only if these goals are espoused and emphasised at general office level. Williamson advances a number of reasons why this might be. In particular, he refers to an important psychological effect of the separation of strategic and operating decision making, under which the general office is committed to *overall* performance. With diverse divisional activities, this is measurable only in terms of profitability which, moreover, is the basis of the reporting system used at general office level. Hence, he argues, the focus of top level on profit-goals is natural for the M-form firm. Moreover, as we have seen, strategic policy formulation is expected to remain freer from 'partisan' (functionally related) concerns. But, suggestive as these arguments may be, profit-maximising behaviour at top level remains only an assumption underlying the M-form hypothesis, and perhaps its strongest assumption. The desirable control properties of the M-form in constraining lower-level behaviour towards an overall objective, and avoiding organisational chaos after rapid and diversified expansion, could in principle just as easily be harnessed to pursuit of growth-maximisation in mature corporations (Mueller 1972).

(7) The superior capital-market properties of the M-form (better funds-metering and better disciplining of poor performance) are presented as improvements on what the external capital market can achieve. Hence the extent of M-form gains in this area depends, in part, on the degree of external capital-market failure, due to problems of asymmetric information, and so forth. This is a natural way of looking at the issue in America and Britain, both of which have large, well-developed external capital markets at the centre of their systems of industrial finance. Other advanced countries, such as France, West Germany and Japan, do not. Moreover, the bank-based systems on which they rely in some cases have features which could offer benefits similar to those of M-form. In West Germany for example, the country's 'universal' banks have widespread representation on the supervisory boards of industrial companies, and control very substantial proportions of shareholder voting rights. They are also virtually indispensable as intermediaries in the provision of any form of external finance. The resulting close

bank–industry relationship has been regarded accordingly as a 'quasi-internal capital market', sharing to some extent the informational and interventional advantages of M-form (Cable 1985a,b; Cable and Dirrheimer 1983). Japanese business groups, both those descended from the pre-war *zaibatzu* and the bank-based groups, have somewhat similar properties (Cable and Yasuki 1985).[8] Where institutional arrangements such as these are present, prior to or independently of M-form, potential M-form gains may be attenuated. More generally, the point is that the extent of M-form gains may depend upon the historical and institutional context in which it is viewed, as well as upon the intrinsic properties of M-form *per se*.

(8) Finally, the M-form may share responsibility for abuses of socio-political power by big business, in so far as it has facilitated the survival and development of vast corporations, often multinational in their scope. It may be no exaggeration to say that M-form has affected the structure of democracy as much as of industry.

2.3 M-Form Diffusion

The Historical Record

Multi-divisional (MD) organisation was first detected and analysed by the business historian Chandler (1962), from case studies on the twentieth-century development of corporate strategy and structure in large American companies. Chandler credits four major companies with the independent, and more or less contemporaneous, evolution of the MD form in the 1920s, though Kocka (1980) has subsequently claimed that the West German company, Siemens, had adopted its main features a decade earlier, before 1914.[9] However this may be, the new organisational form was initially slow to catch on, and its spread in America and elsewhere has occurred primarily in the period since the end of the Second World War, in 1945. According to Williamson and Bhargava (1972), 1945–1950 was a critical period, when M-form first took on quantitative significance in the USA. Many American firms then subsequently adopted M-form as a defensive measure in the 1950s, and the conglomerate variant flourished in the 1960s (in part, no doubt, because US antitrust law had by then made growth by horizontal merger almost impossible.) Rumelt's (1974) data for the US confirm distinct waves of M-form adoption in the middle and late 1950s and in the mid-1960s.

In Britain, Steer (1973) found the 1960s a period of marked internal reorganisation, with a strong trend away from U- and H-form towards M-form. Both his classification of individual companies and (as Table 2.1 shows) his overall estimate of the degree of penetration of M-form by the early 1970s are in broad agreement with those of Channon (1973). Hill (1985b), however, reports a lower overall incidence of M-form (only 61.1 per cent) in questionnaire data for 144 UK companies in 1982. Moreover, Hill also found a much greater incidence of 'corrupted' (M̄) and holding company forms,[10] and noted that many multi-divisionals were far from effectively organised, especially with respect to the complexity of their divisions.

Table 2.1   The Diffusion of M-Form (percentage M-form in sample shown), 1950–1970

	1950	*1970*	*Sample*
United States	23.6[(i)]	78.5[(ii)]	200 from Fortune 500
United Kingdom	14.1	71.5	Top 100
		68.3[(iii)]	Top 200
France	6.1	53.8	Top 100
West Germany	5.0	55.4	Top 100
Italy	7.3	48.0	Top 100
Japan	n.a.	41.5[(iv)]	Top 100 +

Source: Derived from Caves (1980), Table 1; Steer (1973); and Yoshihara *et al.* (1981).
Notes: (i)   Figure relates to 1948
     (ii)   "   "   " 1969
     (iii)   "   "   " 1970–72
     (iv)   "   "   " 1973

In continental Europe, very little penetration had occurred before the 1960s, and the spread of M-form took hold only towards the end of that decade. Various factors have been cited in attempts to explain the lag in adopting M-form in Europe as compared with the United States. They include more limited opportunities for the pursuit of diversification strategies; fewer legal inhibitions on horizontal expansion and the use of H-form structure; the influence of family ownership; and a lack of competitive discipline. In addition, difficulties were encountered in some cases in adapting M-form to European conditions: Thanheiser (1976), for example, notes the difficulties experienced in reconciling M-form with the dual-board system in West Germany, and the rather uneasy compromises that sometimes emerged as a result. But there also appears to have been a pure imitation lag, characteristic of the diffusion process of innovations in general. Certainly, there is considerable evidence that the European

Table 2.2 Strategy and Structure: Incidence of M-form (%) by Strategic Category, 1970

Country	Single business	Dominant business	Related business	Unrelated business
United States[i]	24	62	90	98
United Kingdom	17	73	79	50
France	19	59	64	50
West Germany	9	45	88	56
Italy	0	45	58	60

Source: Derived from Caves (1980), Table 1; Steer (1973); and Yoshihara *et al.* (1981).
Note: (i) Figures are for 1969.

adoption of M-form was in many cases led by US firms, and US-based management consultancies played an important catalytic role (Franko 1976; Dyas and Thanheiser 1976).

Table 2.1 draws together the evidence on the diffusion pattern of M-form for the USA, four major European countries and Japan. The figures should be treated as broad indications only, because of differences in sampling and classification method between the various country studies from which they come, and because of question-marks over the 'purity' of M-form structures in some cases, as noted above. Nevertheless, the importance of the period 1950–1970 in the diffusion of M-form is quite unmistakeable, as is the overall predominance of M-form by the end of that period. Bearing in mind the disproportionately large share of economic activity for which companies in the top 100 tend to account,[11] we see once again how great is the economic significance of M-form.

Models of the Diffusion Process

The Strategy–Structure Model

Both Chandler's original case studies (1962), and his more general, long-term analysis of changes in business opportunities, technology and market organisation (1977), led him to conclude that changes in organisational structure generally follow as a consequence of previous choices of business strategy: thus, 'strategy precedes structure'. In the case of M-form, the preceding strategy was typically one involving extensive diversification. Subsequent empirical work has provided extensive evidence of the strategy–structure link (Wrigley 1970,1976; Pavan 1972; Channon 1973; Rumelt 1974; Dyas and Thanheiser 1976). Table 2.1 summarises this evidence, using Wrigley's (1970) classification of strategies. The relationship is evidently strongest in the USA, where the incidence of M-form increases monotonically with the degree of diversification, and is almost total in the most diversified, conglomerate (unrelated) category. In three other countries it is actually lower for this category than for other diversified categories, but in all cases there is a very striking difference between the undiversified (single business) category and the rest.

The 'Harvard school' studies cited above also reveal that transition to M-form was often gradual. Chandler himself found its emergence in the four pioneering companies a piecemeal process. (More recently, Hoskisson and Galbraith (1985) found that of twelve reorganisations undertaken by six companies, five involved 'quantum' changes and seven incremental changes.) The studies further show that the lag in adjustment from structure to strategy could be substantial: 15 to 20 years for the median firm in France and West Germany, according to Dyas and Thanheiser. Often the timing of the internal reorganisation was precipitated by actual or imminent threat of crisis: thus the old (no longer appropriate) organisation persisted until circumstances enforced a change. In this respect, M-form adoption provides an interesting example of the 'behavioural' principle of 'problemistic search' (Cyert and March 1963).

Recognition of this element of M-form adoption adds a second, 'crisis-response' dimension to the strategy–structure model. The studies cited so far do not provide systematic investigation of the structural adjustment lags. In a more recent analysis of abnormal stock market returns (see below), however, Thompson (1983b) finds a systematic relationship between M-form adoption and previous share price decline in a sample of UK firms. In 25–30 per cent of cases, this decline was 'severe', and Thompson interprets this evidence as supporting the proposition that a performance crisis is a frequent stimulus to M-form adoption. Other evidence tends to confirm that the crisis-response feature of M-form is important but not universal. Thus, Bhargava (1973) identified 60 'crisis induced' divisionalisations out of a sample of 108 cases in the USA, while Hill and Pickering (1986a) classified just over half the M-form adoptions amongst 144 UK firms as 'problem responses'.

In general, the strategy–structure model provides convincing insights into the M-form diffusion process, supported by a wealth of detailed empirical evidence. Of course, in itself it reveals only the *proximate* cause of a firm's reorganisation along M-form lines; to unravel the *fundamental* cause we must investigate the determinants of the firm's previous choice of business strategy. The value of the model is that it tells us where to look.

The Technological Diffusion Model

Teece (1980a) and Thompson (1983a) analyse the diffusion of M-form in a different way, using the approach which researchers since Mansfield (1968) have taken to technological innovations. To justify their method, both authors begin by reviewing various similarities and dissimilarities between organisational innovations, like M-form, and advances in process technology. Both note that patent protection is generally not available for administrative innovations, so that the deterrent to imitation should be less than that for patentable technical discoveries. Moreover, the diffusion of organisational reforms, such as M-form, may be speeded up by management consultants. On the other hand, M-form must be tailored to the needs of individual companies, and its adoption may in some ways be detrimental to the individual interests of senior management (in particular, by circumscribing its opportunities for discretionary behaviour), who must initiate the change. Teece notes that, unlike at least some technical changes which can be introduced gradually, administrative changes are often 'all or nothing' in nature, though, as we have seen, the historical evidence does not wholly support this assertion. The existence of set-up costs and organisational disruption, however, is beyond dispute, and, as Thompson points out, M-form reorganisation calls for input requirements at a high level in the organisation.

In general, all this seems to imply differences of degree rather than kind between M-form and technological innovations. Many technical changes would share at least some of the characteristics of M-form; and while we might not be surprised if there were differences in the *rate of diffusion* (which in any case varies among technological innovations), this does not necessarily imply a difference in the *nature of the diffusion process*, and hence in the way it should be modelled. In any event, Teece and Thompson feel justified in proceeding—and this seems reasonable, on an experimental basis.

The basic model is borrowed from medical science, where it is used to describe the effects of contagion in the spread of epidemic disease. Expressed as a proportion of the total population (n) the number infected at a given time, (M_t), follows a logistic curve:

$$M_t/n = 1/(1 + e^{-a-bt})$$

or, taking logarithms and rearranging:

$$ln[M_t/(n - M_t)] = a + bt. \tag{2.1}$$

The spread of the disease then follows a symmetric, sigmoid time path as shown in Figure 2.3(a), asymptotically approaching the full penetration level A. As applied to the diffusion of innovations, the model may be interpreted as describing an imitation process; adoption takes place after

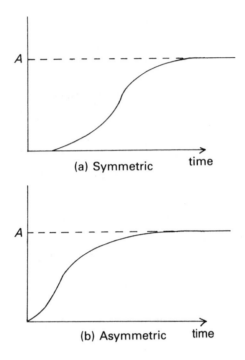

(a) Symmetric   time

(b) Asymmetric   time

Figure 2.3

coming into contact with earlier innovators. Beyond this, the model has no economic content, and it also embodies some debatable assumptions (for example that the profitability of the innovation and the propensity of firms to adopt remain constant over time). However, after adding a stochastic error term to equation (2.1), we can use regression methods to obtain estimates of the parameters a and b (which meausre the position of the curve in relation to the origin and the rate of diffusion respectively), and hope to draw conclusions from the overall performance of the regression equation about the importance of imitation in the diffusion process.

In practice, Teece found the model 'worked well' when applied to data for the US petroleum industry from 1956 onwards, and for principal firms in 17 industries after 1935. In terms of normalised root mean square deviation, his M-form results fell within the limits obtained by Mansfield for technical innovations (3.3–6.7 per cent of sample size, compared with 1.3–8.5 per cent). He concluded that M-form *is* subject to a diffusion process similar to that which describes the adoption of technical innovations. However, M-form diffused much more slowly: whereas the 'half-life' (that is, the number of years before half the sample had adopted M-form) ranged from 0.9 to 15 for Mansfield's cases of technical innovation, in the case of M-form it was 14 and 41 respectively for the petroleum and principal firms samples.[12]

Thompson uses data from 102 UK adopters of M-form over the period 1958–1976 to estimate the logistic and three alternative models. One of these (the cumulative normal model) also generates a symmetric diffusion curve, but the two others (the log-reciprocal and cumulative log-normal) yield positively skewed, asymmetric curves as in Figure 2.3(b).[13] These curves have been considered potentially more appropriate for cheap, simple innovations, where rapid early adoption is more likely (Davies 1979). Thompson finds that the symmetric curves tend to dominate, and this refines Teece's result, suggesting that the similarity is between M-form and *costly* technological innovations, rather than technological innovations in general. Of the symmetric models, the logistic gave consistently best fit. In subsequent cross-section analyses Thompson found firm size and diversification to be significant (inverse) determinants of the length of adoption lag, and this corroborates the strategy–structure school findings. No evidence was found of industry-specific factors in the delay functions, but this may have been due to estimation and data problems.

While these results are interesting in themselves, and usefully corroborate certain other pieces of evidence on the diffusion of M-form, it is not clear how much new light they shed. Lacking economic content, the models offer nothing of the richness of understanding of the adoption process which the strategy–structure approach can give. Moreover, the validity of the principal conclusion—that M-form diffusion proceeds, like that of technical innovations, as if imitation were an important part of the process—is not beyond doubt. This is because the null hypothesis against which the models are tested is that of 'no relationship'. But this is a very weak alternative, and what we really require is a test against the principal competing hypothesis—the strategy–structure model—in order to assess the relative importance of 'imitation' versus other deterministic influences. Ideally, this would require specifying an encompassing model in which both the 'imitation' and the strategy–structure models are nested, to permit model selection via parameter-restriction tests. Though perhaps not the first priority, further research in this direction would seem warranted.

2.4 Tests of M-Form Performance

Tests for Firm-Level Gains

A number of serious problems are encountered while testing for M-form gains. Classifying firms by their organisational form is both judgemental and a time-consuming exercise, so that it is difficult to generate reliable, large-scale samples for statistical work. Moreover, as we have seen, M-form is not the optimum organisational form under all operating conditions, so that crude M-form versus 'other' comparisons may mislead. A further difficulty is that we may expect to observe M-form gains only during the diffusion period, when some firms have yet to adopt M-form who should have done so earlier; otherwise, the scatter of observations will include only optimally-organised firms, and will not reveal differences due to M-form. Thus selection of the time period of the analysis can be critical. But then, the adopting firms' results during the diffusion period are likely to be abnormal: unusually poor pre-adoption if the firm is in crisis, and registering the adverse effects of short-term disruption and transactions-costs in the immediate post-adoption period. In addition, the effects of M-form must be isolated from those of other, extraneous influences which may be in operation over the period under investigation. Finally, care is needed not to confuse the effects of performance on the decision to reorganise with the effects of reorganisation on performance (the causality problem). Full and satisfactory resolution of all these problems is rare in practice, and this must be borne in mind when evaluating the results of empirical analyses.

Essentially the accounting data approach postulates that firm performance is a function of its organisational structure and a set of other variables. Apart from a small number of simulation exercises and non-parametric tests, two main methodological options have been taken in empirical studies to date. One involves estimating regression models of inter-firm differences in accounting profits from cross-section or pooled data, including organisational-form variables amongst the regressors. The other, less common, method involves looking at abnormal stock-market returns using 'residuals analysis'.

The general form of regression model may be written as

$$Y_i = f(X_i) + q(Z_i) + u_i, \tag{2.2}$$

where Y_i denotes the profitability of firm i (variously measured as the profit margin on sales (Π_i/R), or the rate of return on fixed assets (Π_i/K), or shareholders' equity (Π_i/E)); $f(X_i)$ determines the profit-maximising level of profit for firm i; and Z_i is a vector of variables suggested by other, managerial and behavioural theories (Steer and Cable 1978). In principle, M-form should operate through $f(X_i)$ since it is an aspect of firm-level efficiency and hence ought to be captured in the production function. In practice, the organisational-form and Z_i variables are treated symmetrically in most applications. Variables commonly entered alongside organisational form include firm size, growth, variability of returns (risk), degree of owner control, and industry intercepts. The main drawbacks of this approach relate to the well-known problems with accounting data (consistency of treatment of like items between firms, etc) which affect the measurement of Y_i, and to specification problems in determining the correct Z vector. It also makes heavy demands on data availability, especially when Z is complex.

Residuals analysis also involves regression, in this case of the 'market model'[14]. The market model posits a linear relationship between the return (capital gains plus dividends) on an individual security and the return available in the market as measured by the market index. This approach is founded upon the efficient markets hypothesis, which postulates that a share price fully incorporates all available information on the security so that share prices provide accurate signals for optimal resource allocation. The market model can be expressed as:

$$R_{jt} = a_j + b_j R_{mt} + e_{jt} \tag{2.3}$$

where R_{jt} is the monthly share price return for the j'th asset at time t, and R_{mt} is the rate of return on a market index, taking into account dividends and capital gain; b_j measures the 'systematic risk' of asset j (the degree of covariance between the return on asset j and the market as a whole); and $a_j + e_{jt}$ capture unsystematic, company-specific effects. The coefficients a and b are usually estimated by ordinary least squares regression for a set of data where a period around the date of the event of the introduction of the M-form has been deleted. The underlying idea is that the stock-market's evaluation of any abnormal gains (or losses) from an event such as M-form adoption will show up in the difference between actual returns and the returns predicted by 2.3, i.e. in the firm-specific residuals

$$u_{jt} = R_{jt} - \hat{a} - \hat{b}_j \, R_{mt}. \tag{2.4}$$

These can then, for example, be cumulated over a set number of periods before and after the event, averaged over a group of (in the present case) adopting firms, and the resulting series of Cumulative Average Residuals (CARs), examined for discontinuities at the time of the event. Alternatively, 2.3 can be estimated for a period prior to the event, and post-event differences in mean CARs for adopters and non-adopters can be compared.

Residuals analysis is economical on data requirements and avoids the specification and measurement problems encountered in modelling inter-firm accounting returns. Since this type of analysis relies on stock market anticipation of the effects of the event under study, it may be hoped that short-term dislocation costs are discounted, and long-term consequences emphasised. However, it makes strong assumptions about the stability of the parameters a and b over time; about the public availability of information concerning the 'event'; about the capacity of investors to evaluate such information; and about the way stock markets work.[15] A particular difficulty when applying the model to the adoption of M-form,

Table 2.3 Empirical Tests of the M-Form Hypothesis

Study	Sample	Method *Performance*	Model	Result
Armour/Teece (1978)	28 US petroleum industry firms 1955–1973	rate of return on equity after tax (book value)	regression model ($\bar{R}^2 = .23$)	*positive* for sub-period 1955–68; no significant effect 1969–73
Steer/Cable (1978)	82 UK firms 1967–1971	—average rate of return on equity —profit margin	regression model ($.33 < \bar{R}^2 < .51$)	*positive*, but owner-control effect after allowing for M-form
Burton/Obel (1980)	—	profit	computer simulation 2×2 factorial design	*positive*, for each of two levels of decomposability of technology, M-form yields higher profit solution than U-form
Teece (1981)	M-Form innovator and matched competitor in 30 US industries	—rate of return on equity —rate of return on assets	non-parametric tests	—sign test non-significant —Wilcoxon matched pairs test *positive*
Roberts/Viscione (1981)	44 captive finance subsidiaries 134 control company observations in 5 US industries	debt to total asset ratio	before and after comparison	*mixed* (t-test significant in 2 out of 5 cases; Mann-Whitney U-test significant in 3 out of 5)
Thompson (1981)	72 UK firms (from Steer/Cable sample)	share price returns (residuals analysis)	(i) regression model ($0.20 < \bar{R}^2 < 0.33$) (ii) market-model residuals analysis	*positive* (regression confirms S-C result, but residuals analysis suggests bias due to abnormally poor performance of H-forms in control group)

Study	Sample	Performance measure	Method	Result
Cable/Dirrheimer (1983)	48 West German firms of the top 100 (25 M-Form) (1968–72)	rate of return on capital	regression model ($\bar{R}^2 = 0.78$)	*negative* (significant for firms in transition only—neutral 'steady state' effects?)
Thompson (1983b)	138 UK firms 1959–1976	share price returns	(i) residuals analysis (ii) regression models of abnormal returns	*positive* but at best weakly significant; M-form arrests and to some extent reverses pre-adoption decline
Harris (1983)	27 US firms	accounting and financial market returns	various statistical models	*negative*
Bühner (1985)	40 West German firms out of top 300 1966–1981	—rate of return on capital assets —rate of return on equity —Jensen's α	regression model ($0.14 < \bar{R}^2 < 0.65$)	*negative*
Cable/Yasuki (1985)	80 Japanese firms 1968–78	—rate of return on assets	regression model ($0.64 < \bar{R}^2 < 0.71$)	*negative* (non-significant)
Hill (1985b)	128 UK firms		analysis of variance	*positive*: M-form superior to H-form and non-optimal M-form (no comparison with U-form)
Hoskisson/Galbraith (1985)	6 firms matched for 3 industries	accounting returns	time-series analysis over adoption period	*positive* but generally non-significant
Hill/Pickering (1986a)	144 UK firms		correlation analysis	MD not always more profitable. Higher profit more likely where effective decentralisation of operating decisions

Table 2.4 Selected Regression Results, USA, UK, West Germany and Japan

	Armour & Teece	Steer & Cable (S/C)	Thompson	Cable & Dirrheimer (C/D)	Bühner	Cable & Yasuki (C/Y)
	USA 1956–68	UK 1967–71	UK 1967–69	FRG 1968–72	FRG 1966–81	JAPAN 1968–78
DEPENDENT VARIABLE	Π/E	Π/E	Returns per share	Π/K	Π/E	Π/K
INDEPENDENT VARIABLES						
Constant	0.077***	0.077	−0.074	−0.004	5.00***	0.40***
Organisation structure						
Optimal/non-optimal		0.105***	0.123***			
M-form	0.021***			−0.006	−4.09***	−0.005
Transitional	0.024***	−0.046*		−0.0164***		−0.001
Functional + subsids.	0.013			0.020**		
Corrupted-M or Holding	−0.056					
Strategy						
Diversified				0.015**	−1.24	0.007
International					11.64***	
Control						
Ownercontrol ⎰int. ⎱ext.		0.056***	0.088*	0.044*** 0.0004***	−0.01	0.053** 0.048
Bank voting rights				0.020**		
Bank representation		−0.015	0.128			
Management rep.					1.94**	
Bank control						0.001
Business Groups						
Membership						0.002
Main bank borrowing						0.016
Bank borrowing				0.039**		−0.001***

Risk	−0.275		−0.000	−0.2 × 10⁻⁴	−1.11**	−0.114**
Size	0.3 × 10⁻⁶	0.4 × 10⁻⁴***		−0.0 × 10⁻⁶	−1.15****	0.3 × 10⁻⁹
Growth	0.280***	0.028*	0.050*	−0.015*	0.09****	0.002**
Interaction terms						
Structure × Size		−0.2 × 10⁻⁴**				
Owner-control × Growth		−0.007*				
R^2	0.25	0.50	0.33	0.78		
$\bar{R}^2$	0.23				0.63	0.713
F	13.69	7.24			23.27	9.74
n	339	82	72	48	160	89
Other Variables	(i) Capacity utilisation	(i) Industry dummies	(i) Ratio of sales revenue	(i) Public ownership		
				(ii) Industry dummies		

Note: Most authors report alternative models (see text and individual studies). Armour and Teece and Bühner used pooled samples, others are cross-section. Organisation structure coefficients capture deviations from basic functional (U-form) observation, *except* that in S/C, C/D and C/Y, transitional dummy captures deviation from (steady state) M-form. Owner control is dummy in S/C and Thompson, but Herfindahl index of shareholder dispersion elsewhere; internal–external distinction applies only to Japan, and separates shares held within and outside business groups. In C/D, 'Functional and subsidiaries'; is 'Functional/Holding' category. ***, **, *, denote significance at 1, 5 and 10 per cent or better; *t* values reported in individual studies.

as opposed to more conspicuous events such as mergers, lies in the need to date rather precisely the 'announcement' of the event. Bearing in mind the gradual, and sometimes halting, process that M-form adoption can entail, it is clearly difficult to be sure when and what the stock market learns of the reorganisation.

Table 2.3 summarises the results of fourteen different studies of the M-form/performance relationship. Table 2.4 gives more detailed results for a number of models which are sufficiently similar to permit such detailed comparison. Drawing overall conclusions is complicated by differences in sample, period and method, and sometimes by international differences in the external environment. Moreover, no such study can be free of methodological shortcomings and inadequacies of data, and flaws are not difficult to find in those under consideration. Armour and Teece's date for the end of the diffusion period (1968) is questionable, given that in their sample, U-form firms continued to decrease up to 1969 and M-form to increase up to 1972, and no structural-break tests are reported. Steer and Cable's estimates of the magnitude of organisational-form effects (a difference equivalent to nearly 50 per cent of average returns to capital across the sample) are so large as to invite suspicion, and may have been exaggerated by abnormally low returns in the (non-optimal) H-form group in the sample (Thompson 1981). Teece's principal firms analysis may be subject to systematic bias if the firms 'paired' to the M-form innovators in each industry, and themselves subsequent M-form adopters, were affected by pre-adoption 'crisis'. Thompson's (1983b) marginally significant results could reflect on the appropriateness of the market model as an empirical tool for investigating the M-form phenomenon. The poor overall results obtained by Cable and Yasuki, for Japan, could similarly hint at a general unsuitability to the Japanese case of a model developed for other countries.

Following from this, we may hazard the following general statements:

(1) There are a considerable number of results which the authors interpret as supporting the M-form hypothesis, especially for the USA and Britain, where testing has been carried out most extensively.

(2) At the same time, M-form gains are not so overwhelming that they appear robustly in all cases.

(3) The finding, in several studies, of an owner-control effect on profitability in the presence of M-form variables (Table 2.4) suggests that M-form may offer incomplete control over discretionary behaviour; this raises the question of what other sources of M-form gain may be important.

(4) The absence of any positive results for Germany and Japan, where the authors point to institutional features that might attenuate M-

form gains, raises the possibility that M-form is not 'culture-free' in its effects, i.e. that the hypothesis may not apply with equal force in all environments. Resolution of this issue must, however, await further investigation in view of the small number of studies undertaken so far.

Evidence of Systemic Gains

Empirical tests for systemic effects of M-form are much harder to carry out than are tests for firm-level gains, and the existing evidence can only be described as fragmentary. One study offers some information on the relative importance of M-form firms in the takeover process, and on the scope of internal capital markets within M-form firms (Cable 1980).

The predominance of M-form acquirers in UK conglomerate mergers in the 1970s was overwhelming: in 32 out of a sample of 37 merger cases, the acquiring firm was M-form (an incidence of 86.4 per cent, compared with around 70 per cent in the population of largest firms as a whole, shown in Table 2.2). Clearly, this is consistent with the notion of M-form as an effective takeover instrument, although, as we have seen, the social effects of increased takeover threat may not always be beneficial.

With respect to internal capital markets, the evidence suggests that, whatever improvements there might be in intra-firm capital transfer *between divisions*, internal capital markets are of limited significance for inter-industry capital transfer. Using a fairly disaggregated, 67-industry classification of UK manufacturing, Cable found that more than half of all possible pairs of industries were not linked via any known M-form firm's divisions;[16] that over one-third were linked in this way by only one or two firms; and therefore that, in less than 10 per cent of cases, industries were linked by three or more separate M-form firms.

2.5 Conclusion

The multi-divisional corporation is an important economic institution, not least because of the huge amount of economic activity which goes on under its control. Historical evidence clearly shows that the M-form innovation has allowed giant firms to survive, and to solve the problems attendant upon policies of growth and diversification which might otherwise have led to their downfall. What is less clear is whether it can be said to have resulted in behaviour significantly closer to the neoclassical model than would otherwise have been the case. Though early statistical results of the M-form hypothesis to that effect were interpreted as supporting the hypothesis, subsequent evidence has been mixed. Some of this evidence suggests that there may be differences in the extent of potential M-form gains in different national settings and, more generally, that the benefits may depend on context as well as the intrinsic properties of M-form itself. In short, it can safely be said that, though not all M-form adoptions have been entirely successful, M-form has often been a triumph in business efficiency terms. But its effects in broader, economic efficiency terms (which are *a priori* ambiguous for welfare) have yet to be established beyond reasonable doubt.

Notes

1. For detailed analysis of individual cases see Chandler (1962).
2. This is due to 'serial reproduction loss' as messages, instructions, etc. are repeatedly passed from person to person. The phenomenon is sometimes made the basis of children's games, and is of course fundamental to the spread of rumours. It has also been demonstrated in experiments where, on repeated redrawing, the image of an owl becomes distinctly recognisable as a cat.
3. However, in the case of takeover targets, the general office would not be favoured by privileged access to internal information of the kind on which its expertise in evaluating divisional performance is based.
4. Assuming that the supply of managerial resource inputs is not rationed.
5. See e.g. Steiner (1975).
6. For a stimulating and controversial discussion of some relevant aspects of stock market behaviour, see e.g. Shiller (1981), Mueller (1984) and Nickell and Wadhwani (1987).
7. The intuition of this result is that the incumbents can exactly emulate an entrant's behaviour by divisionalising, while avoiding the latter's overhead costs of entry; and they will always prefer to form a new division than to permit entry and allow the entrant to take a profit.
8. Also, Japanese business groups offer a unique combination of advantages of specialisation at company level and diversification at group level, with substantial intra-group trading and inter-corporate shareholding. (Allen 1981). In this way they provide a partial alternative to the M-form as an institutional solution to the problem of combining managerial efficiency and diversification.
9. The US companies in question were Du Pont, General Motors, Standard Oil (New Jersey) and Sears Roebuck. The validity of Kocka's claim is hard to judge, because it is not clear from his account whether the characteristic control apparatus and *modus operandi* were fully present in Siemens at this time.
10. The 'corrupted' (M-form) variant was identified by Williamson and Bhargava (1972) in their expanded classification scheme, and features over-involvement of the centre in divisional affairs. A further (M') category was also included for firms in transition to M-form. Neither M nor M' firms are predicted to show full M-form performance.
11. The top 100 companies in Britain and America accounted for 41% and 33%

respectively of manufacturing net output in 1970 (Prais 1976).

12. Note that these lags between first- and median-firm adoption should not be confused with those for structural adaptation to strategic choice in a given company, reported by Dyas and Thanheiser (1976).

13. In stochastic form, the three alternative models are, respectively:

$$Y_t = a_2 + b_2 t + u_{2t} \text{ (cumulative normal);}$$
$$\ln (M_t/n) = a_3 + b_3/t + u_{3t} \text{ (log reciprocal);}$$
$$Y_t = a_4 + b_4 \ln(t) + u_{4t} \text{ (cumulative log normal);}$$

where Y_t is the normal equivalent deviate (normit) of M_t/n.

14. See Thompson (1981, 1983a,b) for a more detailed discussion of the application of the market model to the measurement of M-form gains, and of the alternative, capital-asset-pricing model.

15. See Mueller (1984) for a stimulating discussion of the stock market's preoccupation with short-run turning points rather than the long-run earning power of individual assets.

16. The number of possible pairs is given by $n(n-1)/2$. With $n = 67$, this implies a total of 2,211.

3

The Corporate Life Cycle

DENNIS C. MUELLER*

3.1 Introduction

Adam Smith's famous discussion of the organisation of production in a pin factory articulated the advantages of the division of labour, the economic gains from specialisation and large scale production. But, Adam Smith expressed considerable scepticism concerning the relative efficiency of that particular form of business organisation we now name the corporation, in which ownership and management are separated (1937, p. 700). Yet it has been this organisational form that has come to rule the day and on a scale and scope that the Scottish sage could hardly have imagined.

This chapter explores the ramifications of this development. It describes the process of evolution of a representative corporation from birth through maturity, with particular emphasis on the innovation records of corporations, and their diversification and merger strategies. Empirical evidence is reviewed pertaining to Adam Smith's concern over the efficiency of the corporate form in the modern capitalist market system.

3.2 The Birth of Firms

In Schumpeter's description of the capitalist system, it is the innovator–entrepreneur who disturbs the economy's circular flow equilibrium (1934, p. 64): development occurs through the introduction of 'new combinations' of product characteristics, production techniques, marketing methods, sources of supply, and organisational forms, i.e. through the introduction of innovations. Innovations lift the economy out of its circular flow equilibrium—they are the source of development; profits are

38

the rewards to the iconoclastic entrepreneur, who brings about economic development.

While in principle these iconoclastic entrepreneurs could reside in a large, established firm, one's preconceptions of the behavioural selection biases of large organisations makes it seem unlikely. Indeed, Schumpeter's iconoclast–entrepreneur seems to have much the same personality traits as Anthony Downs's new bureau heads: 'zealots who have a specific idea they want to put into practice on a large scale' (1967, p. 5). Zealots and iconoclasts seem more likely to be at home in a small, new firm. So it appears Schumpeter also believed, at least as late as 1934. '[N]ew combinations are, as a rule, embodied, as it were, in new firms which generally do not arise out of the old ones but start producing beside them; . . . in general, it is not the owner of stage coaches who builds railways' (1934, p. 66).

Schumpeter does not indicate why innovations are to be expected from newcomers rather than established firms, but more modern treatments of the subject provide at least three explanations. First, the established firm may already be earning a profit (rent) in the industry. The profits to the stagecoach manufacturer from successfully introducing the railroad are the above-normal returns from the railroad *less* the rents on its stagecoach business, wiped out by the railroad (Arrow 1961; Kamien and Schwartz 1982, Ch. 4). The greater the rents on the existing line of business, the smaller the incentive to develop an innovation that will destroy them. For the newcomer, gross and net profit from an innovation are one and the same.[1]

Second, the small firm does not experience the control loss and information distortion problems of the large, rigidly structured company (Monsen and Downs 1965; Williamson 1967, 1970, Ch. 2). These problems are likely to be particularly important with respect to major innovations (Williamson 1970, pp. 157–60). Radical departures appear to emerge most readily out of flexible organisational structures (Abernathy 1978, p. 71 ff.), out of the kind of open, informal, high trust environments that are more readily established in the small firm (Klein 1977, pp. 161–75).

Third, the small firm provides better incentives to management to undertake the tremendous risks surrounding major innovations. When Haloid's top management decided to 'bet their company' on the xerography invention, they put up their own savings as well as the time and energy needed to see the development through. The success of the innovation made them (now the top managers of newly-named Xerox) into multimillionaires, whose pictures were commonly featured in the leading business magazines and newspapers (Forbes 1965). No large corporation offers its middle-management incentive packages that promise such rewards in exchange for taking the kinds of risk involved in the development of xerography. Perhaps this explains why creative R & D personnel—who wish to pursue important, innovative ideas— would typically leave a large firm to start their own company, as for example in transistors (Tilton 1971, pp. 49–55).

These factors help to explain why the independent inventor, the university research team and other outsiders have remained a major source of important inventions.[2] Jewkes, Sawers and Stillerman's investigation of the origin of 61 important inventions attributed only 12 to large corporations (1969). Grosvenor (1929) attributed 12 of the 72 major inventions between 1889 and 1929 to corporate laboratories, and Hamberg (1963) listed large corporations as the source of major inventions in only 7 of the 27 cases he examined for the decade 1946–55.

Thus, the small or newly-born firm is a primary source of new products and innovations, just as new products and innovations are the primary cause for the birth of new firms.[3] Few counter examples come to mind.[4] Rather, the typical large firm today is one which came into existence at the birth of a new product (Kodak), or if the firm entered a mature industry, it did so by introducing an important product or production process innovation (Polaroid).

3.3 The Product Life Cycle

At the beginning of its evolution, the growth and development of a firm is closely entwined with the growth and development of its main product(s). The hypothesis that products pass through a cycle in which the rate of growth of output first expands rapidly, but eventually declines, has been around for a long time. The classic study of product life cycles was by Arthur F. Burns in 1934. Burns studied the output histories of 147 products beginning as far back as 1870, and claimed to observe a general pattern of retardation in output growth rates for each product after some point in time. More recent investigations of 140 products by Polli and Cook (1969), and of 46 products by Gort and Klepper (1982) appear to confirm that products typically do pass through a common pattern of development, although with important exceptions and caveats to be noted. The salient features of this common pattern are as follows:

(1) The rate of growth of output is rapid at first and then declines. Burns observed continual declines in output growth rates for the products he examined, and the same is true on average for the Gort and Klepper sample. But Bela Gold (1964), in a follow-up to Burns's study, found undiminished rates of growth for many products over long time periods. No downward trend in output

growth was apparent in 9 of the 46 products in the Gort and Klepper study over the latter segments of their reported data.[5] Thus, if one envisages a product's life cycle as an S-shaped curve, with output on the vertical axis and time on the horizontal, then the segment of the curve at which its concavity reverses may be a straight line of considerable length (cf. Gold 1964, p. 58).

(2) The number of firms in the industry rises at first, then a 'shakeout' occurs in which there is a rapid exit of sellers. This period is followed by a mature phase in which no systematic pattern of change in the number of firms in the industry is observed (Gort and Klepper 1982; Klepper and Graddy 1984).

(3) Initial entrants are typically small and are often newly formed companies, including spinoffs from existing companies. (Gort and Klepper 1982; Klepper and Graddy 1984; Abernathy 1978; Tilton 1971). Entry is 'know-how' determined, and the critical human inputs are scientific and engineering (Hirsch 1972).

(4) The rate of technological change is at first rapid, but then slows. Early innovations tend to be focused on product design changes, improving quality rather than reducing costs. Many innovations at the early stages come from outside the industry, e.g. from universities or customers. As output grows and 'dominant' product designs are hit upon, innovation is oriented more towards process improvements and cost reduction. Firms inside the industry begin to account for an increasing fraction of innovations.[6]

It is interesting that this process of product evolution appears equally applicable to recent innovations like transistors and xerography as to earlier innovations like automobiles and automobile tyres. For it seems to resemble, in many respects, the process of economic development first described by Joseph Schumpeter at the turn of the century.[7] Schumpeter stressed that each innovation brings with it a 'crowd' of imitators (1934, p. 133), which corresponds well to the rapid growth in number of producers occurring during the early phases of a product's life cycle. The 'shakeout' periods that inevitably come eliminating many early entrants might be equated to Schumpeter's 'perennial gale of creative destruction.'

3.4 The Emergence of Dominant Firms

The innovative entrepreneur's task is to create a firm and, in the case of a new product innovation, to create an industry. If one takes a Knightian view toward profit, and assumes that it is the reward for bearing uncertainty, then the innovator–entrepreneur can be thought of as a creator of uncertainty, disturbing market equilibria by introducing new products and processes, and gambling on his ability to predict the future success of the innovations despite the uncertainty that shrouds that future (Mueller 1976). The task of the management of the established firm is to preserve rents already extant, in order to preserve the first-mover advantages inherited from the founding entrepreneur. It must control uncertainty if not eliminate it (Klein 1977, pp. 12–24). Thus, as the corporation passes from young small innovator in an uncertain dynamic market to mature market leader in a stable growing market, profit creating needs to give way to rent preserving strategies (Klein 1977, Ch. 5).

As an industry matures, competition within the industry shifts from an emphasis on product quality and product improvements to an emphasis on price (Hirsch 1972). Management becomes the critical human input (Hirsch 1972): product design innovations are displaced by process inno-vations; major innovations give way to minor ones; and dynamic goals of improving product quality or production technique are replaced by the static goals of meeting production quotas, maintaining quality control and cost control. Here, cause and effect cannot be separated: the maturing successful firm experiences greater bureaucratisation, slower change in product design, and greater standardisation and specificity in production technique—and the one cannot easily be separated from the other.[8]

Many of these changes are the inevitable accompaniments of size. The small firm is almost by definition decentralised: it can maintain the flat, fluid informal organisational structure that is required to cope with rapid technological change; and it can maintain the high trust and personal relationships that are essential to sustain organisational stability in an uncertain environment (Klein 1977, Chs 5, 6). As the company grows larger, increases in formality and hierarchy become almost inevitable (Klein 1977, Chs 5, 6; Williamson 1975, Chs 3, 7; Abernathy 1978, Ch. 4). With these changes in organisational structure come, not surprisingly, changes in management 'style.' Schumpeter's 'iconoclastic entrepreneur' and Downs's 'zealot' are replaced by managers who are better suited to the formal hierarchical structure now in place, and who both lay down the rules and enforce and preserve them; such managers are described by Downs as 'conservers' (1967, p. 19).

Growth in size typically brings with it another important change in the structure of the firm. The demand for investment funds for the truly successful growing firm outstrip the supply of capital that can be generated internally. The founding entrepreneur–capitalist ownership interests in the firm must be diluted (Marris 1964, pp. 5–11). Thus, growth in size brings with it both an increase in formality and bureaucratisation (separating the leadership of the firm from the firm) and a dilution of the financial interests of the leadership (driving a wedge between management interests and those of pure ownership).

3.5 Maturity: Stable Internal Growth, External Growth and Decline

Firms are born, grow and sometimes die. This cycle of development has suggested to several observers the analogy between the firm and living organisms. Alfred Marshall likened firms to trees that grow to a given size and then cease growing (1920, p. 263). Like the great trees in a forest, many corporations seem capable of surviving indefinitely. But, continuing the analogy, they also lose their vitality and eventually enter a state of stagnation.

The implication is that the firm's returns will decline as the corporation matures and 'stagnates'. John Hiller (1977) has undertaken one of the few direct studies of firm life-cycle effects on company returns. He traced a sample of 144 of the 200 largest US corporations of 1973 back as far as 1929 and measured both average and marginal returns on capital. He found a continual decline in the marginal returns on capital of both young and mature firms over the post-World War II period, but the marginal returns of young firms remained substantially above those of mature companies throughout the period. Interesting also was the finding that average returns on capital, including monopoly rents, remained high for the mature firms in markets with very high entry barriers and were actually higher than those of young firms in these markets at the end of the period (see Table 3.1). Thus, while aging brings with it declining marginal returns, mature firms with protected market positions can maintain high rents on capital over long periods. Hiller's results are consistent with those of other writers concerning the persistence of above-normal returns (Qualls 1974; Mueller 1977a, 1986).

Several studies have examined the stability of market positions, and they all reach the same conclusion: there is a definite regression on the mean effect. Firms with initial market shares substantially above the average tend to lose market share over time, but the market-share erosion process works slowly and in many markets does not work at all. Counteracting it are the first-mover advantages that incumbents have with buyers (Schmalensee 1982), and the learning-by-doing cost advantages of incumbents (Arrow 1962; Rosen 1972; Spence 1981; Smiley & Ravid 1983). Many companies are the leading sellers in their markets from one decade to the next. Thus, although several of the 18 companies Shepherd examined with 1948 market shares of 50 per cent or more experienced substantial declines in their market shares by 1973 (e.g. Du Pont's

Table 3.1 Marginal and Average Returns on Capital for Young and Mature Firms 1945–71

Firm Age	Barriers to Entry	Returns	1945	1950	1955	1960	1965	1971
Young	Very high	Marginal	77.6	63.9	54.1	36.2	23.0	14.1
	Substantial/low	Marginal	56.7	44.2	59.2	48.2	20.5	16.5
	Very high	Average	—	69.7	98.2	81.8	75.9	43.2
	Substantial/low	Average	—	33.7	65.8	83.7	85.9	56.5
Mature	Very high	Marginal	52.6	39.5	28.5	30.7	18.0	9.8
	Substantial/low	Marginal	54.0	35.5	23.2	23.1	14.5	7.9
	Very high	Average	78.5	71.2	59.4	52.4	67.2	53.5
	Substantial/low	Average	34.7	52.3	60.0	45.3	51.6	38.8

Source: Hiller (1977)
Notes: Sample size is 144
   All calculations based on an assumed 10% depreciation rate.

cellophane went from 90 per cent to 60 per cent), 15 of the 18 still had market shares of 50 per cent or more in 1973.[9] Similarly, Weiss and Pascoe (1983) found that 18 of the 23 companies with 1950 market shares of 40 per cent or more in their sample continued to have market shares above 40 per cent in 1975.

In an examination of 350 *roughly* comparable markets in 1950 and 1972, it was found that in 142 of the 350 markets the same company was the leading firm in both 1950 and 1972, and in another 13 the same two firms were industry leaders but with reversed ranks in the two years (Mueller 1986, Table 3). Dominant firms do not always decline.[10]

Substantial evidence also exists indicating that market leadership brings with it above-normal returns. A strong positive correlation exists between profitability and market share.[11] Those firms which have succeeded in obtaining a large market share can earn persistently above normal returns if they retain it. Their rate of growth will be equal to that of their industry and thus may gradually decline over time as the industry's products are displaced. But a leading firm may continue to enjoy an above-normal return and a modest growth rate for decade after decade.

A company can expand more rapidly than its product market without leaving it by increasing its market share. To do so by internal growth means the displacement of existing sellers, with all of the hostile oligopolistic responses one expects from this type of strategy. Thus, those companies which seek to grow more rapidly than their markets are growing, but which do not wish to diversify, can be expected to engage in horizontal acquisitions.

But there is an obvious upper limit to expansion within a market, and antitrust policies (as in the United States) place additional constraints on growth by horizontal acquisitions. Thus, one observes companies shifting toward growth through diversification in all countries since World War II.[12]

With diversification comes the need for further organisational change. While the organisational structure remains essentially hierarchical, the addition of several new products or product lines adds parallel hierarchical pyramids to the firm. The consequence is most usually that the traditional, hierarchical pyramid, what Williamson calls the U-form organisation, is replaced by an M-form structure.[13]

An M-form organisation's top management is incapable of being expert in all of the different product or geographic areas in which its firm operates and thus tends to be expert in none. M-form managers are typically generalists trained in finance, accounting and the law as befits the general services they supply to the firm—in contrast to the backgrounds in engineering, production and marketing that dominated in U-form firms.[14]

While the M-form structure has several advantages in processing information internally,[15] it also is likely to be at a disadvantage in adapting to a rapidly changing environment where new products or processes are acquired.[16] Its structure does not typically provide sufficient incentives to lower level managers to take the sizeable risks required to introduce new products and processes. The top managers have neither the expertise nor sufficient information to make these decisions. (For further discussion of these issues see Chapters five and ten.) The consequence is that one expects the large, M-form organisations to rely on diversification and mergers to achieve growth, with rather little success at innovations and internally generated investment opportunities.

3.6 Diversification: Size, Growth and Profitability

While diversification and mergers can be expected to increase company size, it is less clear that they will increase its profitability. If the M-form managers are no better or worse than acquired firm managers at running acquired operations, and if the informational disadvantages of the M-form outweigh its advantages, diversification and profitability could be inversely correlated.

As expected, both company size and diversification, and company growth and changes in diversification have been found to be positively correlated.[17] But empirical evidence on the relationship between profitability and diversification is mixed and difficult to interpret. A positive correlation between profitability and diversification has been found by Rhoades (1973) and Carter (1977) for the United States. Lecraw (1984) found a positive correlation between profits and diversification among Canadian companies but only when they were diversified into related businesses. Lecraw's finding for Canada was corroborated in a follow-up study by Rhoades (1974) to his earlier work. In 1973, Rhoades published a paper indicating that diversification outside of one's major 4-digit industry is positively related to profitability, but his 1974 study measured diversification in a broader fashion, i.e. as diversification out of the firm's major 2½–3-digit product area. This more broadly measured degree of diversification was *negatively* related to profitability. The present author also found a negative relationship after controlling for the predicted profits of a firm, based on its market share and product differentiation (Mueller 1986, Ch. 7). Miller (1969) found no relationship between profitability and diversification whatsoever.

Particularly difficult to disentangle in these studies is the direction of causality. If diversification takes place to conceal above-normal returns, then diversifying companies have above-normal profits in their base industries prior to any diversification activity they undertake. Similarly, if diversification is motivated by a pure desire to grow larger even without any increase in profitability, the R & D or mergers that lead to diversification must somehow be financed. Those firms earning above-normal returns in their basic product lines are in a better position to finance unprofitable diversification. If the diversification activity does not entirely wipe out the above-normal returns precipitating it, then profits and diversification will again be positively correlated. To test whether diversification *caused* higher profits one would have to measure profits both before and after diversification, not simply correlate *ex-post* levels of each.

Jesse Markham confronted the causality issue in his investigation of diversification, and his observations warrant repeating:

> In almost all models in which profitability and price–earnings ratios entered as statistically significant, they took on a negative sign. This inverse relationship between profitability and both 1970 company diversification and the volume of 1961–70 diversifying acquisitions is consistent with any one of several hypotheses: it may . . . indicate that acquisitive conglomerates sacrifice profitability for growth; it may mean that companies earning relatively low rates of return in their present industries are the most active acquirers of companies in other industries; or, alternatively, it may simply mean that

diversification through acquisiton in 1961–70 was not generally an especially profitable activity.[18]

Thus, while growth and diversification are clearly positively related, the relationship between diversification and profitability is ambiguous both with respect to sign and causal interpretation.

Given that firm size and diversification are positively correlated, one might expect to find the same ambiguous relationship between firm size and profitability as exists between diversification and profitability. But, the correlation between size and diversification is not so strong as to make the relationship between profitability and size a foregone conclusion. A brief look at this literature is therefore warranted.

Early studies by Crum (1939), Stekler (1963) and Stigler (1963) reached the conclusion that above some rather minimal size, profitability and size are unrelated. Given that a greater fraction of economic profits is likely to appear as costs in small firms where owners and managers are more often one and the same (Stigler 1963, pp. 59–61), these early findings seemed to reduce the notion that big firms are able to earn higher profits.

Hall and Weiss (1967) selected a sample of companies they believed to be sufficiently large to be above minimum efficient scale and found a positive correlation between profitability and the log of assets (more accurately, a negative correlation between profitability and one over the log of assets), after controlling for other variables. Their paper has become the standard reference for the conclusion that profits and absolute size are positively related. But the Hall and Weiss findings were soon challenged by Marcus (1969), and Weiss himself has expressed some doubt concerning the result in personal communication with the writer, since he has not been able to reproduce the original findings. Gale (1972) did get positive coefficients on firm size in all six of the equations he estimated, but the variable was significant in only two. While generally taking on a positive sign in the present author's work, it also was typically insignificant (Mueller 1986, Chs 6 and 7).

Outside the United States, all observers have found either no relationship between profitability and size or a negative one. Singh and Whittington (1968) found no significant differences in the average profitability of UK firms across different size classes. Samuels and Smyth (1968) found a negative relationship between profitability and size for quoted UK companies. In France, studies by Morvan (1972) and Jenny and Weber (1976) both find profitability and firm size to be negatively related. Jacquemin and Saëz (1976) found a negative relationship between size and profitability within a sample of large European and Japanese companies (see also Jacquemin and Lichtbuer 1973). Outside the United States, there is no evidence whatsoever that, beyond the smallest size class, bigger firms earn higher profits; within the United

States, the evidence is ambiguous.

No company management chooses to diversify without weighing the consequences of this decision. Firms need not diversify and grow so large that they become members of the top 500, or 200, or 100. If size and diversification do not bring with them increases in profitability (and especially if there is a decline in profitability) the following questions arise: Why do managers choose to expand and diversify when they could remain small or, more accurately, medium sized? What are the implications of non-profitable corporate expansion for the allocation of capital in society and the overall efficiency of the economy?

A frequently discussed motivation for diversification is to reduce the variability in a firm's profitability,[19] and the preponderance of empirical evidence confirms that size and diversification are negatively related to profit variability.[20] But it is also now well-established that shareholders can achieve superior diversification in their holdings of shares than it is possible for firms to achieve through diversification of real assets.[21] If management seeks to maximise ownership's welfare, then diversification which does not increase the returns on the combined activities is not a defensible strategy.

Reduction in the variability of a firm's profits may be in the management's interests. If the profitability of a management's dismissal rises in a period of relatively low profitability, then smoothing profits over time—even with some sacrifice in mean returns—may reduce managerial risks.[22] Moreover, managers and owners may not be able to trade away their shares in their companies to achieve diversified portfolios of shares; management's ability to protect itself from dismissal is directly related to its own shareholding (Mueller 1986, Ch. 7). Thus, while diversification may be an inefficient way to reduce the risks of outside owners, it may be attractive to managers whose wealth and income are heavily dependent on their company.

The other managerial motive for diversification is to avoid slow or declining growth prospects facing a firm in the mature phases of its life cycle. Weston and Mansinghka (1971) show that the companies engaged in the most intensive conglomerate merger activity in the sixties had lower than average profit rates in the late fifties—such merger strategies were described as 'defensive diversification'. While this motive for diversification is aptly named 'defensive diversification', it is really separate from the risk reduction motive just discussed. The management of a company in a mature or declining industry knows with near certainty that its company is destined to stagnate and decline if it does not diversify. Diversification in this situation is to avoid the inevitable, not to protect against the unknown. The question raised by the literature on profitability, size and diversification is whether this diversification activity serves any social purpose beyond preventing the decline of certain firms.

3.7   Returns on Investment and the Theory of the Firm

If growth and diversification by mature companies do not increase their profitability, then the returns on investment of these firms should be below the opportunity cost of capital for their owners. Further evidence on the efficiency consequences of corporate growth and diversification can be found in estimates of the returns on investment for large, mature companies.

What is at issue, with respect to the efficiency of the allocation of capital, are the *marginal* returns on investment. Thus, the many studies examining average returns on capital across firms and industries are, unfortunately, largely irrelevant to the question of whether—on the margin—mature firms invest optimally.

Several studies have appeared in recent years, however, which are relevant to the issue at hand. In a pioneering paper in 1970, Baumol, Heim, Malkiel and Quandt (hereafter BHMQ) estimated the returns on investment out of ploughback and new debt and equity issues. They concluded that:

> the rate of return on equity capital is higher by a substantial margin than that on the other two forms of new capital. Depending on the lag involved, the rate of return on equity capital ranged from 14.5 per cent to 20.8 per cent. The rate of return on ploughback, however, ranged from 3.0–4.6 per cent; while the rate of return on debt ranged from 4.2–14 per cent. Thus, it appears that the rate of return on new equity is substantially higher than the rate of return on ploughback; while the rate of return on new debt is somewhere between the rates of return to ploughback and equity (p. 353).

Relevant to the question of whether capital is being allocated efficiently are both the relative differences in returns across the various sources of finance and the absolute level of the returns on ploughback. If reinvested cash flows during the fifties earned on average only a 3–4.6 per cent return, then they earned substantially less than the return their shareholders could have obtained by buying the equity of other firms. Fisher and Lorie's (1964) estimates of returns on the market portfolio of common shares for the fifties are in the range from 13–18 per cent.

If firms in early phases of their life cycle make heavier reliance on the external capital market than mature companies, then the BHMQ results would also tend to corroborate a life cycle hypothesis. Grabowski and Mueller (1975) tested this hypothesis directly. They estimated returns on investment out of all sources of finance for firms, which were founded after World War II, or sold products predominantly in the early phases of their life cycle. These estimated returns ranged from 13.7–26.3 per cent for funds invested in the fifties and early- to mid-sixties. In contrast, the range of estimates for mature firms was from 9.2–12.5 per cent. Although the latter are higher than the returns BHMQ estimated, they are all below the Fisher and Lorie estimates of stock market returns.

John Hiller (1978) also compared his estimates of marginal rates of return on investment to the Fisher and Lorie stock market returns estimates. Depending on choice of depreciation rate, he found that 57–68 per cent of his sample of 144 companies had estimated marginal returns on investment significantly below the Fisher–Lorie index for five or more consecutive years over the fifties and sixties. His results, like those of BHMQ and Grabowski and Mueller, are inconsistent with the neoclassical theory of the firm as in Modigliani and Miller (1958), which assumes that managers are constrained in their investment decisions to choose only projects earning rates of return at least as great as those available to their shareholders elsewhere.

The BHMQ article has been followed by studies for Canada and the UK. McFetridge's study of 205 large Canadian companies for the period 1961–70 is most comparable to BHMQ's in methodology (1978). He presents a range of estimates depending on lag structure chosen and on whether intercepts are included. In all 12 equations presented, the estimated returns on equity exceed those on ploughback, with the differences being as large as 7.8 per cent on ploughback as opposed to 23.6 per cent on equity. Nevertheless, the standard errors on the estimated coefficients are large enough for the differences between the coefficients on ploughback and new equity to be (typically) insignificantly different from zero, at the 5 per cent level, using two-tail tests (but not always if 10 per cent level or one-tail tests are used). McFetridge concludes, 'Managerial earnings retention policies are not a source of inefficiency' (p. 223).

While the differences in estimated returns on equity and ploughback in McFetridge's study are not statistically significant, they are nevertheless economically significant. For the specification which McFetridge favours (i.e. including an unweighted constant), his estimated returns on ploughback range between 2.7 per cent and 6.8 per cent. These returns must be considerably below what shareholders could have earned in the Canadian stock market during the sixties. The fact that large absolute differences in coefficients prove to be statistically insignificant implies only that the standard errors of the coefficients are large, in turn implying that many firms earn even lower returns on ploughback than the average returns reported by McFetridge. Given that this average is itself below the opportunity cost of capital for Canadian shareholders, McFetridge's study indicates rather clearly that many Canadian firms earn substantially lower returns on reinvested retained earnings than their shareholders could earn in the market. Certainly, for the shareholders of these firms, managerial retention policies are a source of inefficiency.

Brealey, Hodges and Capron (1976) propose several modifications to the BHMQ estimating procedure and present estimates for 816 UK companies over the 1949–63 period. They note that, on average, new equity accounts for less than 1 per cent of assets (p. 474). Moreover, most firms issue no new equity in a given year. Thus, it is not surprising that the standard errors on this variable's coefficients are large, and it is difficult to establish statistically significant differences in estimated returns across sources of finance. Furthermore, the returns on ploughback occasionally exceed those on new equity.

Brealey, Hodges, and Capron castigate BHMQ for estimating average returns rather than marginal returns, whereas it is marginal returns that should equal the cost of capital according to neoclassical theory.[23] They therefore attempt to estimate true marginal returns by placing a control on the size of investment for each firm. They do this by, first, regressing returns on risk and the ratio of total investment to initial size and then regressing the residuals from this equation on the three sources of finance. The results from both stages are interesting. In accordance with neoclassical theory, Brealey, *et al.* assume that '[i]f companies accept all projects with positive net present values, one might expect that the average return would be high when a large volume of projects is undertaken,' but find 'contrary to expectations, [that] the average return *declines* with the volume of investment' (p. 475, italics in original). 'The second-stage results show sharp divergencies in the estimated returns on the different kinds of finance, with the return on new equity substantially and significantly higher than on plowback' (p. 475). Thus the results from both stages of the Brealey *et al.* estimating procedures are inconsistent with neoclassical theory. But the authors cannot accept this implication. 'Our reluctance to accept this finding stems from an unwillingness to accept the stage-one implications that companies either systematically overestimate the returns on large projects or require a lower return on them' (p. 475). But this reluctance is difficult to fathom. If managers do invest ploughback funds in projects with lower returns than their shareholders can earn elsewhere, then they are *not* using a criterion of accepting only those 'projects with positive net present values.' Moreover, the bigger the investment project is the lower will be the returns on average. Brealey *et al.*'s first-stage results confirm still further what is apparent in their second-stage results: that there is significant overinvestment out of ploughback among large companies. Brealey *et al.* dismiss the plausibility of one set of results that are inconsistent with neoclassical theory, because they are obtained from another set of results that are inconsistent with neoclassical theory. In so doing, they illustrate clearly why it is that neoclassical theory remains so immune to empirical falsification.

Geoffrey Whittington (1972, 1978) adopted a different methodology than BHMQ and thus his results for the UK are somewhat difficult to compare with theirs. By controlling for past profitability and growth he eliminates characteristics of the firm, which one expects to be related to the relative profitability of their investment. His results nevertheless indicate small but statistically significant higher returns for those UK companies which issued new equity.

The studies by BHMQ (1973), Grabowski and Mueller (1975), Hiller (1977, 1978) and Whittington (1972, 1978) indicate that different firms earn significantly different rates of return on investment. The papers by BHMQ (1970, 1973), Grabowski and Mueller (1975), Hiller (1977, 1978), and McFetridge (1978) indicate that for many firms the return on their investment was significantly below the neoclassical cost of capital, even during an era of economic prosperity like the fifties and sixties. When prosperity turned to depression in 1973, the *mean* marginal return on investment for large firms fell to zero, as companies continued to plough back cash flows and even cut dividends to do so (Brainard *et al.* 1980). These studies suggest that a substantial volume of investment occurs each year at returns significantly below the opportunity cost of capital.

Unfortunately, by first posing the question of capital market efficiency as one of differences in returns across sources of finance rather than differences across types of firms, BHMQ diverted the profession's attention away from the central issues. Do some firms overinvest? If so, what are their characteristics? While the results reviewed in this section suggest answers to these questions, more research specifically directed at answering them is clearly needed.

3.8   The Effects of Mergers

Mergers provided the quickest way to grow and the most popular avenue to diversification (Berry 1975; Scherer and Ravenscraft 1984); they are highly visible, lumpy investment decisions, whose effects on company size, growth, and profitability ought to be easy to determine. Unfortunately, they are not, and there are several reasons for this. First, many of the acquired companies are small and/or privately owned and thus do not publish income and balance sheet data. Thus, it is impossible to adjust for the acquisition's effect on the acquiring firm's profitability and size. Second, even when both companies are public, a variety of accounting conventions are used to combine the income and balance sheet data of the merging companies. Readjusting the data to make them comparable across firms is no easy task, nor is it made easier by the firms themselves. Although one expects corporate management to maintain separate income and balance sheet records of its acquisitions for at least the first few years after they occur (and indefinitely for diversification mergers), companies virtually never publish separate income and balance sheet statements for their acquisitions, which would allow one to determine how successful the acquisitions have been. Indeed, demands from security regulation and antitrust authorities for the publication of accounting data by industry or product line—the kind of data that would make monitoring the effects of diversification mergers rather easy—have been resisted most strenuously by corporate managers. These difficulties with accounting data have led many to turn to stock market data in order to evaluate merger effects. But these data have their limitations also, as will be seen below.

Merger Effects on Market Shares and Internal Growth

Mergers can increase efficiency by lowering a firm's costs, or increasing the quality of its products. Both consequences should increase the firm's market share or the market share of the unit acquired (Mueller 1986, Ch. 9). Only two studies have made direct estimates of the effects of mergers on market shares. Goldberg (1973) measured changes in market shares for 44 companies concentrated in markets with heavy advertising. He tracked the merging companies for one to eleven years after the merger but found no significant change in their market shares following the mergers.

Mueller (1985; 1986, Ch. 9) examined the market shares of companies acquired in conglomerate mergers between 1950 and 1972 and pairs of companies engaged in horizontal mergers during the same years. The changes in market shares for these firms, between 1950 and 1972, were compared with those of non-merging companies in the same industries. The companies, acquired through conglomerate mergers or involved in horizontal mergers, were found to have experienced significant losses in market shares following the mergers relative to non-merging companies. For example, while the average non-acquired company had a 1972 market share that was 88.5 per cent of its 1950 value, the average company acquired through a conglomerate merger had a 1972 market share of only 18 per cent of its 1950 value.

Where market share data are unavailable, an indirect test of whether mergers have increased efficiency can be made by seeing whether the merging companies increased their overall size relative to similar companies following the mergers. This test was conducted for merging pairs of companies in seven countries.[24] In each case a merging pair was matched to a pair of non-merging firms—of similar size to the merging pair and drawn from the same industry(ies). The growth rates of the merging and control group companies were measured over the five years preceding the merger and the three or five years (depending on data availability) after the merger. In no country did the merging firms exhibit an increase in their internal growth rates relative to the control group firms in. the years following the mergers. In Holland and the United States, there was a statistically significant relative decline in growth.

Two additional studies of mergers in the United States, Hogarty (1970b) and Lev and Mandelker (1972), observed either lower than predicted sales or slower internal growth rates for merging firms following the mergers. These findings regarding post-merger sales and growth rates are consistent with those of Goldberg and Mueller using market shares. Eleven separate studies spanning seven countries have failed to find any evidence of increased internal efficiency based on sales data. Five of the eleven have presented evidence suggesting a decline in efficiency.

Merger Effects on Profitability

Several studies of the first two merger waves in the United States exist.[25] Although severely dated, as judged by today's statistical standards, the results are sufficiently consistent across studies that one can draw, with some confidence at least, one conclusion as to the effect of these early mergers on profitability—that is, they did not lead to increases in profitability on average. Some students of this period even believe that the merging companies' profits fell following the mergers; this conclusion is somewhat remarkable, because the first two merger waves in the United States took place at a time when horizontal and vertical acquisitions were allowed. Many companies were created which had dominant market positions at that time and have remained dominant until today. It is difficult to believe that some of these mergers did not result in sufficient increases in market power to generate extra profits. However, the reductions in profits, due to losses in efficiency among the other mergers, were apparently sufficiently great to offset these gains.

The profitability of merging firms before and after mergers was compared in the seven-country international comparison cited above. No significant change in profitability was observed in the United States, and the results in Europe divided evenly between a tendency to observe slight increases in profitability (Belgium, the Federal Republic of Germany, and the United Kingdom), and a tendency to observe slight declines (France, Holland, and Sweden) (Mueller 1980, Chs. 3–8, 10). As with the results in the United States for the first two merger waves, the significance of these results for Europe arises in that a more consistent and dramatic positive effect of mergers on profitability has not been observed. Had profit increases been observed in all countries, one would still be left with the question of interpreting whether they were due to market power or efficiency increases. That horizontal mergers reduce market power seems unlikely. Thus, one must conclude that in three countries efficiency seems on average to have declined by enough to offset, or more than offset, any beneficial increases in market power from the mergers. In Belgium, West Germany and the United Kingdom, the efficiency losses of some firms following the mergers, if there were any, were on average smaller, or no greater, than the gains in market power for the other merging firms in the sample. Here, the results of the previous section should be recalled: if mergers improve the efficiency of the merger partners, their costs fall and their sales should expand relative to other firms. In none of the three countries in which there is evidence of an increase in profitability following the mergers, is there evidence of a relative increase in sales. Thus, the increases in profitability in these countries do not appear to be due predominately to efficiency gains.

The most exhaustive study, to date, of merger effects on profitability is by David Ravenscraft and F. M. Scherer (1986). They gathered data on roughly 6,000 lines of business acquired between 1950 and 1977. Their results indicate no improvement in the profit-to-assets ratios of the acquired companies, when assets are measured at pre-acquisition book values, and significant declines in returns when acquired assets are restated as the purchase price of the acquired company. Ravenscraft and Scherer find that acquired companies are more profitable than otherwise similar non-acquired firms, and that their profitability declines steadily after they are acquired.

Geoffrey Meeks's study (1977) also deserves special attention because of the number of mergers studied (more than 1000) and the care he took to adjust the basic accounting data to make the observations comparable. Meeks concluded that mergers in the United Kingdom have resulted, on average, in modest *declines* in profitability.

Similar to Meeks's study in terms of labour input, but different in methodology, are the case studies of individual mergers in the United Kingdom by Cowling and his associates (1980). These studies demonstrate how mergers can increase efficiency and they develop a methodology for testing this fact. But no consistent pattern regarding changes in efficiency is apparent in the mergers in these group studies: if mergers improve the operating performance of the merging companies, it is not readily apparent from the evidence available in studies using accounting data.

Merger Effects on Shareholder Returns

A plethora of studies has appeared in the last two decades, which measure the effects of mergers as the deviation of a company's returns from those predicted by the CAPM around a merger's announcement

Table 3.2 Returns to Acquiring and Acquired Firms' Shareholders

Study	Time Period (Country)	Returns Prior to Merger Announcement, Acquiring Firm	Returns in Announcement Day (d), Month (m), Year (y), Acquiring Firm	Post-Merger Returns in Days (d), Months (m), Years (y) after Merger, Acquiring Firms	Acquired Firms' Returns	Sample	Control Group
Hogarty (1970b)	1953–64 (USA)			(y varies from +1 to +11)		43 nonconglomerates engaged in heavy merger activity	Firms in acquiring company's base industry
Lev and Mandelker (1972)	1952–63 (USA)	.135^b(y = -5,-1)	.083(y = 0)	-.05(y = +1 to +5)		69 firms making large acquisitions	Non-merging firms matched by industry and size
Halpern (1973)	1950–65 (USA)		.063(m = -7,0)^e		.304(m = -7 to 0)^e	78 mergers by nonconglomerates	Market portfolio
Mandelker (1974)	1941–63 (USA)	.048^b(m = -34,-1)	.003^b(m = 0,6)	-.015^b(m = 7,46)	.120*	241 large mergers	Market portfolio
Ellert (1976)	1950–72 (USA)	.233*(m = -100 to -1)^c	-.018*^{d}	-.016(m = +1,48)		205 mergers challenged by Justice Department or FTC between 1950 and 1972	Market portfolio
Franks, Broyles, Hecht (1977)	1955–72 (UK)	-.048(m = -40,-1)	.001(m = 0)	-.014(m = 1,2)	.179	70 mergers by breweries and distilleries	Market portfolio
Dodd & Ruback (1977)	1958–78 (USA)	.117*(m = -60,-1)	.028(m = 0)	-.059^b(m = 1,60)	.206*	136 tender offers	Market portfolio
Kummer & Hoffmeister (1978)	1956–74 (USA)	.170^b(m = -40,-1)	.052^b(m = 0)	.006^b(m = 1,20)	.187*	88 cash tender offers	Market portfolio
Langetieg (1978)	1929–69 (USA)	.136*(m = -64 to -1)	-.028(m = 0 to +5)	-.262(m = +7 to 78)	.128*	149 mergers of all kinds	Market portfolio and industry index
Bradley (1980)	1962–77 (USA)		.04*(d = 0,5)	.01^b(d = 6,40)	.36*-.49*	161 tender offers	Market portfolio
Dodd (1980)	1971–7 (USA)		-.011(d = -1,0)	-.072*(d = -10,140)^f	.340*	71 mergers	Market portfolio
Kumps & Wtterwulghe (1980)	1962–74 (Belgium)		-.047(y = 0)	-.014(y = 1,3)		26 mergers of all kinds	26 non-merging firms matched by industry

Study	Period (Country)					Sample	Control group
Jenny & Weber (1980)	1962–72 (France)		$.116^*(y = 0)$	$-.095^b(y = 1,3)$		43 mergers of all kinds	43 non-merging firms matched by size and industry
Ryden & Edberg (1980)	1962–76 (Sweden)		$-.040(y = 0)$	$.011^b(y = 1,3)$		23 mergers of all kinds	23 non-merging firms
Cosh, Hughes & Singh (1980)	1967–9 (UK)	$-.069^*(y = -5,-1)$	$.187^*(y = +1)$	$-.169^b(y = 1,5)$		63 mergers of all kinds	63 non-merging firms matched by size and industry
Mueller (1980)	1962–72 (USA)		$.088^*(y = 0)$	$-.084^b(y = 1,3)$		219 mergers of all kinds	219 non-merging firms matched by size and industry
Firth (1980)	1969–75 (UK)	$.014^b(m = -480, -1)$	$-.063(m = 0)$	$.001^b(m = 1,36)$	.363	434 mergers of all kinds	Market portfolio
Asquith (1983)	1962–76 (USA)	$.132^b(d = -480, -1)$	$.002(m = 0)$	$-.072^*(d = 1,240)$	$.133^*$	196 mergers of all kinds	Market portfolio
Asquith, Bruner, & Mullins, Jr. (1983)	1963–79 (USA)		$.028^*(m = 0)$		$.175^*$	214 early mergers by firms beginning merger programs after 1963	Market portfolio
Bradley, Desai, & Kim (1983)	1962–80 (USA)		$.024^*(m = 0)$		$.318^*$	161 successful tender offers	Market portfolio
Malatesta (1983)	1969–74 (USA)	$.043^*(m = -60, -1)$	$.009(m = 0)$	$-.079^*(m = 1,12)$	$.168^*$	256 mergers of all kinds	Market portfolio
Magenheim & Mueller (forthcoming)	1976–81 (USA)	$.184^*(m = -24, -4)$	$-.003(m = 0)$	$-.422(m = -3,36)$		78 mergers of all kinds	Market portfolio

Notes: Returns are measured as the difference between merging companies' returns and control group returns in all cases. In those studies in which the data were centred around the date of final consummation, the series were displaced backwards by 6 months to allow for the fact that announcements generally precede mergers by 6 months.

[a] Post-merger returns include gains (losses) in announcement day (d), month (m), or year (y) whenever possible.

[b] Reported data do not allow calculation of statistical significance.

[c] Month 0, in the Ellert study, is the month in which a complaint is filed.

[d] Announcement of merger, in the Ellert study, is measured as period from judicial complaint through settlement.

[e] Halpern's figures for acquiring firms are for the largest of two companies involved in a merger. Acquired firms' figures are for the smallest of the two merging firms.

[f] Dodd reports figure for 10 days before announcement until 10 days after merger is approved. Calculation is based on assumption that there are, on average, 6 months (26 weeks times 5 working days) between a merger's announcement and its approval.

date.[26] Table 3.2 summarises the rate of return evidence from 22 of these studies, and—in order to facilitate comparisons—the returns for both acquiring and acquired firms have been computed as the differences between merging company returns and control group returns. Thus, for example, the returns for the 43 non-conglomerate companies that engaged in heavy merger activity over the 1953–64 period, which Hogarty (1970b) studied, average 5 percentage points lower than the industries in which they were based.

The easiest results to interpret are those for the acquired firms: the returns on their shares rise sharply at the time the mergers are announced; occasionally this rise commences one or two months prior to announcement. The average time span between announcement and completion of the merger is six months, and when the merger is completed the acquired firm disappears. The gains to acquired firm shareholders over this short period are positive and large. The median gain for the studies surveyed in Table 3.2 is 0.187.

More difficult to interpret are the results for the acquiring firms—in part, this difficulty arises because the acquiring firms do not disappear when the merger is completed. Thus, the question arises with respect to acquiring firms as to what period of time is appropriate to measure the *effects* of the mergers as reflected in shareholder returns. Table 3.2 divides the shareholder returns' results for acquiring firms into three time periods: a period prior to the merger, ending in the month or year before the announcement, the period immediately surrounding the merger or its announcement, and a post-merger period. From this array, a fairly uniform pattern actually does emerge across the several studies.

A sustained and substantial rise in the returns on the acquiring companies' shares occurs prior to the mergers. The immediate reaction of the market to the mergers is mixed, and sets off a steady decline in returns following the mergers. This pattern re-occurs with some exceptions throughout the studies. Eleven of the twelve studies in Table 3.2 that report on the period prior to the mergers found positive, abnormal returns to acquiring firm shareholders. The one exception is the Franks *et al.* (1977) study of UK brewers and distillers, but even they found that the brewing and distilling industry from which their entire sample was drawn was earning above normal returns in the pre-merger period. The remaining two studies and all eight US studies found positive acquiring firms' returns over long intervals preceding the mergers. Moreover, the magnitudes of the increases in abnormal returns are substantial. The median increase is 0.124.

In contrast, the median increase in shareholder returns around the time of the merger is only 0.009. The mergers come during a long time span in which acquiring firm shareholders are doing quite well, but the mergers themselves do not result in much of an improvement in shareholder returns. Following the mergers, a majority of the studies (14 out of 19) report declines in returns. The median post-merger decline is -0.05.

The main issue, of course, is what the total effect upon acquiring firm shareholders has been. This question is difficult to answer for two reasons: first, since the mergers occur during (or more accurately at the end of) a long period of return increases, it is not clear whether those increases observed at the time of the mergers reflect the market's response to the mergers, or the mere continuance of the existing trend; Second, while the decline in returns following the mergers does appear to have been precipitated by them, it is not evident how long after the mergers one must track them to measure their full effect. Several studies observed continuous declines in acquiring company returns throughout the entire post-merger period under investigation, e.g. Mandelker (1974), Dodd and Ruback (1977), Langetieg (1978), Jenny and Weber (1980), Cosh *et al.* (1980), and Mueller (1980). Given the consistency of this pattern, and the ambiguity of any increases observed coincident with the mergers, it would be rash to judge the anticipated effects of the mergers on the basis of evidence of returns *only* at the time of the merger. This reasoning suggests that a prudent estimate of the market's expectation of the effects of mergers on acquiring firms should be formed by adding the returns figures for the announcement period (month, year) to those for the post-merger period, omitting those studies (Halpern 1973; Asquith *et al.* 1983; Bradley *et al.* 1983) which did not report post-merger returns, as well as those reporting just a couple of months after the merger announcements (Bradley 1980; Franks *et al.* 1977). Of the remaining 17 studies, 12 have negative returns to acquiring firm shareholders over the combined announcement period and post-merger interval. The median of these returns is -0.034.

An Interpretation

The motives for mergers are many, and no single explanation can explain all. An eclectic posture, as Steiner (1975, pp. 180–4) adopts, is the most prudent. Yet, the pattern of results observed above is broadly consistent with the view that managers undertake acquisitions to maintain or increase the site of their firms, in spite of incurring transaction costs and other inefficiencies that lower company returns. To acquire another firm, a cash offer for shares, and/or an exchange of stock or debt, must be made. The most propitious time to undertake an acquisiton is thus when one's cash flow and/or stock price is abnormally high. The timing of acquisitions at the end of sustained periods of abnormal positive returns for the acquiring firms is, thus, fully consistent with the hypothesis that mergers occur not out of the recognition of some synergy between acquirer and acquiree—since such recognition can occur presumably at any time—but out of enhanced capacity of firms to expand at certain points in time.

The fact that the mergers do not bring about synergistic gains is indicated by the negative returns observed in 12 of the 17 studies that report both announcement period and post-merger returns. Although these losses to acquiring firm shareholders are small, in percentage terms, this does not diminish their economic importance for either the theory of the firm or public policy. If management persists in undertaking acquisitions with negative mean returns, then some motive other than stockholder welfare must be driving their decisions.

If it is assumed that the combined market values of the acquiring and acquired companies reflect the market's estimation of the future returns of the combined enterprise, then, for public policy purposes, the relevant question is whether the combined impact of the mergers on share returns is positive or negative. To make this calculation, one must take into account the different relative sizes of the acquiring and acquired firms. Unfortunately, none of the studies report these data even as averages, and only a couple attempt the calculation themselves (e.g., Halpern 1973; Firth 1980). In an earlier study (Mueller 1980), it was found that acquiring companies averaged ten times the size of acquirees. Thus, to compare acquiring company returns with those of their acquirees, the former would have to be scaled by a factor of 10. This would make the median acquiring firm return -0.34 (in Table 3.2), which roughly doubles the positive 0.187 median return of the acquired company shareholders. While such a calculation is admittedly rough, it does serve to highlight the fact that too much weight should not be given to the large positive returns of the acquired firms in judging the total effects of the mergers. The effect of the mergers on acquired firm returns is certain: once the merger goes through, it is the premium above pre-merger market price. Since the gain is concentrated in a period of a few months, it is easy to measure and therefore positive and significant. In contrast, the effect of the mergers on the acquiring companies' share prices reflects the market's appraisal of the future impact of the merger. When the market's reaction is drawn out over a long period of time, and the acquired firm is small relative to the acquirer, the measured effect on the acquiring firm's shareholders is essentially small and difficult to disentangle from other events. This problem is particularly likely when, as seems to be the case, the mergers come upon an independent, upward trend in acquiring firm returns.

3.9 Conclusion

The pattern of evolution for the individual corporation, which has been described in broad outline, parallels the development pattern of corporate capitalism over the past century—at least within the United Kingdom and the United States. Leslie Hannah for the UK (1976) and Alfred D. Chandler, Jr., for the USA (1962) both describe the pattern of corporate development in their respective countries (since 1850) in terms of stages or phases of development that parallel the stages of a firm's development described above.

Today, the United States, the United Kingdom, their Anglo-Saxon sisters (Australia, New Zealand and Canada) and the industrialised countries of Western Europe are all in a mature and stagnant stage of economic development: unemployment is high, and productivity gains are low; one market after another is lost to Asian competition; pessimism regarding the economic future abounds.

Are these passing phases in capitalism's development, as perhaps the thirties was, to be followed by a new burst of growth and development, or are they symptomatic of more fundamental problems inherent in modern, managerial capitalism? If the latter is the case, does the material of this chapter shed light on the nature of these problems and any possible remedies?

Definitive answers to these questions are obviously impossible to give. The present author believes that the characteristics of managerial capitalism described above do provide some insight to what has been happening. When Schumpeter first outlined the salient characteristics of capitalism, at the beginning of the twentieth century, there was but one way to construct a 'private kingdom'. One had to build it from the bottom up. This option still exists today, but now there is a second route to the top of a corporate empire: climb the hierarchical ladder within an existing giant. Those who succeed in reaching the top of a giant corporate hierarchy command an organisation which they could never hope to build in their own lifetime. Many of those who strove, a century ago, to build their own businesses would strive today to get ahead in businesses others have built, or, increasingly, to take over an ongoing enterprise.

A century ago, most great fortunes were made by those who founded and built the first generation of corporate giants. But even then there was opportunity for some to get ahead simply by helping to put the great trusts together. Both the Mellons and the Carnegies grew wealthy during the first merger movement. Since the first great merger movement, promoters' profits have received a place of prominence in any list of causes for mergers (Stigler 1950; Markham 1955)—and they remain an important contributing factor. Today, an industry of investment bankers, consultants and lawyers exists to facilitate and encourage the merger process.

Increases of 50 per cent in the market values of target firms are commonplace today; 100 per cent premia are not rare. Substantial gains are possible and fortunes can and are made overnight. The development of the modern stock, bond, commodity and foreign exchange markets has given to those with a penchant for plunging—alternative options for making a quick fortune. Risk taking today often consists of speculation on changes in asset values rather than on one's ability to create asset value. It may be a coincidence that the two Western nations with the most highly developed capital markets and the most active markets for corporate control have had the slowest economic growth since World War II. But this chapter has reviewed evidence suggesting why these phenomena may be causally related; if they are, then fundamental reforms will be needed to revitalise capitalism and stimulate the birth and growth of new firms, as well as the sustainment of mature ones.

Notes

* This essay contains much material originally published in D. C. Mueller *The Corporation: Growth, Diversification and Mergers*, Chur, Harwood Academic Publishers, 1987. For a more complete discussion of topics, this monograph should be consulted. Thanks are due to the publisher for permission to reprint this material. Thanks are also due the Thyssen Foundation of West Germany for financial support in writing the essay, and Paul Geroski, Alexis Jacquemin and Steven Klepper for helpful comments on the original manuscript.

1. A good example of how the existence of even modest rents can deter incumbent firms from innovating (or imitating) is the UK dry-cleaning industry after World War II (Shaw 1973).
2. For surveys of this literature, see Hamberg (1966), Mueller and Tilton (1969), Kamien and Schwartz (1982, pp. 64–70) and Scherer (1980, pp. 415–18).
3. The innovations need not accompany the firm's founding. Haloid was a small, fifty-year-old company when it acquired the rights to the Carlson patent, which led to its rebirth as Xerox. Texas Instruments moved into transistors.
4. As so often is the case, mergers can provide an exception to the rule. Litton Industries was started in 1953 by a group of managers, who left Ford to build a company via acquisitions. If innovation is involved in the growth of Litton, it would seem to be in the management's ability to finance one merger after another without the aid of other innovations—a feat successfully accomplished until the conglomerate merger bubble broke at the end of the sixties. The story of Litton's rise is recounted by Harris (1958), Rieser (1963), Seligman and Wise (1966), and *Business Week* (16 April, 1966). The decline is described in Rukeyser (1968), *Business Week* (27 January, 1968), and *Forbes* (15 February, 1968 and 1 December, 1969).

5. Electric shavers after 1935, jet propelled engines after 1951, fluorescent lamps after 1942, freezers after 1949, outboard motors after 1939, penicillin after 1949, phonograph records after 1918, tyres after 1914, and zippers after 1926. (See Klepper and Graddy 1984, Table 4.)

6. Mansfield *et al.* (1971, pp. 173–81; Abernathy (1978, Ch. 4); Buzzell and Nourse (1966); Harvey (1968); Utterback (1979).

7. Schumpeter's early description of economic development has also inspired Nelson and Winter's recent evolutionary theory (1982). For a recent attempt to model the Schumpeterian process rigorously, see Reinganum (1985).

8. Harvey (1968); Klein (1977); Abernathy (1978); Gort and Klepper (1982); Klepper and Graddy (1984).

9. Shepherd (1975, p. 309, Table B.2). A greater attrition of market positions is apparent between 1910 and 1935 (see p. 308, Table B.1), but Shepherd is surely correct in his conjecture that the market shares of 1910 were artificially high, having been brought about by the great trust-creating merger wave in the preceding two decades. In 1948, by way of contrast, there had been no appreciable merger activity for 19 years.

10. The hypothesis that dominant firms do decline has, as its intellectual antecedent, the classic paper by Worcester (1957) and, as its factual bellwether, United States Steel Corporation. For a critical reappraisal, see Geroski (1985).

11. See Imel and Helmberger (1971); Gale (1972); Shepherd (1972, 1975); Gale and Branch (1982); Ravenscraft (1983); Smirlock, Gilligan and Marshall (1984); and Mueller (1985b).

12. On Europe, see Hughes and Singh (1980), Channon (1973), Pavan (1972), Gorecki (1975) and Dyas and Thanheiser (1976); on the United States, see Berry (1975) and Scherer and Ravenscraft (1984).

13. For a comparison of the M- and U-forms, and a discussion of their relative merits, see Chandler (1962, 1977), Williamson (1970, 1975, 1979, 1981), Caves (1980), Teece (1988) and Chapter 2 in this volume.

14. On the differing backgrounds of chief executives, see Beam (1979) and Sussman (1979).

15. See references, Note 13.

16. Williamson notes that large corporations may have difficulties coming up with important innovations (1975, pp. 184–87).

17. See studies of the United States by Gort (1962) and Berry (1975), of Canada by Caves *et al.* (1980) and of the United Kingdom by Hassid (1975, 1977).

18. Markham (1973, p. 160) cites Gilbert (1971) in further support of the multiple interpretation to the profitability–diversification correlation.

19. See discussions in Scherer (1980, pp. 104–8) and Jacquemin and deJong (1977, pp. 90–94, 114–17).

20. Prais (1981, p. 97) discusses why the relationship should hold and shows size and profit variability to be negatively related in a hyperbolic fashion using data for the United States from Stekler (1963) and for the United Kingdom from Whittington (1971). See also, for the United States, Winn (1977); for the United Kingdom, Singh and Whittington (1968), Samuels and Smyth (1968); for France, Morvan (1972); and for large European and Japanese firms, Jacquemin and Saëz (1976). An exception to this general finding is Smyth, Boyes and Pesau (1975).

21. See Levy and Sarnat (1970), Smith (1970) and Azzi (1978). The recent work of Roll (1977) and Levy (1983) demonstrates that the optimally diversified portfolio should contain *negative* positions in some shares. No firm can make negative investments in real assets.

22. See Caves and Yamey (1971) and, with respect to diversifying mergers, Amihud and Lev (1982).
23. BHMQ regress *changes* in profits on investment and thus do estimate a marginal return on total capital, albeit, for large investments, their estimates may also contain inframarginal rents. Should the latter occur, their estimates for a given firm would exceed the true marginal returns. Thus, if the BHMQ-type estimates are below the neoclassical cost of capital—as they are in the BHMQ, Grabowski and Mueller, and McFetridge studies—accurately measured marginal returns must *a fortiori* also be lower.
24. The countries were: Belgium, the Federal Republic of Germany, France, the Netherlands, Sweden, the United Kingdom and the United States.
25. See the surveys by Markham (1955), Nelson (1959), Reid (1968), Eis (1969) and Hogarty (1970a), and references therein.
26. See Sharpe (1964), Lintner (1965) and, for applications of the procedure to mergers, Halpern (1973) and Mandelker (1974). See Chiplin and Wright (1987) for a review of studies.

4

Agency Costs of Internal Organisation

STEVE THOMPSON

4.1 Introduction

An agency relationship occurs where one party (the principal) rewards another (the agent) for taking actions on his/her behalf. The essence of their relationship is that it involves the delegation of (at least some) responsibility for decision making to the agent. In practice, the prevalence of uncertainty means that many (perhaps even most) economic relations involve an agency element. For example, it was noted above (pp. 7–8) that problems of informational asymmetry and opportunism influence the costs of exchange and make it prohibitively difficult to write fully specified contracts. Most incomplete supply contracts give the supplier some discretion in interpreting his/her role, at least over the interval between renegotiations.

The agency theory approach is part of a wider—'New Institutional'[1]—interest in contracting as the determinant of economic organisational forms. This development also embraces the transactions cost-minimisation framework of Williamson (1975) and the property rights theories (see Furubotn and Pejovich 1972). Indeed, all the current strands in 'New Institutional' economics share an important ancestor in Coase's (1937) contractual view of the firm. They differ primarily in emphasis, and should be seen as complementary rather than rivalrous.

It is seen in Chapters 2 and 10 of this volume that Williamson has sought to identify the sources of transaction costs and to compare the properties of differing organisation types in reducing them. The work of the *property rights school* (see Alchian and Demsetz 1972, Alchian 1984) has placed importance upon the distribution of the bundle of resource restrictions in determining the costs of co-operation between the owners of property rights. The distinctive focus of agency theory, by contrast, is on the specific role of contractual provisions in modifying behaviour. It emphasises the importance of contract design in ensuring that agent discretion is exercised in the interest of the principal. More specifically, it is concerned with the choice of contractual—i.e. institutional—forms which minimise the overall costs of the agency relationship.

This chapter aims to review the major contributions of agency theory relevant to a comparison of internal and market organisation of activities. Following an introduction to some basic concepts of agency theory, and a study of its scope, there is a more detailed analysis of the costs arising from a crucial agency relationship in modern corporations—that between the firm's senior managers and its shareholders. The influential model of Jensen and Meckling (1976)—which has been the starting point for a number of subsequent analyses—is examined in some depth.

The author then turns to the devices which operate to control managerial discretion: the roles of hierarchy and the managerial compensation contract, and the importance of markets—both managerial and corporate control—in disciplining executive behaviour. Finally, by examining control further down the organisational hierarchy and considering the corporate headquarters/divisional management relationship in an agency context, he considers some cases where agency costs are apparently lowered by contracting *outside* the internal hierarchy.

4.2   Principals, Agents and Agency Costs

Agency costs occur because contracts are costly to write and enforce. They include, after Fama and Jensen (1983a):

> [T]he costs of structuring, monitoring and bonding a set of contracts among agents with conflicting interests, plus the residual loss incurred because the cost of full enforcement of contracts exceeds the benefits. (p. 327).

While some categories of agency cost are bourne disproportionately by one party or another—for example, monitoring costs are usually met by the principal and bonding expenditures by the agent—their sum falls upon the relationship as a whole. This combined cost, externality or third-party effects aside, must be subtracted from the potential benefits made available to the parties by their economic association. It follows that all parties have a potential interest in finding the contractual solution which minimises agency costs.

As noted above, since Coase (1937) it has been possible to view the firm as a nexus of contracts involving factor supply. The structuring of the contractual relations determines the firm's organisational form. From an agency perspective, the survival of any particular organisational type in a competitive environment indicates its relative success in economising on agency costs. (Jensen 1983). As Jensen and Smith (1985) explain:

> Since most goods and services can be produced by any form of organization, different organizational forms compete for survival in any activity just as different species compete for survival in nature. . . . Absent fiat, the form of organizations that survives in an activity, is the one that can deliver the product demanded by consumers at the lowest price while covering costs. (p. 97).

In a complex organisational form there may be many hierarchical layers, each containing individuals who function as principals in their dealings with subordinates and as agents to their superiors in the hierarchy. However, some relations have been singled out to describe broad organisational types. For example, the relationship between the firm's senior executives and the suppliers of its equity capital—who normally have prior claim to any residual surplus—is particularly important. Certain generally recognised types of firm—the sole proprietorship, the partnership, the labour-managed firm, the modern corporation, etc.—may be distinguished primarily by the implications of their different restrictions on the saleability of residual claims (Fama and Jensen 1983a, b).

4.3   The Scope of Agency Theory

Principal–agent difficulties are a subset of a larger category of contractual problems which arise where informational asymmetries are present. For example, whenever the behaviour of at least one party to a contract is unobservable *ex post*, and yet influences pay-offs to both parties, there is always the potential for that behaviour to be modified to the detriment of the other's welfare. This is the classic 'moral hazard' insurance problem (Arrow 1963). However, opportunism is not restricted to the post-contractual stage. Where there is an *ex-ante* information asymmetry, the better informed party can utilise this in selectively enjoining contracts— the 'adverse selection' problem of insurance markets (Arrow 1963).[2] Some relationships may embody even elements of pre- and post-contractual opportunism. For example, where parties to a continuing relationship make specific investments in skills, etc., the process of contract renewal may become characterised by opportunistic threats of 'hold-outs', etc. (Barney and Ouchi 1986, Klein, Crawford and Alchian 1978).

While any economic definition of an agent's role would be considerably wider than a purely legal one (Ricketts 1987, p. 116), the analysis loses focus if it is applied to all situations involving information asymmetries. In the present context the term 'agency' is reserved for those situations where an agent is directly remunerated for assisting a principal. These include such relations as those involving shareholders and managers (Fama and Jensen 1983a, b), clients and their professional advisers (Watts and Zimmerman 1983), employers and employees (Harris and Raviv 1978) and landowners and sharecroppers (Shaban 1987). These contracts tend to be of an enduring—or at least recurrent—nature. However, more ephemeral transactions also bear elements of agency: for example, a cab driver exercises discretion, as he uses his specific driving skills and route knowledge, in the interests of the passenger.

Following Jensen (1983), it may be useful to identify two distinct strands in the agency literature. The first, which he terms *principal–agency theory*, has followed the lead of Spence and Zeckhauser (1971), Ross (1973) and Mirlees (1976) in seeking to specify formal mathematical models of contract design. Typically, these start by making general assumptions on the preference structure of the parties, the nature of uncertainty present and the informational distribution between the parties. Then, they describe that optimal contract which maximises the welfare of the principal whilst securing the assent of the agent by leaving him/her at least as well off in the relationship as outside it.

The second approach, or so-called *positive theory* of *agency*, tends to be less formal and to rely more upon *ad hoc* reasoning. Following, in particular, the contribution of Jensen and Meckling (1976), this *positive theory* tends to concentrate on the ways in which agency cost minimisation shapes observable contractual relationships. This typically involves some sacrifice of analytical rigour to allow the analysis to handle the complexities of real organisational and financial arrangements.

The rest of this chapter, because of its primary interest in the internal organisation of modern corporations, will be largely concerned with contributions from the *positive* or applied side of the agency literature. Nevertheless, it must be recognised that both approaches are equally valid and mutually supportive.[3]

4.4   Owner–Manager Conflict

As early as 1932, Berle and Means showed that shareholdings in large US corporations had become so widely dispersed that effective control lay with the management. This observation—although one recently questioned from different perspectives by Fama and Jensen (1983a) and by Leech (1987)— stimulated a whole generation of managerial theories (Baumol 1959, Marris 1964, Williamson 1964, Galbraith 1967, etc.), each of which set out an alternative to shareholder wealth maximation. In turn, the managerial models have given rise to many empirical attempts to isolate and quantify the impact of control type on firm conduct and performance. However, the large body of evidence which has been generated gives no clear guide in selecting a preferred alternative from the set of managerial theories offered. Indeed, the empirical evidence provides, at best, only very limited support for the general managerialist proposition that, *ceteris paribus*, profitability should be higher in owner-controlled companies.[4]

The disappointing absence of consensus in the empirical literature has been variously ascribed to difficulties in deriving unambiguously testable hypotheses from the managerial theories and to problems of measurement and omitted variables in the data sets employed.[5] However, another weakness of the managerial theories—particularly when viewed as long-run models—is the assumption of a 'passive' acceptance (Edwards 1987) by shareholders and managers of an inefficient outcome. The departure from profit maximisation is viewed as being Pareto-inefficient, but apparently none of the affected parties look for any institutional improvement which, with suitable compensating payments, could raise the wellbeing of all.

O.E. Williamson, himself one of the principal managerial theorists, recognised this deficiency. Williamson (1970, 1971) suggested that part of the reason for the reorganisation of large firms from unitary form to multidivisional form—see the chapters by Cable (Ch. 2), Buck (Ch. 6), Stephen and Thompson (Ch. 9), in this book—was to curb the pursuit of managerial goals. Under an M-form arrangement, the elite staff have little incentive to sanction inessential expenditures at the divisional level, whilst the divisions are run by managers remunerated according to divisional performance. This entails, according to Williamson, the return of the M-form to behaviour closer to profit maximisation—as noted by Cable on page 17.

The principal–agent approach is not in conflict with this stress on organisational structure. It does emphasise, however, the variety of devices—including hierarchy itself—which may be used to reconcile the behaviour of managers (and others in the firm) with the interests of equity owners.

Most recent contributions on agency costs within the firm have drawn substantially on the insights of Jensen and Meckling (1976). They consider the case of a firm which is 100 per cent owned by its single controlling manager. The analysis centres on the impact on the manager's wealth and utility of the sale of some proportion of the equity to outsiders. (The resulting diversification benefits to the owner, together with any loss of utility associated with ownership *per se*, are ignored.) For simplicity, the model assumes no debt, no taxes and no financial claims other than voting equity.

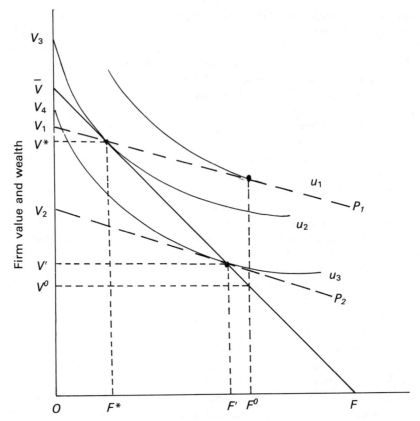

Figure 4.1 The Basic Jensen–Meckling Model

Some activities of the firm provide direct utility to the owner–manager as well as contributing to the firm's income stream. If X is a vector of such activities, providing income to the firm $P(X)$ at cost $C(X)$, then the net benefit to the firm is given by:

$$B(X) = P(X) - C(X)$$

If the impact of X on managerial utility is ignored, the optimum vector of activities, X^*, is given by:

$$\frac{dB(X^*)}{dX^*} = \frac{dP(X^*)}{dX^*} - \frac{dC(X^*)}{dX^*} = 0$$

However, if the manager indulges his tastes for preferred activities then he chooses $X \geqq X^*$, with $F \equiv B(X^*) - B(X)$ giving the dollar cost (F) of this choice to the firm.

When costs and benefits are treated in present value terms, the 100 per cent owner faces the budget constraint $\bar{V}F$ in Figure 4.1. The position of $\bar{V}F$ depends on the size of the firm and the management wage contract—both assumed to be given. Its slope is -1, since the additional net cost of any non-pecuniary benefits produces a corresponding reduction in the value of the firm. The utility-maximising owner–manager will adopt an equilibrium such as F^*V^*, in which $\bar{V}V^*$ wealth is sacrificed to obtain non-pecuniary benefits F^*.

Now consider the sales of equity to an outsider with the former owner remaining as manager. If the outsider took 100% of the equity and if he consumes managerial perquisites to F^*, at zero monitoring costs, the firm value of V^* could be realised. However, if there are costs to restraining the managers, the level of F will rise and the equity price will fall. For example, suppose the manager sells a fraction $(1-\alpha)$ of the equity for $(1-\alpha)V^*$: this will shift the manager's budget constraint to V_1P_1 with slope of $-\alpha$. In the absence of action from the new shareholders, the manager's equilibrium would shift to $V^\circ F^\circ$.

Jensen and Meckling show that with full anticipation by potential equity buyers, the outsiders will be prepared to pay only $(1-\alpha)$ times the post-sale value of the firm. This entails that the whole of the fall in value is borne by the owner. In Figure 4.1 this is shown by the tangency of U_3 and V_2P_2 occurring along $\bar{V}F$.

In view of the implied fall in firm value $(\bar{V}V^1)$ the owner will presumably sell only if diversification or liquidity benefits merit it. However, Jensen and Meckling show that control devices—including monitoring and bonding—which reduce managerial discretion may also raise the value of the firm. Let B, in Figure 4.2, represent the corresponding equilibrium in Figure 4.1 and let monitoring expenditure, M, reduce F—albeit at a declining rate—i.e. for $F = F(M, \alpha)$ assume $\delta F/\delta M < 0$ and $\delta^2 F/\delta M^2 > 0$. If these expenditures generate a new budget constraint BCE, the spending of M (i.e. $D-C$) raises the value of the firm from V' to V''.

To summarise, the Jensen–Meckling model shows:

(i)   that the full anticipation of post-sale managerial opportunism leads to the seller bearing its cost *ex ante*;

(ii) that control devices which limit such managerial scope will be worthwhile until their marginal cost equals their marginal benefit; and

(iii) that maximisation, of the joint pay-off to buyers and seller requires minimising the sum of control costs and residual loss.

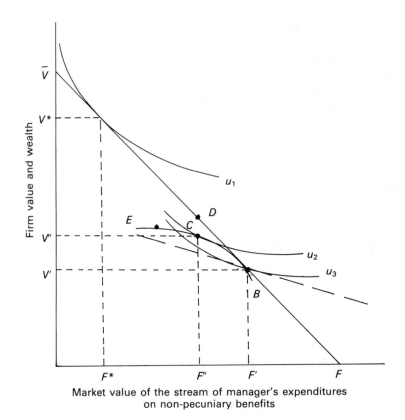

Figure 4.2 The Jensen–Meckling Model with Control Devices

At the same time, however, the basic Jensen–Meckling model assumes away a number of important elements in owner–manager relations:

(i)   the costs of monitoring and disciplining managers depend not merely upon α but on the distribution of outside voting equity (Cubbin and Leech 1983);

(ii) expressing everything in current value terms assumes away uncertainty aspects—including project riskiness;

(iii) when debt is included as an alternative source of finance, the risk of projects selected can produce wealth transfers between debt and equity owners.

Furthermore, the typical modern corporation has already achieved a transfer of equity to a dispersed set of outsider owners. The relevant agency cost issues concern the continuing relationship between these shareholders and the firm's management, which might or might not hold a substantial equity interest.

4.5   The Control of Managerial Behaviour

In formal terms—as legally adopted in its articles of association—a public limited company is controlled by the votes of its shareholders. However, the dispersed nature of shareholdings in most corporations creates the familiar 'public good' problem of free riding: each individual owner–voter has little incentive to engage in costly information-gathering and voting when he or she only stands to benefit by a minute fraction of the returns to better corporate governance. In consequence, the shareholder's meeting is widely considered to be an ineffective control device under normal circumstances (Stiglitz 1985). At the same time, however, it remains the ultimate source of authority over the firm and serves to legitimise the other control devices. These are considered in turn.

Hierarchical Monitoring

The very creation of a hierarchy—or multi-level principal–agent problem— normally involves the establishment of some kind of monitoring system. Fama and Jensen (1983a) suggest that the existence of specific knowledge—which they define as knowledge which is costly to transfer across agents located at different places within an organisation—requires delegation of decision making. However, to reduce the scope for agents to take actions which conflict with organisational goals, they suggest that delegation is usually limited to *decision management*—that is, the initiation and implementation of decisions. The superior hierarchical layer retains the function of *decision control*—that is, the ratification and monitoring of lower level decisions. This argument closely parallel's Williamson's (1975) analysis of decentralisation to divisional management as a device to prevent control loss—see Chapters 1 and 2 in this volume.

Fama and Jensen (1983a, b) point out that separating decision control from decision management introduces a system of 'checks and balances' into the hierarchy. In particular, the ratification of decisions should be made by those with no direct involvement. For example, the function of outside (i.e. non-executive) directors on a board of management is to assist in making unbiased decisions. In some contentious areas of decision making— for example, on the executive compensation committee—the outsiders may have a dominant position. However, whilst outside directors may check any 'excessive' managerial consumption of perquisites (Brickley and James 1987) and represent general shareholder interest, their lack of specific information—and limited incentive to acquire it—may reduce their overall effectiveness.[6] This probably accounts for the lack of statistical evidence linking outside directors and firm performance (e.g. in Steer and Cable 1978).

Management Remuneration

Agency theory suggests that incentive packages for managers are not simply a 'tax-efficient vehicle for delivering pay' (Lambert and Larcker 1985b) but they fulfil a function in reducing the costs of managerial behaviour. In particular, a suitable incentive arrangement can encourage effort levels and attitudes to risk and time horizons which benefit shareholders. Three basic types of compensation have been identified: fixed annual salaries; market-based payment schemes; and accounting-based payment schemes. These are examined below.

Fixed annual salaries may still involve an incentive element since each renegotiation allows the board to give *ex-post* rewards for performance. Furthermore, annual salary improvements may be particularly important in motivating younger managers at relatively lowly positions in the firm, although Jensen and Smith (1985) point out that salary adjustments may become relatively unimportant for those nearing retirement.

Market-based remuneration schemes—including stock options, stock appreciation rights, leveraged stock ownership plans, etc.—have the advantage of linking managerial pay directly with shareholder welfare. Stock options are an especially useful component of any package as their value rises with the volatility of the share price since the holder has the option *not* to exercise his right. Stock options may be used to help any reluctance of risk-averse managers to invest in risky projects or to extend the firm's leverage. However, option schemes need to be adjusted for dividend pay-outs if they are not to cause a bias towards retentions. It is also argued (e.g. by Lambert and Larcker 1985b) that market-based incentive schemes should carry a deferred compensation element, in order to encounter any managerial ability to manipulate the share price in the short run.[7]

Accounting-based payments—including profits bonuses—may reward effort, but they suffer from the disadvantage that accounting numbers are subject to executive manipulation. Healy (1985) found that US executives were able to accelerate or retard their recognition of certain expenditures (e.g. maintenance) to make better use of available bonus schemes. This suggests that accounting-based schemes may be unreliable unless compensation is deferred. Of course, market-based remuneration may be inappropriate for managers in unquoted companies and those occupying relatively junior positions.

The evidence on the effectiveness of compensation schemes is ambiguous. Empirical studies by industrial economists—see Ciscel and Carroll (1980) for a review—have generally (but not invariably) found that size is the major determinant of executive compensation, with performance having a minor effect if any. On the other hand, studies using an efficient markets framework—see above in Cable's chapter, pp. 29–34, for a description of 'events' methodology—have reported positive announcement effects for the introduction of incentive schemes (e.g. Brickley *et al.* 1985, Tehranian and Waegelein 1985 and Larcker 1983).

A particularly interesting study by Lambert and Larcker (1985a) reported a significant impact on the stock price associated with the announcement of 'golden parachute' agreements. (These give US executives generous payouts in the event of a change in the control of their corporation. The intention of the payments is to discourage executives from seeking to thwart takeover or merger approaches—so keeping up the sanction of the capital market, and maintaining the chance of a lucrative bid premium!) Since the average gains to the stockholders easily exceeded the maximum cost of any payouts to managers, it appeared that the net value of the firm was responsive to managerial incentive arrangements.

A disadvantage with the 'events' studies, including that of Lambert and Larcker, is that it is difficult to rule out reverse causation. For example, managers could time the introduction of an incentive scheme to coincide with good performance. If the market believes this, the announcement effect is simply a signal. Similarly, the timing of a 'golden parachute' package may indicate to the market management's awareness of the increased probability of an impending takeover bid. If so, the share price increase may be merely a reflection of the anticipated bid premium.

One plausible rationalisation for the different results reported for the 'events' and econometric studies is given by Murphy (1985). He suggests that it is reasonable to specify the compensation of executive i at time t (*Compit*) as depending on firm performance over time (*Performit*) thus:

Compit = ai + *a Performit* + *eit*

Murphy points out that such a relationship captures firm—and executive—specific factors in the constant term (ai). However, most compensation studies are estimated as cross-sectional relations. This, Murphy suggests, incorporates an omitted variables factor. For example, in Figure 4.3 let A be a highly-paid executive in a large low-performance firm and B be a lower-paid executive in a smaller, high-performance firm. A pooled cross-sectional regression generates an incorrect negative performance coefficient. Murphy's own empirical study of US executive remuneration reports a positive effect for both size and stock performance *after* employing separate dummy variables to capture firm and personal effects.

Market Curtailment of Agency Costs

The existence of an efficient outside market for any resource will tend to discourage resource owners' acquiescence in its employment in non-

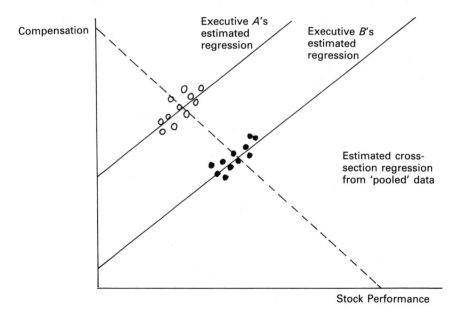

Source: Murphy (1985) p. 23.

Figure 4.3 Scatterplots and Regression Lines Portraying the Relation Between Compensation and Stock Market Performance for Two Hypothetical Executives

value-maximising ways. A viable managerial labour market, for example, will encourage managers to safeguard their reputations (and hence earning power) by attending to the success of their firms. Similarly, an unrestricted capital market might be expected to facilitate changes in the control of corporate assets where existing managerial teams have departed too far from the maximisation of shareholder wealth. These market-based checks to agency costs are examined in turn.

The Managerial Labour Market

Fama (1980) notes that a major part of the wealth of a typical senior executive consists of human capital. However, the rental generated depends to a considerable extent on the success or failure of the manager's firm. This, Fama suggests, does more than encourage individual managerial effort, it also stimulates mutual monitoring since inseparabilities create a problem for the outside market in assigning abilities/efforts to individual managers. Furthermore, even if managers succumb to the pleasures of corporate perks or an easy life, in a way the market has not anticipated, Fama suggests there will be an *ex-post* long-term *settling up*.

Strong and Waterson (1987) point out that Fama's analysis rests upon very strict—and as yet unsupported—assumptions about the managerial labour market. Indeed, Hirschey (1986) likens Fama's model to the strong form of the efficient capital market hypothesis which requires that all information—publicly available or not—is utilised in security pricing. Hirschey suggests that information asymmetries and the existence of firm-specific human capital (which creates quasi-rents, Frank 1984) will limit the efficiency of the labour market. However, he also suggests that this may create an incentive to acquire, or even to sell off, firms where managerial talents are mispriced.

Some evidence of the rationality of the labour market is provided in the financial literature. Coughlan and Schmidt (1985), in a study of US corporations between 1977 and 1981, found that executive termination (positively) and executive compensation (positively and negatively) were related respectively to abnormally poor share price performance. Lambert and Larcker (1985b) found that acquisition activity appeared to increase execution compensation, but that most of the gains went to those making acquisitions which increased shareholder wealth. Finally, an attempt was made by Johnson *et al*. (1985) to estimate the capitalised value of the specific skills of US chief executives by looking at the stock price response to the announcement of their sudden death. Interestingly, the average response to the death of a non-founding executive was significant and negative and that for a founder figure significant and positive!

A more thoroughgoing investigation of the hypothesis on managerial labour market control would need to investigate international variations. National disparities in termination practice and managerial mobility in general—perhaps influenced by differences in compensation arrangements, pensions and housing markets—might be expected to give rise to different degrees of effectiveness.

The Market for Corporate Control

A second, market-based check on managerial behaviour comes from the threat of takeover. Where senior managers have specific human capital investments in the firm, their wealth is threatened by its acquisition and their subsequent displacement. The merger and takeover market may be thought of as an arena where managerial teams compete for the control of corporate assets (Manne 1965).

The effectiveness of the market for corporate control has been the subject of considerable debate in both the industrial economics and finance literatures. If observed takeovers represent the displacement of inefficient managers by profit-conscious rivals, this should be reflected in performance comparisons. However, the empirical evidence contains ambiguities, reflecting, in part, differences in the approach of the researchers. Each of the major strands in the empirical literature is considered in turn:

(1) *Characteristics of victims.* A number of studies have sought to identify the inferior performance, if any, of acquired firms. Most find the typical victim's profitability to be below average (see survey in Chiplin and Wright 1987) but a minority—including Meeks (1977) and Levine and Aaronovitch (1981)—find little, if any, difference. However, most studies report that the typical victim was smaller than average and that size appears to be a defence against takeover.[8]

(2) *The impact of mergers on accounting rates of return.* Those studies which have compared pre- and post-acquisition rate of returns for raiding firms have generally concluded that mergers actually reduce profitability—although perhaps by not very much—for example, in UK studies, by Singh (1971), Utton (1974) and Meeks (1977). This literature is reviewed in some detail in Mueller's chapter above. There are formidable data problems associated with using reported returns—not least in adjusting for 'goodwill' and for the impact of any further changes in accounting procedures—and these appear to have encouraged most recent researchers to adopt other methods of investigation.

(3) *Real cost comparisons.* An illuminating—if labour-intensive—approach to evaluating mergers has been to examine their impact on real output costs. The most comprehensive example is the series of case studies of mergers edited by Cowling *et al.* (1980). These found no widespread evidence of substantial efficiency gains across a range of UK industries.

(4) *Stock market tests.* A very large group of studies has looked at the impact of merger and takeover announcements on the share prices of both the acquiring and acquired firms. Again, the methodology employed has normally involved a comparison of actual share-price returns with those predicted using estimates from the market model. The underlying assumption is that an informationally efficient stock market will capitalise the anticipated net future gains from the merger in the price of the acquiring firms.

In the United States, where most studies have been conducted, the *short-run* consequences of merger announcements are reasonably clear. Recent reviews (Jensen and Ruback 1983, Lev 1983 and Mueller 1987, and Chapter 3 of this volume) of the many empirical investigations agree that the shareholders of the acquired firm make a substantial gain (perhaps 18 to 30 per cent), whilst those of the acquiring firm do not experience any significant change.

Since the US antitrust laws ensure that few acquisitions are horizontal—and so rule out market power gains—the generation of a net increase in shareholder wealth on merger announcements has been taken as evidence of their beneficial effects. At the same time, the acquisitions market appears to be so competitive that all the gains go—via a bid premium—to the owners of the acquired firm. European announcement effect studies tend to confirm the American evidence, although some (including Firth 1979, 1980) report substantial negative wealth effects for the acquirer.

When the longer-term share price performance of the acquiring firm is examined, the picture becomes less clear. Dodd and Ruback (1977), for example, report that acquiring firms typically enjoy positive abnormal returns for a long period (average 43 months) *prior* to the merger announcement. Since a high share price facilitates takeover finance, it may not be implausible to consider mergers to follow, rather than precede, an improvement in acquirer performance.

Dodd and Ruback and several others (including Mueller 1980 in the USA and Cosh *et al.* 1980 in the UK) also report substantial long-term declines in average share-price returns *after* the merger. There is no consensus in the literature on the appropriate interval across which post-merger returns should be assessed, and the studies use different periods. It is clear, however, that subsequent negative returns for the acquirer may cancel out a large part of—or even outweigh—the immediate gains to the victim's shareholders.

The Role of Debt Bonding

It is well-established in the finance literature (e.g. Modigliani and Miller 1958, Fama and Miller 1972 and Smith and Warner 1979) that there is a potential conflict of interest between a firm's shareholders and its suppliers of debt. The latter usually receive a fixed return and so are primarily concerned with the firm's security. However, some activities—such as increased dividend payments or investment in riskier projects—may raise the value of a firm's shares within a fully diversified portfolio but also increase the probability of firm failure. Managers are not merely disinterested onlookers to any debt-owner/shareholder conflict of interest. They must be expected to have firm-specific investments in human capital which will ordinarily give them an interest in reducing the probability of failure. This bias may, of course, be checked where the managers have an offsetting equity interest—either an actual one or a potential involvement through a stock option scheme or an employee share-ownership plan.

When managers increase the leverage (or debt–equity ratio) of their firms, they are *bonding* or *pre-committing* themselves to achieve sufficient cash flow to meet the increased interest bill. (In the event of failure, the managers' specific investments in the firm are at risk.) Their discretion to follow preferred goals is reduced and, in consequence, the value of equity claims on the firm may rise (Grossman and Hart 1982, Jensen and Meckling 1976). Kim and Sorensen (1986), in a recent study of the financial structure of US corporations, report that the degree of leverage is positively related to the extent of inside ownership, as the bonding argument implies.

The bonding function of debt helps explain its use in a number of recent innovations in corporate finance. *Leveraged buyouts* (Thompson, 1988) and *going-private deals* (De Angelo *et al*. 1984) typically create a new company with a high level of debt. Since the management normally has a substantial human and equity capital stake in the venture, it has much to lose in the event of failure. This bonds the management to expend effort to meet the terms of any corporate plan agreed with the outside financiers. Jensen (1987) has recently hypothesised that for similar reasons mergers financed by debt will be more successful than those based on cash or equity payments.

The reduction of agency costs through borrowing may not be limited to bonding effects. Stiglitz (1985) suggests that those lending to the firm, including banks, may be better placed to control the activities of its managers than are equity owners—not least, because of the sanction of refusing to renew loans. Cable (1985a) demonstrates the importance of banker involvement for the performance of German firms. Thompson and Wright (1987) find evidence of an active financier role in those UK companies which have recently experienced a management buyout.

The monitoring function of the capital market—both loan and equity— is also useful in explaining why companies pay dividends. Since capital gains are usually more lightly taxed than dividends, a growing firm might be expected to retain its earnings and let shareholders enjoy a tax-efficient income by partial liquidation of their equity holdings.[9] Easterbrook (1984) points out that by paying out dividends, managers increase the frequency with which they must subject themselves to capital market scrutiny. This reduces managerial discretion and so lowers agency costs.

4.6 Intra-Firm Agency Costs

Most of the discussion of agency cost issues in the literature has concentrated upon the shareholder/senior manager relationship. At lower levels in the firm the intra-organisational relations between monitor and monitored are somewhat different because the former, who is not necessarily a residual claimant, need not be presumed to have any interest in maximising the value of the firm. Therefore the internal design of the organisation needs to structure superior–subordinate relations in such a way as to minimise agency costs.

The multi-divisional form of corporate organisation, which is examined extensively elsewhere is this volume, appears to have been adopted by most large corporations in the USA and Western Europe. Accordingly, the corporate HQ/divisional management relationship seems to be a particularly important one for examining intra-firm agency problems. These agency cost issues are considered below.

Remunerating Divisional Management

In Williamson's (1971a, 1975) analysis of the M-form, it is assumed that the profit orientation of divisional management is maintained by suitable incentive remuneration. However, divisional executives—so-called 'middle management' in many firms—are likely to require different compensation arrangements than their senior colleagues. In particular, market-based schemes will be less important. First, the division has no shares of its own and those of the whole corporation may reflect the contribution of many sets of divisional managers. Secondly, because of divisional managers' more junior positions they will tend to have much lower holdings of accumulated wealth—including investments in the firm's shares.

Payment schemes to divisional managers are likely to be comprised of annual salaries and accounting-based incentive payments. The former may not be very effective where managers have little opportunity for further promotion. There is some evidence (e.g. Channon 1973) that European M-forms have relied more upon fixed salaries than their US counterparts. The recent spread of employee share-ownership plans (ESOPs) (Estrin *et al.* 1987) may be putting an end to this.

The effectiveness of performance-based remuneration schemes is likely to depend on the decomposability of a firm's divisions. Where there is a high degree of overlap—e.g. shared facilities or inter-divisional trading—the earnings figures for each division may depend crucially upon accounting rules and their application by corporate headquarters. (Solomons 1965). This will limit the use of performance-based compensation.

Monitoring Divisional Management

It is a part of the M-form hypothesis that the location of strategic and operating responsibilities at corporate headquarters and divisional levels, respectively—i.e. the separation of *decision control* and *decision management* in Fama and Jensen (1983a) terms—improves the quality of executive decision making. Corporate HQ has no obvious incentive to sanction uneconomic expenditures by the semi-independent divisions. At the same time, however, it can use its superior position to obtain information—via internal audits, etc.—which might not be available to the outside market (Williamson 1975). Furthermore, there may be alternative channels of internal information—e.g. inter-divisional committees, promotion-hungry managers, etc.—existing outside the formal hierarchy.

However, the general spread of multiproduct M-forms also reduces the market and accounting information available to assist in monitoring middle managers. As independent widget-makers disappear, it becomes harder for the corporate staff to monitor its widget division. Furthermore, it would defeat the objective of separating strategic and operational management if elite staff were to become expert in the details of the widget market to better appraise divisional results. This probably accounts for the adoption of general performance targets by M-form conglomerates and the frequent recourse to divestment where these are not met (Scherer 1984).

The Management of Cash Cows

An efficiently functioning internal capital market need not create equal opportunities for divisional management teams. The existence of a *product life cycle*—discussed by Mueller in Chapter 3—means that some product divisions may generate substantial profits without offering corresponding re-investment opportunities. Jensen (1986) refers to this as the generation of '*free cash flow*'. In an independent firm, growth-minded managers may respond by diversification, by investing in projects which do not offer an opportunity cost return. These possibilities are discussed by Mueller (1987, and Chapter 3 above), and by Stephen and Thompson in Chapter 9. However, within an M-form, capital allocation is determined by corporate headquarters. Hill (1984) reports that divisions are frequently run as 'cash cows' to finance development elsewhere.

The motivation of divisional management in cash cows appears to be particularly problematic. Since the division's product will normally belong to a low-growth, technologically mature industry, the opportunities for rapid development are limited. This is likely to restrict the scope for managerial promotion. At the same time, managers may feel resentment if their efforts are funding growth elsewhere in the organisation and opportunities for better-placed colleagues.

The important requirement for the management of cash cows would appear to be the writing of an appropriate incentive-based remuneration contract. Evidence from the United States (Jensen 1987) suggests that divestment activity is concentrated upon low-technology, cash-generating divisions. These are also the target of leveraged buyout activity in the USA and management buyouts in the UK (Thompson 1988). Indeed, Jensen (1987) argues that much of the market for corporate control in the 1980s has been dominated by trade in 'free cash flow' generating entities. This activity, which incurs all the costs associated with control changes, constitutes at least prima-facie evidence that M-forms find it difficult to devise suitable incentives for cash cow management.

The Limits of Internal Organisation

The substitution of external market control for internal direction may be a means of reducing the agency costs of hierarchy. In particular, the decomposition of firms into separately-owned units re-unites residual claims and control at the operational level. Management buyouts, new company spin-offs and 'going-private' deals—where managers buy back their firm's equity (De Angelo *et al.* 1984)—are frequently observed examples of transactions which re-concentrate shareholdings in the hands of management. It was seen above that where such deals are financed by debt, the bonding effect may further lower agency costs. These issues of firm decomposition are taken further in Chapter 9.

4.7 Conclusion

The principal–agents theory offers important insights into the control and structuring of firms and thus into the organisation of economic activity. In particular, the *positive theory* of *agency*—with its emphasis on the need for agency cost minimisation under competitive conditions—has had considerable success in explaining the properties of alternative organisational forms. However, it is important to remember that because the approach rests on an evolutionary 'survival of the fittest' assumption—a 'useful tautology', as Jensen (1983, p. 331) puts it—it has to produce testable hypotheses and not merely *ex-post* rationalisations. Otherwise, mere existence equates with superior efficiency, and agency theory degenerates into 'apologetics for corporate capitalism' (Strong and Walker 1987, p. 202).

A particularly valuable contribution by the theory of agency has been to re-examine the relationship between the firm and its capital suppliers. This has drawn attention to the distinctive differences in the relations between senior managers and the suppliers of debt, and the relations between the same managers and their shareholders.

This approach highlights the apparent neglect of debt in earlier treatments of the separation of ownership and control issue. In turn, emphasis on the financing of the firm has encouraged economists to incorporate financial structure as a variable in models of firm behaviour.

Notes

1. The 'new' is used to distinguish these post-Coase developments from the older American institutionalist school of the 1930s. The latter, which was based around the work of Commons and Veblen, was largely eclipsed by the dominant neoclassical thought of the 1940s, 1950s and 1960s. It has enjoyed something of a revival, in the last decade or so, in the *Journal of Economic Issues*.

   Williamson (1975, p. 3) suggests that the work of J.R. Commons does provide a link between the two institutional approaches. It was Commons (1924) who first emphasised the importance of the transaction as the basic unit of analysis.
2. The role of *screening* and *signalling* devices can be interpreted as a means of obtaining and conveying information, respectively, to reduce costs in the face of adverse selection (Arrow 1973, Spence 1974). Whilst the terms 'moral hazard' and 'adverse selection' have achieved widespread usage, Arrow (1987, p. 38) cautions that they have a specific meaning in insurance which is not necessarily met in the general context. Barney and Ouchi (1986, p. 439) use the terms 'pre-contractual opportunism' and 'post-contractual opportunism', so avoiding this difficulty.
3. For example, the highly theoretical models of Grossman and Hart (1982) have generated important insights into the role of debt in disciplining managers. Furthermore, as Strong and Walker (1987, p. ix) have noted recently, financial economics is one of the relatively few parts of the discipline where theoretical concepts tend to be absorbed into practice with a relatively short delay.
4. Reviewed in Lawriwsky (1984 Ch. 2).
5. A particular problem with most empirical studies concerns the definitions of 'owner' and 'managerial' control. Most studies assign firms to a 'managerial' sub-sample where no clearly defined individual or group has $\geq$ x% of the shares (in general, $x \leq 20$). This procedure both ignores the overall distribution of voting equity and tends not to capture the influence of institutional holdings (Lawriwsky 1984). Leech (1987) develops a probabilistic voting model which suggests that small groups of shareholders—insiders and/or outsiders—may achieve a controlling coalition of voters. Cosh and Hughes (1987), in a recent study of giant US and UK firms, show that such a more sophisticated analysis of voting power casts doubt on the general applicability of the managerialist position.
6. There are clearly very considerable international differences in the importance of outside directors. In West Germany, where banks play a very important role in financing industrial companies, bank representatives sit on the supervisory boards of a majority of large firms. Cable (1985a, pp. 119–20) reported that

bank representatives actually act as board chairmen in 20 per cent of the leading 100 companies.

A recent comparative study for the USA and UK, by Cosh and Hughes (1987), indicates that American non-executive directors (NEDs) are more important than their British counterparts. Cosh and Hughes found that NEDs constitute 37 per cent of the average UK board compared to 65 per cent of the mean for US boards. Furthermore, UK NEDs are more likely to be former executives of the company itself and, unlike their US equivalents, most unlikely to be the representatives of family shareholding interests (Cosh and Hughes 1987, pp. 93–6).

7. Given that most corporate chief executives will tend to be close to retirement, they may possess a more short-term perspective than their shareholders. Lambert and Larcker (1985b) review an innovative compensation package which aims to remedy this. In this package, the market-related part of executive compensation depends on a comparison of the firm's share performance with that of other major corporations, based on a ten-year period which extends for three years beyond the executive's own retirement (pp. 17–18).

8. However, the available published studies were conducted *before* the merger wave of the 1980s. This appears to have contained a sizeable number of very large transactions.

5

The Contingency Theory of Organisational Control

DAVID OTLEY

5.1 Introduction

The study of organisational functioning has developed from a variety of perspectives, but the integration of the insights obtained into a more coherent theory of organisations remains problematic. Nevertheless, a considerable body of empirical research has been performed which now provides an important foundation for the generation of more comprehensive theories.

A major theoretical paradigm of organisation theory during the 1960s and 1970s was the contingency approach. In contrast to previous work which had taken a universalistic view, seeking to discover the one best form of organisational structure, researchers in the new paradigm had noted that particular organisational forms appeared to be best suited to certain circumstances. The contingency theory of organisational structure thus attempted to specify and test the organisational forms that were best suited to given conditions.

More recently, researchers interested in the processes of organisational control have further developed the approach. Management accounting researchers, in particular, have long been concerned with responsibility accounting and the control of organisational activities, although their work has been traditionally based on classical organisation theory. Since 1975, however, much of their work has adopted a contingency perspective, taking ideas originally concerned only with organisational structure and applying them to the processes of control that take place within such structures.

Thus a more complete picture of the ways in which organisations accommodate themselves to external exigencies is being built up. Such processes of adaptation are important, as it is apparent that organisational change can be a lengthy and traumatic process. If the rate of adaptation required by the economic environment exceeds that which can be reasonably accommodated by an organisation, failure may ensue. Conversely, adaptive organisational forms tend to be inefficient under conditions of relative stability, and a balance therefore needs to be maintained between flexibility and efficiency.

In this chapter, the contingency theory of organisational structure will be outlined, and some of the major empirical results noted. This will be followed by a survey of the contingency theory of management accounting, to extend the perspective presented from one of structure alone towards one which involves the processes that occur within a given structure. Both organisational structure and the mechanisms used to establish internal control are linked in the attempt to develop effective organisational responses to environmental conditions. Structure and process are the two sides of the same coin, and modern developments indicate that they are being studied increasingly in conjunction. As such, contingency theories form part of the management control approach: this is concerned with the links between the establishment of corporate strategy and the implementation of such strategy by the day-to-day operations undertaken by first-level employees. The guiding perspective used in this chapter is therefore one drawn from the management control systems approach (Lowe and Machin 1983).

5.2 The Contingency Theory of Organisational Structure

Early theories of how an organisation should be best designed and managed were universalistic in nature: that is, they attempted to specify the best way in which a particular task could be organised, regardless of other circumstances. More modern theories are usually contingent in that they relate prescriptions about what should be done to other features of the organisation and its environment. Further, earlier theories tended towards treating organisations as closed systems operating in isolation from other organisations and from society more generally. The problems engendered by such a closed systems perspective became recognised during the 1950s and were overcome by the development of open systems approaches which explicitly attempted to model the connections that existed between an organisation and the wider environment in which it was set. Finally, there has always been a tension between approaches that treat organisations as designed artefacts, constructed to achieve defined purposes, and approaches which treat them as naturally occurring phenomena, displaying rationality and purpose only to a limited extent.

Some of the main characteristics of the rational and natural approaches to the study of organisations are set out in Table 5.1. However, despite

Table 5.1   Rational and Natural Views of Organisations

	The organisation as a designed artefact	The organisation as a natural phenomenon
Basic question asked	How can organisational effectiveness best be achieved?	How can organisational behaviour best be explained?
Existence of goals	Goals exist, but they may be multiple, conflicting and perhaps displaced.	Goals are an inappropriate concept. Behaviour is better explained in terms of power and processes of interaction.
Control	Overall guidance of the organisation towards objectives	Exercise of power and influence by groups.
Typical theories	• Classical management • Contingency theory • Sociological structural functionalism	• Open system • Sociological action theory
Major stress	• Formal organisation • Organisation design	• Informal organisation • Unanticipated results
Orientation	Normative	Descriptive
Role of management control	Rational and neutral procedures used to help ensure overall effectiveness	Tools used by one group to enable them to dominate other groups

the dichotomous nature of this presentation, it has to be recognised that human economic organisations display both sets of characteristics: they are designed to achieve certain economic purposes, yet simultaneously develop in ways that are unplanned and unexpected. Purposes can become displaced, and parts of the organisation may show great resistance to the implementation of planned changes. Theories of organisation design must therefore recognise these dual aspects of organisational activity.

Scott (1981) has suggested that the development of organisation theory can be viewed as a progression from rational to natural models: firstly, within a closed systems perspective and, more recently, within an open systems perspective. Some major studies representing each of these stages are set out in Table 5.2, and a more comprehensive discussion can be

Table 5.2 Dominant Theoretical Models and Representative Theorists 1900–1970

Closed systems models		*Open systems models*	
1900–30 rational models	*1930–60 natural models*	*1960–70 rational models*	*1970– natural models*
Taylor (1911)	Barnard (1938)	Woodward (1958)	Hickson *et al.* (1971)
Weber (1947)	Roethlisberger and Dickson (1939)	Lawrence and Lorsch (1967)	March and Olsen (1976)
Fayol (1949)	Mayo (1945)	Thompson (1967)	Meyer and Rowan (1977)
	Dalton (1959)	Perrow (1967)	Pfeffer and Salancik (1978)
	McGregor (1960)	Pugh *et al.* (1968,1969) Blau & Schoenherr (1971)	Pondy and Mitroff (1978)

Source: Scott (1981, p. 409) with addition by Boland and Pondy (1983)

found in Otley (1984). Yet organisations display *both* rational and natural characteristics. Thompson (1967) has also argued that they display the characteristics of both closed and open systems, in that they constantly strive for rationality (closure) in the face of uncertainty (openness). It therefore appears that each stage in the development of organisation theory has the potential to teach us something about the functioning of organisations, but that no single theory yet has a monopoly of understanding. The theory appears to be at a point where it is able to recognise these conflicting tendencies within itself; however an integrated theory incorporating both closed and open system perspectives and rational and natural characteristics has yet to emerge.

The central feature of the open systems approach is that it seeks to study the activities of an organisation in the context of the wider environment in which it is set. Its basic premise is that an organisation is profoundly affected by, and dependent upon, its environment, and that its ultimate survival is determined by the degree to which it is able to adapt and accommodate itself to environmental contingencies. Initially, the chain of causation was seen as running solely from the environment to the organisation, essentially determining what should be the most appropriate organisational response; later, the interaction was viewed as being two-way with the organisation influencing its environment as well as vice versa.

A major development was the recognition that the work situation involves both social and technological factors, with overall performance being influenced by both of these factors and their interaction. An early study was conducted by Trist and Bamforth (1951) into the effects brought about by the introduction of the longwall system of extracting coal in British coal mines. This partly mechanised system of production replaced traditional manual methods, but involved a reorganisation of both task and social arrangements within a mine. However, the expected technological benefits were much reduced by the social frictions engendered by the new system. A new approach to job design, the socio-technical systems approach, which recognised the importance of both social and technical elements in organisational functioning, was developed and proved to be a major influence over the subsequent thirty years.

The concept of the organisation as a social system was also to increase in importance. Initially, much work was based on an organic analogy: the organisation was viewed as a living organism that was open to its environment, and survived by an interchange of both material and information with it. The total organisation was broken down into sub-systems, each having its own primary task (function) to perform. The role of the theory was to guide organisational design, in integrating the activities of these differentiated sub-systems, into a coherent pattern of organisational activity leading to effective performance. Work in this tradition includes Rice's (1958) study of an Indian textile plant, Katz and Kahn's (1966) study of the social psychology of organisations and Lawrence and Lorsch's (1967) analysis of the interaction between an organisation and its environment. The major issue, with regard to this work, is the pre-eminence that is given to the total organisation and to its survival, over its parts and the individuals who comprise it. It is essentially a form of sociological structural functionalism and is subject to the usual criticisms of that position—see Silverman (1970) for a comprehensive and understandable discussion.[1]

The study of the impact made by the environment on the organisation led to a major change in the thrust of organisational research: namely the development of the contingency approach. Lawrence and Lorsch's (1967) study suggests that different organisational principles were appropriate in different organisational circumstances and, indeed, in different parts of a single organisation. Burns and Stalker (1961) had already noted the appropriateness of mechanistic (i.e. formal and bureaucratic) and organismic (i.e. less formal and more flexible) forms of organisational structure to stable and dynamic technological environments respectively. Successful adaptation to a rapidly changing environment required a more flexible form of organisation than that provided by the classical bureaucracy— previously regarded as the most effective form of organisation. A study by Woodward (1958, 1965), designed to lend empirical support to classical management theory, had found it necessary to recommend different principles of management depending on the nature of the production process (i.e. unit, batch, mass or process production); and classical design principles were found to be dependent upon the production technology being used. Chandler (1962) discovered a link between the corporate strategy adopted by a firm and the organisational structure most conducive to its effective implementation; growth by diversification was best achieved by the adoption of a multi-divisional form of organisational structure. All these results indicated that there was no single form of organisational structure that was optimal in all circumstances: many factors, both internal to and external to the organisation, impact upon the choice of structure. An excellent insight into this organisation theory literature is provided by Pugh's (1984) book of readings.

However, it is important to recognise that, although the contingency framework provided a means of reconciling the results of a growing body of empirical research, there was little consensus on its theoretical foundations. In its present state, the contingency theory of organisational structure may best be described as (Burrell and Morgan 1979):

> a loosely organized set of propositions which in principle are committed to an open systems view of organization, which are committed to some form of multi-variate analysis of the relationship between key organizational variables as a basis for organizational analysis, and which endorse the view that there are no universally valid rules of organization and management.

The extent of the theoretical diversity can begin to be seen when the major contingencies, believed to affect organisational design, are listed. These include the nature of the production technology, the stability of the product–market environment, whether product markets are homogeneous or heterogeneous in nature, and the organisation's corporate strategy. When more recent empirical studies are considered, almost any factor that appears to explain some variation in observed organisational arrangements appears to have been seized upon by some researcher. The most complete empirical studies are perhaps those of the Aston group (Pugh and Hickson 1976, Pugh and Hinings 1976 and Pugh and Payne 1977) where variables such as origin and history, size, ownership and control, charter, technology, location, resources and interdependence with other organisations have been used to characterise organisational context. The results of this work have been mildly disappointing in that only size has been shown to have a consistent and major effect on structure; otherwise, only quite low correlations have been found, and connections with any underlying theory have been tenuous.

A more comprehensive theoretical basis for organisational design, which includes consideration of the social processes that occur within an organisational structure, has been put forward by Galbraith (1977). Organisations are seen as having three major choices to make: first, there is the choice of domain which involves choosing goals and determining strategy; second, there is the choice of organisational structure; and third, there is the design of the organisational processes which affects the integration of the individual into the organisation. These two latter choices form the principal means of co-ordinating activities, with the precise form of co-ordination used being dependent upon the degree of uncertainty confronting the organisation. The greater the level of uncertainty, the greater the need for information to be processed, and this creates overload on senior managers who must devise means of reducing the number of decisions referred to them.

For Galbraith, the fundamental managerial activity involves managing the number of exceptions to the routine decision-making procedures which need to be handled by senior staff. A manager's initial response will be to move from personalised, central control to forms of control exercised through a hierarchy of authority. Subsequent responses will include instituting rules and procedures, using staff specialists, and narrowing spans of control. When these possibilities are exhausted, two basic choices remain. One possibility is for the organisation to *reduce the amount* of information (to be processed by environmental management) by creating slack resources or by recombining units from a functional grouping into task-oriented groupings by the creation of more self-contained tasks. Alternatively, it can attempt to *increase its capacity* to process information by either improving the vertical information system, or by creating lateral relationships such as task forces or matrix structures. Thus, the design of control systems and other processes of organisational co-ordination complement structural approaches as a means of assisting in objective attainment.

As uncertainty increases, techniques of management control shift from behaviour control (i.e. specify exactly what should be done)—first by personal means and then by impersonal means reinforced by hierarchical supervision—to short-run output control, with centralised co-ordination, and then to long-run output control, with decentralised co-ordination. Finally, the uncertainty to be managed may be so great as to prevent even output goals being set, and the major form of control shifts to control over organisational inputs, especially personnel training and selection (Merchant 1986).

It can be seen that the choice of appropriate controls is influenced by the nature of the environment faced by the organisation as well as its chosen strategy and technology. But there is still the opportunity for a considerable degree of managerial choice. Control systems design involves juggling with several interdependent variables that include the type of information system used; the organisational structure adopted; the personnel selection and training techniques used; and the evaluation and reward systems that are developed. The choices made in the design of each sub-system will affect the other sub-systems involved. For example, in *adhocracies* (Mintzberg 1979),[2] the organic structures adopted, together with their laterally-based information systems, can be extremely stressful and they require personnel who have considerable commitment as well as specific technical and social skills. To reduce personal stress and role ambiguity, reward systems in these organisations need to stress intrinsic and social rewards rather than focusing on immediate output (Hopper and Berry 1983).[3]

It is evident from the previous discussion that organisation theory is not a unified subject of study, but rather an untidy collection of empirical studies and insights from researchers having a variety of perspectives. Burrell and Morgan (1979) argue that all theories of organisation are based upon both a philosophy of science and a theory of society. In terms of their analysis, the work outlined above falls into a small area of functionalist sociology characterised by a high degree of emphasis on objectivity (as opposed to subjectivity) and a fairly high degree of emphasis on regulation (as opposed to radical change).

In the next section, more recent work on control processes within organisations will be reviewed. This approach, too, begins from a similar theoretical position but can be seen as trying to move beyond its restricted starting position, albeit sometimes unsuccessfully. Increasingly, in particular, a more subjectivist stance on the role and impact of organisational control systems is being taken.

5.3   The Contingency Theory of Management Accounting

The development of contingency theories of organisational structure in the mid-sixties was paralleled by their application to accounting control systems in the mid-seventies. Although some of the initial work applied findings merely from the organisational literature to problems of accounting information systems (AIS) design, other studies were more innovative. Increasingly, there has been movement towards an emphasis on organisational processes, in addition to structure, and a recognition that control systems design is an area of considerable complexity requiring new research approaches.

Initially, three main classes of contingent variable were identified, drawn directly from the organisational literature: environment, technology and organisational structure. Relevant features, of the environment affecting AIS design have been suggested, for example: its degree of predictability, the severity of competition faced in the market place, the number of different product markets involved, and the degree of hostility it exhibits.[4] Technological variables include the nature of the production process, its degree of routineness, how well means–end relationships are understood and the amount of task variety that exists. Suggested

Table 5.3   Major Contingent Variables and Studies

ENVIRONMENT
Type of competition	Khandwalla (1972)
Toughness of operating environment	Otley (1978)
Hostility	Gordon and Miller (1976)
Dynamism	Gordon and Miller (1976)
	Waterhouse and Tiessen (1978)
Turbulence	Amigoni (1978)
Heterogeneity	Gordon and Miller (1976)
Complexity	Amigoni (1978)
	Waterhouse and Tiessen (1978)
Uncertainty	Gordon and Narayanan (1984)
	Govindarajan (1984)
	Merchant (1985a)

TECHNOLOGY
Production technology	Woodward (1958, 1965)
Work unit technology	Daft and Macintosh (1978)
	Macintosh (1981)
Routineness	Waterhouse and Tiessen (1978)
Task complexity	Piper (1978)
Automation	Merchant (1984)
Predictability	Merchant (1985b)

ORGANISATIONAL STRUCTURE
Differentiation	Lawrence and Lorsch (1967)
Interdependence	Otley (1978)
Type of interdependence	Hayes (1977)
Centralisation/autonomy	Bruns and Waterhouse (1975)

SIZE
Size	Williamson (1970)
	Pugh and Hickson (1976); Pugh and Hinings (1976)
	Merchant (1981,1984)
Ownership	Jones (1985)
	Wright *et al.* (1983)

CORPORATE STRATEGY
	Dermer (1977)
	Govindarajan and Gupta (1985)
	Merchant (1985a)

MANAGERIAL STYLE
	Hopwood (1972)
	Otley (1978)
	Hirst (1981)
	Brownell (1983)

CULTURE
	Flamholtz (1983)
	Markus and Pfeffer (1983)

---

structural factors include size, interdependence, decentralisation and resource availability. A summary of the major studies conducted and the major variables involved is given in Table 5.3.

But it is unrealistic to suppose that a complete theory of control systems design will emerge immediately. Further, recent research has uncovered a much more complex situation than was originally envisaged. As Emmanuel and Otley (1985) conclude in their recent text on accounting for management control:

> It is clear that the package of controls used by an organization interact in a very complex manner, and that there is a great deal of managerial choice and judgement involved in developing an effective control package.

In this section we shall therefore outline some of the major findings of the contingency theory of management accounting. However, it must be emphasised that most of the connections suggested are only tentative, and that a considerable amount of empirical research still needs to be undertaken before confident prescription is possible.

Environment

It is perhaps self-evident that the nature of an AIS will be affected by the external environment, for the purpose of a control system is to assist the organisation to adapt to the environment which it faces. However, it must be stressed that formal control systems are only one of many mechanisms that may be used to assist in attaining overall control.

Khandwalla (1972) was one of the first accounting researchers to examine the effect of the external environment on management control practices. He concluded that the sophistication of an AIS was influenced by the intensity of the competition faced by the firm. Moreover, different types of competition—for example price, marketing or product competition—had very different impacts upon the uses made of accounting information in manufacturing firms.

A similar conclusion was reached by Otley (1978) who studied the effects of different environments faced by unit managers within a single firm. Senior managers were found to use budget information in quite different ways in 'tough' environments compared to 'liberal' environments. Whereas a rigid style of performance evaluation that emphasised the attainment of budget targets was effective in a liberal environment, a more flexible style was required in a tough environment.

In a seminal theoretical paper, Gordon and Miller (1976) identify three main environmental characteristics hypothesised to affect control systems—namely dynamism, heterogeneity and hostility. A high level of dynamism (or rate of change) will require frequent control reports—both financial and non-financial information—which emphasise forecasts rather than past actual results; heterogeneity (or the number of different product markets served) will lead to a decentralised control system with quasi-independent responsibility centres; in the face of severe competition or market hostility, a more sophisticated AIS is required, again incorporating non-financial information about critical threats.

Waterhouse and Tiessen (1978) see the environment as having the two important dimensions that affect AIS design: the simple–complex and the static–dynamic. These are very similar to the dimensions identified by Thompson (1967) in his analysis of the effect of environment on the organisational structure. Other accounting researchers have taken up these ideas and they can be seen in studies such as that of Hayes (1977). Thus the contingency theory of organisational structure can be seen to have had a profound impact on the approach taken by accounting researchers—see Otley (1984) for a more comprehensive review.

Amigoni (1978) developed a different framework in which he assesses the appropriateness of different accounting control tools, ranging from financial accounting and ratio analysis, through financial simulation models and responsibility accounting, to strategic planning devices. He identifies two major contingent variables, namely the degree of structural complexity of the enterprise and the degree of turbulence in its environment. Whereas increasing structural complexity leads to the *addition* of new accounting tools to those already in use, environmental discontinuity will often require the *replacement* of tools which have become obsolete by new ones.

Gordon and Narayanan (1984) hypothesised a tripartite association between perceived environmental uncertainty, organic forms of organisational structure and the use of external, non-financial and *ex-ante* information for control purposes. Their analysis showed strong correlations between these three variables, but—after controlling for the effect of uncertainty—information systems and structure were not significantly related to each other. This supports the view that both structure and control systems are dependent upon the state of the environment rather than control systems being determined by structure.

Another study which focused on environmental uncertainty and also considered performance outcomes was that of Govindarajan (1984). He found no direct connection between evaluative styles, reward systems and effectiveness until the mediating effect of uncertainty was considered. Under conditions of high uncertainty, a correlation between more subjective methods of evaluating performance and effectiveness emerged—again supporting the contention that effective controls are contingent upon environmental circumstances.

Environmental 'stress', 'restrictiveness' and 'aggressiveness' have also been referenced by researchers. All of these aspects of the organisation's environment involve factors such as the availability of opportunities and the extent to which the firm is manipulated or controlled by other organisations such as competitors, suppliers, customers and government bodies (Khandwalla 1972; Pfeffer 1981). It can be argued that the existence of powerful interest groups in the organisation's environment increases the level of uncertainty it faces. Similarly, a high degree of heterogeneity, or other forms of complexity, may also increase uncertainty at the centre, if only through inadequacies in information processing. Thus the major factor underlying control systems design that has been identified appears to be environmental unpredictability in its various guises (Otley 1980). The considerable body of work conducted by organisation theorists on the effect of unpredictability on organisational and information systems design—summarised in such work as Galbraith (1977), Mintzberg (1979) and Pfeffer (1982)—has yet to be fully incorporated into accounting and control systems research.

Technology

One of the longest established relationships between a contingent variable and control systems design has been its connection with production technology. Woodward's (1958) work which linked different structural arrangements with particular types of work flows has been paralleled in AIS design. It has been long recognised by accountants that the nature of the production process determines the amount of cost allocation rather than cost apportionment, that can take place. The level of accuracy that is possible in costing unit and small-batch production cannot be carried over into process production, because the bulk of costs are incurred jointly by a mix of final products. There is thus a technological constraint on AIS design due to product interdependence.

Production technology has an important effect on the type of control information that can be provided, and recent work has indicated other aspects of technology that impact on the information that should be provided to aid effective control. For example, Piper (1978) demonstrates that the complexity of the task faced by an organisation is relevant to defining an appropriate financial control structure. In his study of four retail organisations, task complexity (defined by the range of products sold, the diversity of the range, seasonal variations and variations in the type of outlet) affected the financial control structure adopted *via* the intervening variable of organisational structure.

Technology is specifically introduced as a major contingent variable for effective AIS design by Daft and Macintosh (1978). Following Perrow (1967), two dimensions of technology were studied (the number of exceptions that arise in the production process and the search procedures used to resolve such exceptions) which correlated highly with measures of information systems style (i.e. the amount, focus and use made of data), although it should be noted that no attempt was made to assess effectiveness. More recent work by Merchant (1984) has indicated a positive association between the degree of automation in the production process and the formality of budget systems use. Finally, Merchant (1985b) has found some weak evidence to suggest that the propensity of production managers to create budgetary slack is inversely related to the degree of predictability of the production process.

Waterhouse and Tiessen's (1978) definition of technology again follows that of Perrow (1967), but is reduced to the single dimension of organisational routineness. Organisational sub-units are seen as having predominantly operational functions (defined similarly to Anthony's (1965) operational control) or managerial functions (which include both Anthony's management control and some of his strategic planning activities). It is suggested that managerial functions can be best understood by focusing on environmental variables, whereas the structure and processes of operating units will be more directly related to technological variables.

The AIS is thus viewed as one type of control mechanism which is primarily dependent upon the control needs of each organisational sub-unit. The definition of a sub-unit is dependent upon organisational structure which, in turn, is contingent upon both environment and technology. However, the evidence linking technological, organisational and managerial variables with overall effectiveness is still weak, and even the definition of the variables involved is often vague.

Organisational Structure

Literature on organisation theory has concerned itself with the effect of contingent variables, notably environment and technology, on organisational structure. However, we are concerned here with the effect of organisational structure on the design of the AIS and other control arrangements; evidently, these direct effects may be difficult to disen-tangle if there is also an effect mediated by organisational structure. This has been a source of some confusion in the management accounting literature, with some authors tracing the effect of contingent variables through organisational structure and others focusing upon their direct effects—see Otley (1980) for a critique. Nevertheless, it is of value to consider the direct impact of organisational structure on control systems design, whilst recognising the possibility of other indirect effects.

The need for accounting control systems to be consistent with organisational structure is well-accepted in management accounting texts. An organisational structure describes authority and responsibility relationships, and has an evident connection with the design of responsibility accounting systems. However, the traditional textbook description of the design of such systems has serious limitations: typically, they are designed to fit perfectly structured hierarchies of managerial authority, and to achieve control by linking ideas of controllability and traceability to the formal hierarchy of responsibility. However, interdependency of activities, joint responsibilities and the use of other integrative devices may cloud the precise determination of responsibility (Chenhall *et al.* 1981). A review of the potential dysfunctional aspects of responsibility accounting, which arise from attempting to operationalise the principle of controllability, is provided by McNally (1980).

An essential aspect of formal organisational structure is the segmentation of activities into parts that can be handled by individual managers. Such differentiation allows sub-units to devise their own ways of coping with their own specific circumstances. However, a complementary process of integration is necessary to co-ordinate the activities of the different sub-units, and the AIS often plays an important role in this process. The degree of integration necessary depends upon the amount and type of differentiation adopted. Thompson (1967) has developed a categorisation of organisational interdependence which distinguishes between pooled, sequential and reciprocal interdependence. Pooled interdependence refers to quasi-independent operating units which require only a limited provision of central services, typically finance. Subsequential interdependence occurs when there is a one-way flow of goods or services between sub-units, such as production flows in vertically integrated manufacturing firms. Reciprocal interdependence occurs when the outputs of one sub-unit become the inputs of another, and vice versa.

Hayes (1977) used this categorisation of interdependence, together with two other major contingencies (environmental relationships and internal factors), to examine sub-unit performance within an organisation. He concluded that his data supported the contingent hypothesis that the performance of sub-units was explained by different combinations of these contingent variables. However, this study has been extensively criticised (Tiessen and Waterhouse 1978) and the results should be treated with care.

Bruns and Waterhouse (1975) have argued that a manager's budget-related behaviour is contingent upon various aspects of organisational structure, such as centralisation, autonomy, and the degree to which activities are structured. This leads them to conclude that different control strategies are appropriate in different kinds of organisation: for example, they suggest that a decentralised and structured organisation operating in a stable environment seems particularly suited to the use of budgetary control. Their analysis culminates in the description of two modes of control strategy, administrative and interpersonal, which are associated with different kinds of organisational arrangements.

Unfortunately, the analysis of the effects of organisational structure alone can be misleading because of the direct effects of other contingent variables upon control arrangements. Otley (1980) has suggested that structure is itself a form of control, and that it may be more profitable to consider the effects of all other contingent variables on the control 'package' implemented by an organisation, rather than treating structure as a contingent variable in its own right. Such an approach clarifies contingent analysis, although it emphasises the complex interaction of all the elements in an overall control package.

Size

Organisational size is an important variable affecting both structure and other control arrangements which has figured extensively in the work of both organisation theorists and economists. For example, Williamson (1970) has argued that as an organisation grows it will initially organise on a functional basis. However, increased growth by means of diversification and the consequent exposure to more diverse product–market environments prompts the reorganisation of activities into semi-autonomous divisions. This allows the AIS to be used to measure and compare divisional performance using similar accounting measures to those which determine overall firm performance.

More recently, Merchant (1981) focused on the differences found in corporate-level budgeting systems. His results showed that in larger organisations (where there was greater diversity and decentralisation of decision-making) there was greater participation in budgeting, despite less personal interaction between managers, and a general attitude that meeting the budget was important to managers' career progression. Perhaps the most significant finding was that performance was highest in the larger firms when an administrative approach to budgeting was used, in contrast to smaller firms where the best performance was associated with a more personal approach. This supports the contingency notion of the need for a fit between size and the way in which a budget system is operated, and it is consistent with the findings of Bruns and Waterhouse (1975).

Merchant (1984) extended this study to the departmental level where size, functional differentiation, and the degree of automation in the production process all led to greater formality in the budgeting process. Once again, performance was higher in those departments where the expected fit between context and budget use was found, than in those departments where it was absent. However, performance was negatively correlated with the requirement to explain budget variances, which led Merchant to suggest that performance should perhaps be considered as an independent variable affecting style of budget use, rather than vice versa, as previously suggested by Otley (1978). This possibility will be considered further in the subsequent section on budgetary style.

Merchant's work clearly suggests a contingency relationship between size and budgetary system characteristics at both the corporate and departmental level. It should be noted, however, that departmental size is controllable, to some extent, by the organisation in its determination of organisational structure.

Further evidence of the impact of size on control techniques can be found in Jones's (1985) study of the role of management accounting systems following merger or takeover. Differences in control practices that existed in small, medium and large companies prior to merger or takeover almost entirely disappeared afterwards, as the new subsidiary was required to conform to the practices laid down by the acquiring company. It may be that pressures for conformity to corporate control systems limit the ability of subsidiary companies to design and operate the control systems best suited to their individual environments. (See Chapter 10 for further discussion.) If so, attention needs to be paid to the alternative control arrangements that replace them. With the tendency towards corporatism in many areas of economic activity, where ownership is concentrated into fewer large corporations, more complex information handling systems will be required to cope with the increasing levels of complexity and diversity.

Strategy

Consideration of corporate strategy has not been prominent, rather surprisingly, in studies of control systems design, despite Dermer's (1977) argument that differences in corporate strategies should logically lead to differences in planning and control systems design. Chandler (1962) demonstrated a link between corporate strategy and organisational structure, but this has not been carried through to the design of other control mechanisms until recently.

Govindarajan and Gupta (1985) examined the relationship between business strategy, style of evaluation and effectiveness. Strategy was measured along a spectrum ranging from 'pure harvest' to 'pure build': the former being characterised by a high market share and the maximisation of earnings and cash flow, whilst the latter represented a mission to increase market share in high growth markets, often resulting in poor short-term profits and net cash outflows. They found that when greater reliance was placed on long-run criteria of evaluation, and managerial bonuses were determined by subjective (non-formula) methods, effectiveness was enhanced for 'build' strategies but diminished for 'harvest' strategies. However, the relationship between reliance on short-run criteria in bonus determination and effectiveness was virtually independent of business unit strategy.

Merchant (1985a) used a similar method of categorising strategy, but his findings do not support those of Govindarajan and Gupta, in that he found strong evidence that spending decisions in conditions of rapid growth were more constrained by short-term criteria such as monthly income targets. Such a relationship seems highly plausible, as resources are often in short supply during periods of rapid growth, and it may be that the studies are not, in fact, inconsistent. It may be quite possible to attempt to manage resources very carefully in conditions of rapid growth whilst, at the same time, attempting to increase market share in a competitive environment.

The effect of strategy on control systems design is still unclear, therefore: in the short term, a strategy can be seen as a response to an environment; in the longer term, the environment is itself determined by strategic decisions about the markets and environments in which the firm wishes to operate. Studies of control systems need to clearly specify the time span of the controls which they examine, for variables, such as structure and strategy, which can be considered as given in the design of short-term controls, become responses themselves when a longer perspective is taken.

Culture

Flamholtz (1983) has developed a schematic model of an organisational core control system consisting of four elements (planning, operations, measurement and evaluation-reward systems). This is located within the framework of an overall organisational control system which includes factors such as organisational structure, dominant organisational culture and values, and is set within an external environment.[5] Flamholtz argues that the process of exercising control is much more complex than traditional management accounting theory suggests, and that accounting controls must be viewed as a part of a more comprehensive control system. He also warned of the dangers of ignoring organisational culture in control systems design; control systems which are inconsistent with an organisation's value system are likely to create resistance and to produce motivations aimed at defeating the purposes of the core control system.

Another piece of work which recognises the importance of organisational culture and power relationships within organisations is that of

Markus and Pfeffer (1983). They, too, argue that the language and symbols of control systems, and the goal assumptions incorporated within them, must correspond to the dominant organisational culture, otherwise the controls may engender sufficient resistance to cause them to fail. The introduction of new control systems that alter existing power relationships, may be thwarted by those who consider their position to be threatened by the new system. These conclusions were substantiated by evidence from a number of case histories of the introduction on computerised accounting and control systems which were unsuccessful despite their technical sophistication.

The idea that control systems are dependent upon power relationships *within* organisations can be extended to the view that they are also dependent upon power relationships *between* the organisation and its environment. Pfeffer and Salancik (1978) have developed a resource dependence framework that attempts to explore the impact of important resource dependencies upon organisational strategy and control.

Work on the impact of culture upon control systems design is evidently at a very early stage, but it is of clear importance. Perhaps the most effective control processes are those which operate by generating a corporate culture that is supportive of organisational aims, objectives and methods of working, and which is consistent with the demands of the environment in which the organisation operates.

Style of Control

The managerial styles of decision making and accounting information use have also been considered as significant variables affecting the effectiveness of control systems, both in theoretical speculation (Gordon and Miller 1976; Dermer 1977) and in empirical work. When accounting data such as budgets are used as standards, against which performance is subsequently evaluated, rewards become directly connected with budget achievement. The problem of designing and operating an effective system of budgetary control is primarily that of constructing a set of performance measures which, if achieved, will result in the desired overall performance for the organisation. There is usually little difficulty in motivating managers to aim at achieving the specified results; what is difficult is ensuring that the results are achieved in the intended manner.

The difficulties inherent in specifying and rewarding appropriate managerial *behaviour* have led to a concentration on the monitoring and rewarding of *results* (i.e. output controls). The most commonly used measures of performance involve accounting measures of results, and they use budgets as the standard against which performance is assessed. If rewards are sufficient to motivate managers to attain the performance targets, it is likely that the targets themselves will come under considerable pressure, and also that accounting reports of actual performance will be biased or manipulated to give the impression of good performance, even when it does not exist. Finally, and most seriously, actual behaviour may be modified so that desired results appear to be attained, although they may be achieved in an undesirable manner.

Despite these problems, accounting measurement procedures are used, and recognised to be of value, in a wide variety of organisations. Some of the problems associated with the use of accounting-based performance measures appear to be avoided by managers using the imperfect accounting information in more complex ways than is suggested in the technical accounting literature.

One important study is that conducted by Hopwood (1972), who distinguished between a rigid (budget constrained) style of accounting information use and a more flexible (profit conscious) style. His study indicated that the rigid style was associated with high degrees of job-related tension, poor relationships with both peers and subordinates, and dysfunctional behaviour such as the manipulation of accounting data, whereas the more flexible style had no such associations. He therefore concluded that the flexible style of budget use was likely to lead to more effective organisational performance. However, his study was conducted using cost-centre managers in an organisation having a high degree of inter-dependence between operating units. In such circumstances, accounting information is only an imperfect surrogate for true performance, and its effective use appeared to require a great deal of managerial judgement.

A subsequent study by Otley (1978) deliberately selected an organis-ation in which accounting information represented a more adequate basis for performance evaluation (i.e. quasi-independent profit centres). In this situation the use of the rigid style of evaluation did not lead to an increase in the types of harmful consequence observed by Hopwood, and it appeared to lead to the most effective performance. Thus, as accounting measures of performance become less appropriate when the degree of interdependence between operating units increases, it is necessary to use accounting information in a more flexible manner as a mechanism of managerial control. However, Otley's study indicated, in addition, that the style of information use adopted by a manager might not be an independent variable. The rigid style of evaluation seemed to be selectively operated only at the more successful operating units; less successful units were evaluated in a more flexible manner. It may therefore be that performance affects the selection of managerial style rather than vice versa.

More recently, Hirst (1981) sought to place these results in a wider context, by noting that accounting standards of performance will be a less complete description of adequate performance in conditions of high uncertainty. He argued that only a relatively low reliance on accounting data for control is appropriate in conditions of high uncertainty. The study by Govindarajan (1984) also suggests that a manager is likely to be evaluated in a more subjective manner if his unit faces a high degree of uncertainty. Again, it is significant that the style of information use adopted was regarded as resulting from environmental conditions rather than from individual personality traits. This study clearly supports Hirst's conclusion that too high a degree of reliance on accounting measures of performance, under conditions of high uncertainty, is likely to prejudice effective performance.

The central findings of these studies, which are relevant to the impact of accounting controls, are twofold: firstly, it is the way in which accounting information is used by managers and the rewards that are made contingent upon such information that are critical in determining the impact of the control system; secondly, the impact of high reliance on accounting data is contingent upon circumstances such as the degree of knowledge that is possessed about how managerial behaviour contributes to effective performance and also the uncertainty that exists in the external environment of the organisation. When faced with high degrees of internal and external uncertainty, what is required may be a reward system that is supportive of innovation and avoids penalising the occasional failure, for only then will managers feel able to devote their efforts towards achieving success rather than avoiding failure.

5.4   Conclusion

Although the contingency theory of management accounting has built upon the earlier contingency theory of organisations, and has identified a variety of potentially influential variables, only a small amount of substantive evidence has been gathered concerning their effect on the operation of organisational control systems. The initial empirical studies assumed a simple linear model with contingent variables affecting control systems design only via organisational structure. Other studies ignored structure altogether and looked for the direct impact of hypothesised contingent variables on the design and use of control systems. Neither strand of the literature paid much attention to organisational effectiveness as a criterion of evaluation: the studies were primarily descriptive and contented themselves with observing associations between contingent variables and features of control systems design.

This approach was criticised as being too limited by Otley (1980). The lack of concern with organisational effectiveness prevents most of the empirical studies from being used as a basis for prescription. However, even if studies were designed to include effectiveness measures, there is the important issue of whether the control systems' design influences, or is influenced by, the performance of the organisation. Both effects seem likely, but it will require longitudinal studies of control systems use to clarify the matter further.

The distinction between organisational structure and the processes of control operated within that structure also seems arbitrary: control systems are probably best considered as a 'package', involving elements of both structure and process. In this control package, each element—organisational structure, accounting information systems, management information systems more widely defined, reward and incentive systems and other control arrangements (such as personnel selection and training)—is likely to interact with other elements. Such a view was expressed long ago (see Horngren 1962) and also echoes the sentiments often expressed by industrial managers who indicate that the form selected for a control system is often intended to cope with known deficiencies in organisational design. Other companies adopt particular forms of organisational structure and operating procedures to avoid the expense of running complex management accounting and information systems. Reward and incentive systems can be used where other arrangements impact only weakly on individuals, such as the common practice of rewarding salesmen on a commission basis. Finally, the selection and training of personnel is an important control mechanism by which individuals, who are thought to fit in well with the aims of the organisation, are selected so as to avoid the necessity of complex control systems.

The contingency theories discussed in this chapter are not yet based on sufficient evidence to provide a firm basis for prescription. Many factors have been suggested that have a strong impact upon organisational functioning, but their precise effect and relative importance has yet to be elucidated. In particular, the impact of specific *combinations* of controls, used in conjunction, has yet to be investigated in detail. However, the contingency framework of control systems design, in conjunction with the organisational design literature that preceeded it, provides valuable guidance in conceptualising important issues concerned with the internal organisation of firms and in particular with respect to control system design (Otley, 1984).

Notes

1. The essence of structural–functionalist approaches is to place emphasis upon the inter-relatedness of the different parts of an organisation. As in a natural

system, the parts are viewed as operating in such ways as to ensure the maintenance of the organisation as a whole. For further discussion see Silverman (1970, Ch. 3).

2. An adhocracy involves a highly organic organisation structure, with little formalisation of behaviour. Specialists are deployed in small project teams to do their work, with there being an emphasis upon mutual adjustment and liaison within and between teams. Adhocracies are also characterised by frequent changes to their internal shape. Mintzberg (1979, Ch. 21) addresses more detailed aspects of adhocracies.

3. Intrinsic rewards are those which relate to the satisfaction an individual derives from doing a job and achieving a target *per se*, as opposed to extrinsic rewards which concern the payment received, etc.

4. Environmental hostility relates to the problems caused for a firm through its interface with competitors, trade unions, government, etc., for example as a result of government legislation which adversely affects the firm. Hostility is to be contrasted with dynamism which refers to conditions of generally rapid change.

5. Evidence suggests that organisations possess cultures and value systems which influence adaptation to change, and which may persist over time even with changes in personnel. (see, for example, Arrow 1974 and Srivastava 1983).

6

Internal Organisation in Different Economic Systems

TREVOR W. BUCK

6.1 Introduction

The purpose of this chapter is to extend the application of post-Coasian developments—in the theory of the internal workings of the firm—to economic systems beyond the capitalism for which they were originally intended. In so doing, it should become evident that the insights about internal organisation, discussed in earlier chapters, have a wide relevance. Of course, very large organisations exist outside market capitalism and have the same concerns and problems: for example, two of the world's largest industrial corporations (in terms of employment)— Coal India and IRI (Table 6.1)—are state-owned; and, in addition, centrally-planned economies have problems of internal control, to put it mildly.

This chapter is divided into two main parts: first, it presents a general consideration of traditional internal organisation within the three main forms of economic system: second, it analyses one recent major organisational reform within each of these three economic systems. It

Table 6.1 The World's 'Top 4' Industrial Corporations, 1986 (Employment)

Corporation	Employees ('000)	Sales ($m)	Net Income ($m)
General Motors	876	102,814	2,945
Coal India (state-owned)	669	2,065	(65)
IRI (Italy, state-owned)	484	26,758	(664)
IBM	404	51,250	4,798

Sources: *Fortune* (1986) 4 August (pp. 173, 179). *Fortune* (1987) 27 April (pp. 188, 198).
Note: Brackets denote losses

should be emphasised that a detailed review of all aspects of internal organisation in three economic systems is impracticable; by the same token, it is not possible to consider all recent developments in the theory of internal organisation, regardless of whether they have any current practical application or not. For a review of theoretical developments notwithstanding practical application, see Radner (1986).

6.2 Internal Organisation in Three Economic Systems

The output of an industrial plant can be allocated in three ways:

- *Markets* Industrial output is sold on markets to the highest bidders. Outputs are chosen to secure profitable sales.
- *Plans* Industrial output is determined and directed by Ministries and other central planners towards those users that are deemed to need it most.
- *Clans* Outputs are chosen by all members of an enterprise on the basis of one member, one vote. Such democracy, or self-management, may include potential customers in the allocation process. The description 'clan' was coined by Ouchi (1984).

Although actual economic systems invariably combine all three of these means of resource allocation in complex hybrids, it is useful to consider the internal economic organisation of industrial enterprises within each system separately.

Markets

In a static market economy, with no uncertainty, the concept of internal organisation is completely redundant since all resources are allocated in spot market transactions between individual buyers and sellers. Where uncertainty does exist, individuals can reduce it or trade it via insurance contracts, market research, advertising, etc. If, however, uncertainty is radical and not susceptible to marginal calculations, individuals may build contingency clauses into their contracts, or else buyers and sellers may commit themselves in the market according to their subjective expectations regarding future prices, without rigorous analysis.

Although market transactions can be extremely sophisticated, perhaps linking together different transactions and contingencies, they are characterised in general by *horizontal* contacts between buyers and sellers, and by negligible *ex-ante* co-ordination of transactions. When misjudgements occur—for example, sellers anticipate demands that never materialise—resource allocation is achieved retrospectively or *ex post*. Dealers who anticipate correctly are adopted by the market while others must adapt or leave. The costs of such adjustments may be high for certain industries.

Internal organisations do develop in even the purest market economies, however, for reasons familiar to anybody who has considered the standard question in micro-economic theory: 'Why do firms exist?'. Where a 'firm' is defined as an industrial organisation, within which resources are allocated mainly through administrative methods, an answer to this question before Coase (1937) would have relied upon *technological* factors like Adam Smith's division of labour, specialisation and economies of scale. In these terms, firms outcompeted individuals through production cost savings in transport and fuel, for example, by having long production runs within one organisation.

Gradually, however, the importance of technology has declined in the explanation of why firms exist. First, Knight (1921) argued that firms could handle uncertainty better than individuals, and the first step was taken along the path towards explaining the existence of firms in terms of information and *transactions* costs rather than technology. (Transactions costs comprise the costs of gathering information, processing it, reaching decisions and disseminating it, either in markets or within hierarchies.)

Coase (1937) extended Knight's ideas and showed that, in circumstances characterised by radical uncertainties, transactions costs could be reduced by buyers offering vague, long-term contracts to suppliers, rather than relying on a series of precise, short-term contracts. Suppliers would, however, submit themselves to the *authority* of the buyer on points of detail within the general terms of the contract, with certain limits. So, for example, labour could be hired by a firm on long-term, general contracts without any explicit agreement on specific duties. Redundancy or dismissal is quite rare and, apart from overtime variations and minor bonuses, remuneration typically does not reflect the firm's performance or labour's contribution to it. In return for fixed pay, however, employees are generally expected to obey the employer's instructions. Williamson (1985) considers that internal resource allocation is generally preferable to external market contracts whenever transactions involve inputs to production that have few alternative uses (asset specificity), that are required frequently (recurrence) or that are characterised by complexity and uncertainty which puts sellers in a dominant position (small numbers opportunism). While internal organisation may constitute what Williamson calls a preferred 'governance structure', however, this does not guarantee superior performance. (Some of the problems inherent in all vertical hierarchies are discussed below, and the reforms designed to counter them are examined on p. 117 ff.)

Before going on to consider plans, however, it should be noted that modern economists are not unanimous in seeing markets and internal hierarchies as alternatives, and higher profits from 'preferred governance structures' as an unalloyed benefit, see Putterman (1986, pp. 5–29). On one view, all hierarchies may be seen as just a 'nexus' (or meeting point) of individual market contracts. Alternatively, hierarchies may be preferred because they confer more power on certain controlling interest groups, not necessarily shareholders.

Plans

This section is rather longer than the last because 'plans' are common to centrally-planned economies (CPEs) and also to predominantly market economies.

Central plans involve control by a 'visible hand', as opposed to markets, and resources are predominantly allocated and controlled by administrative means. The firm in a market economy can therefore be seen as a CPE in microcosm; at the other end of the spectrum, the entire economy of the USSR has been characterised as 'USSR Incorporated'. The literature in comparative economic systems is therefore a rich one for those who wish to understand what happens inside firms.

Central plans involve rejecting the *ex-post* resource co-ordination of market economies in favour of conscious, *ex-ante* attempts at rationality. Of course, just as markets in practice become 'corrupted' by hierarchies within organisations, so observed behaviour within CPEs often seems to bear little resemblance to the central plan, often based on horizontal, decentralised decisions.

In the purest theory, however, central planners (at no cost to themselves) collect accurate information on production possibilities. This information is then combined with the relative preferences of the central authorities to produce optimal plans which are smoothly transmitted to industrial enterprises in the form of directives that are instantly obeyed to the letter.

Just as separate market dealings involve transactions costs in the form of collecting information on prices, seeking out buyers and sellers, and devising and monitoring contracts, so do administrative hierarchies perform less than perfectly in practice. In particular, the existence of significant transactions costs, together with the possibility of self-interested behaviour by members of a vertical hierarchy, gives rise to the twin problems of adverse selection and moral hazard. Both terms are borrowed from the world of insurance, where buyers typically have more information than sellers. With the control of vertical hierarchies, this situation is usually reversed.

Adverse selection occurs before a contract is agreed, although sequential contracts remove this distinction. With adverse selection, one party to a transaction has information unavailable to the other which is crucial to the value of a contract. The buyer or the seller without the information is forced to accept uniform prices and cannot tailor contracts to the individual. With life insurances, for example, a buyer may submit an application form truthfully, but not voluntarily disclose a subjective feeling of being unwell. Within an administrative hierarchy, principals (employers, i.e. buyers) may find it difficult to select agents (employees, i.e. sellers); and even if an employment contract comes up for renewal, a principal may find it difficult to judge whether previous outcomes were attributable to the agent's performance or to other contributory factors. Agents may distort, concede or simply not fully disclose information voluntarily, in order to encourage employers to renew contracts for another period on the same terms, as for other colleagues at similar levels in the hierarchy. In a CPE, for example, the director of a state farm may conceal incompetence by overstating output. If all state farm directors overstate farm output, and principals in the Ministry of Agriculture are unable to expose fictitious returns, good directors are unable to demonstrate their special qualities and will be paid the uniform wage for all directors. But they are likely to resign if their talents are appreciated better elsewhere, and state farms will be left with all the weak directors.

Moral hazard also involves asymmetric information, but usually occurs after a contract, in response to its terms. With insurance, for example, a householder may deploy fewer precautions against theft if the contents of the house are insured. More generally, moral hazard is a problem for principals who share with agents (Strong and Waterson 1987, p. 21) '. . . the same information up to the point at which the agent selects an action, but thereafter the principal is only able to observe the outcome or payoff, not the action itself.' So, for example, the director of a state farm in a CPE—charged with managing the farm's resources to promote the achievement of the central plan—may achieve gross output targets, but only by neglecting to maintain machinery or to rotate crops properly.

Both adverse selection and moral hazard are likely to be significant where agent's decisions are non-routine—perhaps requiring a subjective evaluation of uncertain events—and where other factors besides the decisions and efforts of agents contribute to outcomes. But in addition these two phenomena, which are associated with uncertainty, vertical hierarchies must cope with the communications decay that occurs between different levels, and the bounded rationality of the decision makers, especially at the top of the hierarchy. Even with perfect information, head office must use rules of thumb to make practical decisions in reasonable time. Conscious of the potential importance of moral hazard and adverse selection at lower levels, bounded rationality at the top, and communications decay in between, the heads of bureaucracies within CPEs or inside capitalist corporations can resort to a number of possible remedies.

'Clan'-type remedies are discussed later but, broadly, the heads (or principals) of a vertical hierarchy may 'harden' the constraints on agents' behaviour by strengthening *administrative* procedures and/or introducing *market* (or quasi-market) elements. The concept of constraint hardness was developed by Kornai (1986).

Hard administration can involve stricter inspection, penalties and rewards (financial or otherwise) in relation to targets, budgets or other performance indicators. Inspectors are, however, human beings and subject to the peculiar 'moral hazards' of their job: extortion and 'capture' by the agents under inspection (Hemenway 1985). It is possible to design circumstances in which inspection is likely to secure more compliant behaviour from agents but the eternal problem remains of, 'Who monitors the monitors?'

The main advantage of administrative procedures, compared with the discipline of markets, is that conscious administration is likely to be more humane and to involve less drastic *ex-post* adjustment. By the same token however, it is difficult to identify and isolate responsibility for one section's performance when this depends inevitably on decisions made at more than one level of the vertical hierarchy: this suggests that higher levels will claim the credit for good performance at lower levels and cover up poor performance. The application of penalties and rewards by administrative means is therefore likely to be more inert than the dispassionate influence of product and capital market competition devoid of administrative attempts at rationality.

Market-related remedies for the problem of bureaucracies can focus on the organisation (decentralisation) or the individual (motivation), although in practice the two will interact.

Decentralisation refers to the delegation of authority and responsibility from higher to lower levels in a vertical hierarchy. In its weakest form, decentralisation means spending discretion within a budget or cost centre. In its strongest form, it implies total spending and selling freedom for profit centres tantamount to independent subsidiary companies. Between these two extremes lie the profit centres for M-form divisions which are empowered to make selling and spending decisions (up to a certain limit) of a routine, operating nature, while strategic decisions are retained at the top of the vertical hierarchy, e.g. the head office of a corporation. (The strengths and weaknesses of divisionalisation are discussed below, but at this stage it is pertinent to note that, whatever the benefits, any act of decentralisation must make *ex-ante* resource co-ordination at the centre more difficult, as decentralised choices are made at lower levels within a vertical hierarchy.) Decentralisation is invariably

linked with market-type motivation: within the M-form corporation, for
example, an internal labour market employs bonuses and promotions to
reward compliant behaviour on the part of divisional agents. Similarly,
Williamson (1985) argued for the relative efficiency of internal capital
markets, whereby profitable divisions are rewarded with large shares of
the corporation's investment programme.

Any quasi-market rewards and penalties within a vertical hierarchy
must, however, confront the problem of managers who have to behave
'entrepreneurially', whatever the economic system. Entrepreneurial
behaviour amounts to *arbitrage* operations across markets, technologies
and time. Even the director of a state farm in a CPE will have to
specialise in obtaining cheap raw materials, land and credit, unless the
state takes all these decisions at the centre, which is rare in any CPE. The
director may also have to generate sales revenue beyond procurements by
the state's retail sector, and the directors of Research Institutes are
responsible for the design of innovations whose benefits exceed costs.
These entrepreneurial decisions require judgement regarding uncertain
costs and revenues, and it will be very difficult to design an optimal
contract and monitor entrepreneurial performance when exogenous
factors, like chance, play a significant role. With more routine activities,
it is relatively easy to take a small sample of an agent's efforts to monitor
performance. With arbitrageurs, however, it is very difficult to check the
quality of inputs obtained (however cheaply), and the inspection of
samples of agent's behaviour yields little information. Market economies
solve the problem by making the entrepreneur a major claimant on
residual profits, thus rewarding successful arbitrage and the monitoring of
more routine operations within the corporation's hierarchy. In many
circumstances, the monitoring of relatively routine operations by
arbitrageurs will involve lower transactions costs than the monitoring of
arbitrageurs by the workforce in general. This issue will be addressed in
part (3).

CPEs are obviously unwilling to accept entrepreneurs as residual
claimants (although rewards based on measured profits, in relation to
planned profits, are common): pure residual claims would be unbounded
from above, would drastically change the distribution of income, and pure
profit making by local and national monopolies could be exploitative.
Above all, however, private residual claims on profit would lead to
decentralised decisions that would make central, *ex-ante* resource co-
ordination even more hazardous.

It goes without saying, therefore, that the problems and costs of
administration can never be eliminated; of course, the same can be said
of markets. In Section 6.3 a recent reform in a CPE is analysed—
although, bureaucracies can also have recourse to 'clan' solutions.

Clans

Self-management involves the sort of decision-making that exists within many families or *clans*, whereby all important decisions are made by the workforce or by a managerial committee with delegated powers and perhaps a rotating or elected membership. These 'important' decisions would certainly have to include the distribution of profits to members, investment levels, the product mix and the size of the membership. Capital may be supplied out of enterprise ploughback in the case of the worker-managed firm (WMF) or by an outsider like the State (with no powers of control) in the labour-managed firm (LMF).

It should not be assumed, however, that markets and plans rely upon a Hobbesian view of human nature dominated by fear and self-interest, whereas clans have John Locke's perspective of men being basically decent, social-minded and quite capable of ruling themselves. Certainly, many idealistic advocates of co-operation borrow Locke's vision from the seventeenth century, but clans have, in many circumstances, a hard-boiled, economic basis as an effective governance structure.

Clans dispense with the *vertical* monitoring, common to bureaucracies within CPEs, and to market capitalism, where residual claimants and their agents perform the task. Vertical monitoring is replaced within clans by *horizontal* monitoring by each clan member, who recognises that compliant behaviour by each member will raise distributed profits per member. More idealistically, self-management may improve enterprise performance by reducing any 'alienation' in a vertically-monitored workforce and by promoting 'self-actualisation'.

Horizontal monitoring within clans potentially dispenses with problems of moral hazard and adverse selection, since all members share profits and there are no principals and agents—only principals. At the same time, however, WMFs and LMFs are associated with critical problems like Ward–Vanek effects and under-investment (WMF) and over-investment (LMF), where members have truncated time-horizons (Jensen and Meckling 1979). Institutions can be designed to overcome all these problems, albeit at the expense of an equal distribution of enterprise profits and/or loss of some membership control.

The most persistent threats to self-management, however, are associated with the transactions costs of participatory decision-making and free-riding by individual members.

Williamson (1975, p. 46) pointed out the burdensome transactions cost implications of 'all-channel' communications within a self-managed firm. At the absurd extreme, a separate workers' council meeting must be convened for every single decision, whereas in any vertical hierarchy, senior positions can act as a central focus for information transfers.

Although they concede that residual-sharing by employees may reduce shirking through horizontal monitoring, Alchian and Demsetz (1972) assert that this is more than matched by free-riding and additional shirking, since '[i]f this were not so, profit sharing with employees should have occurred more frequently in Western societies . . . ' (p. 786). It is however possible that, within clans, there may operate an equivalent of the 'Marglin' effect, first developed in relation to social rates of time-preference (Marglin 1963). In the case of a firm, the active monitoring, encouragement and criticism of colleagues by one member has a demonstration effect on others who realise that their attitude and behaviour has external benefits. It is widely appreciated that free-riding is infectious, too, and therefore less likely.

As regards Alchian and Demsetz's quote from 1972, the numbers of self-managed firms and profit-sharing schemes in the West have increased steadily, but there are still many reasons why clan-like firms may find it difficult to compete in large-scale production. It is an empirical matter whether self-management generates more flexibility and lower costs through horizontal monitoring, while Ward–Vanek effects and inefficient investment levels can be eliminated—though at a cost. For whatever reason, however, clan-like firms have tended to remain small, compared with capitalist or state firms, and it seems likely that the explanation can be found in terms of risk and the kind of operation susceptible to self-management. In WMFs, it has been suggested that the labour membership is likely to vote for lower investment and higher distributions than a capitalist firm because the impossibility of tradeable shares makes it difficult for members to hold a diversified portfolio of assets. Already dependent upon the WMF for employment, members may be reluctant to put more eggs in the same basket.

Beyond risk sharing, however, it is possible to explain the size and prevalence of clan-like firms by reference to modern theories of entrepreneurship (see Barzel 1987), discussed in the previous section. Briefly, it is proposed that the entrepreneur often assumes the role of residual claimant in a capitalist firm because the entrepreneur's non-routine arbitrage operations are more costly for the workforce to monitor, through moral hazard and adverse selection, than are the more routine operations of the workforce by the entrepreneur. In addition, the entrepreneur tends to become a capitalist lender to the firm, because the entrepreneur's own capital serves as a bond for the workforce. In many sectors of the economy, however, it is vital that *all* members of a firm act entrepreneurially and therefore become candidates for residual claims. For example, professional members of accountancy, architecture or law practices must seek out clients that are expected to provide profitable assignments. Even a taxi-driver must judge where and when to seek out profitable fares, when to rest, when to re-fuel, and must perform minor, non-routine repairs to the cab itself, see Russell (1985).

It seems no coincidence, therefore, that self-management (or partnership) has dominated those service sector functions where all members must be arbitrageurs to a significant degree, and where technology has not created a predominance of easily-monitored, routine tasks. In addition, self-management will be particularly appropriate where value-added is a high and stable proportion of total revenue: this will be the case where firms require relatively little capital and where revenue is stable as a result of sales to a wide portfolio of customers. These circumstances prevail in exactly the sort of small, service sector activities envisaged above.

It is suggested that this entrepreneurial perspective promotes an understanding of recent market-based reforms within self-managed economies and the introduction of market and clan-like elements to market capitalism and CPEs. These issues are addressed in the next section.

6.3   Reforms in Different Economic Systems

Market Reform

It was noted above that market capitalism is best suited to those industries where the *ex-post* costs of market adjustment are low and where entrepreneurs and their agents can easily monitor the more routine tasks of other employees in an internal hierarchy. However, all tasks can be viewed as having a potentially entrepreneurial component: even workers with the most mundane, routine duties may be able to recommend ways of raising revenues and reducing costs. It may therefore be considered worthwhile for capitalist firms to introduce *profit-sharing schemes* to reduce costs and increase productivity through the horizontal monitoring of the firm as a '*clan*'. A different view of such schemes is that they sharpen the *market* element within firms by linking individual performance (profit) to rewards, although this argument probably applies only to those executives whose behaviour as arbitrageurs significantly affects profit. Finally, profit sharing may be seen as doing nothing towards solving problems of moral hazard and adverse selection, being merely a *bureaucratic* device to appease unions or to pay employees (especially senior executives) in a tax-efficient way.

This section will consider profit sharing from each of these perspectives and provide an empirical survey. Broadly speaking, profit sharing can take the form of profit-related pay (PRP) in the form of cash, and/or the issue of shares or share options (donated by the firm or sold to employees on favourable terms) that may be available to the whole workforce or only a select few. Of course ownership does not guarantee control, and PRP does not even confer any ownership on employees, thus having little 'clan' potential. With profit sharing in the form of shares, however, large employee shareholdings may accumulate, and powers of control must inevitably accrue to groups with significant shareholdings. Self-management is defined in terms of control, not ownership, but general residual profit-sharing may be considered as one step towards the 'clan'. Presumably, if profit sharing does enhance horizontal monitoring, the effect of this 'clannishness' will be to increase company profits—though perhaps only in the long run, as a feeling of 'belongingness' develops and conflict declines.

In the short run, however, profit sharing (especially PRP) may be expected to sharpen the individual's contract by trading risk or by making rewards depend upon performance. This perspective emphasises that profit shares are only handed out in return for something.

Even if profit sharing leaves profits and productivity unaffected, it may be possible for the shareholders to *trade risk* with employees. In return for a share of residual profits, employees would have to bear a share of risks in addition to any existing overtime variations and any uncertainty of employment. It must be emphasised that, as opposed to PRP, losses may be shared as well as profits, especially when shares are held by employees. Employees at the margin may be significantly averse to such additional risk-bearing as a result of the risks they already bear, their relatively low incomes, and their undiversified asset portfolios.

Risks and expected profit may be *changed* if individual rewards are related to profit, since significant increases in profits and reductions in variability are dependent upon the realisation that profit can be influenced by individual action. However, if the effects of individuals' efforts are swamped (e.g. by currency variations, shifts in energy prices and political instability), then the employee will tend to free-ride with a sense of lacking control over, and responsibility for, company profits. It may be possible to restrict profit sharing schemes to those senior executives whose entrepreneurial decisions have a significant impact on company profit, but this may create jealousies within the firm. The only alternative is to sharpen the contracts of individual employees in general through the delineation of very local profit centres or by making profit shares dependent upon some local performance 'trigger'.

As with any 'clan' effect, the market-enhancing effect of profit-sharing can be expected to raise company productivity and profits. On the other hand, if profit-sharing reinforces the *bureaucratic* element implicit in any capitalist firm, profits may be expected to fall. The bureaucratic element that could be strengthened by profit sharing depends on which group is most powerful within the internal organisation of the firm. Profit sharing may represent an opportunity for shareholders, through their hierarchy of control, to shift a proportion of their risks onto employees: for example, employees must suffer automatic income reductions when profits fall. Alternatively, profit sharing may involve little more than creating the illusion of co-operation by shareholders and their managerial agents. For example, it is reported that each employee in Cadbury Schweppes's UK confectionery division receives £1 for every £1m of Cadbury Schweppes pre-tax profits (Incomes Data Services 1986, p. 25). At the other extreme, powerful unions may use profit-sharing proposals as just another opportunity to bid up employee remuneration. More realistically, senior executives may be the dominant group within the hierarchy; in this case, they can devise executive profit-sharing schemes to suit their own pockets. It follows that if profit-sharing schemes reinforce the power of dominant groups within corporate bureaucracies, profits should fall in the long run.

This wide range of possible outcomes is reflected in the diversity of empirical evidence on profit sharing in practice. Surveys of employees' attitudes to profit sharing have generally shown positive, 'clannish' responses (see, for example, Bell and Hanson 1984) but corporate performance, in terms of profitability, has not yet shown any general tendency to improve with profit sharing and/or PRP (see Blanchflower and Oswald 1987, Baddon *et al.* 1987).

It seems clear that profit-sharing can only be a complement to, not a substitute for, the effective management of a corporate internal hierarchy. It is possible, however, that the benefits in terms of profit will be manifested over the long term. Important research remains to be done in the area of executive share incentives and profitability.

Reform in Centrally-Planned Economies (CPEs)

Significant economic reforms were proposed, during 1987, for the world's largest industrial CPE: the USSR. Many of these planned reforms were concerned with the internal organisation of industrial enterprises. A new Individual Enterprise law extended the number of occupations that may be carried out privately on the market by individuals and their immediate families. This activity includes the sale of services and goods to State enterprises. Although the hiring of non-family labour is expressly forbidden, and therefore private hierarchies are unlawful, the new laws do permit and encourage the formation of private workers' co-operatives of between five and fifty partners. Proposed reforms of State enterprises include the election of enterprise managers and 'self-accounting', whereby enterprises are supposed to finance all expenditures from their own revenues.

Often in the past, similar proposals have been heard, however, and certainly full self-accounting would require a massive reform of the USSR prices of most inputs and outputs. For the purpose of this chapter, it is useful to look at one CPE, Hungary, that embarked on a similar process of economic reform in 1968. That process is still incomplete—an outcome which has undoubted significance for the USSR. It is particularly interesting to review one actual Hungarian reform that is now being proposed for the USSR: the encouragement of work partnerships (VGMKs in Hungary) within State firms that may perform services within the State firm itself or outside. Such a review should reveal some of the subtle strengths and weaknesses associated with any attempt to mix markets and clans within the CPE.

It was noted above that vertical hierarchies, whatever their strengths in relation to resource co-ordination, are plagued by the agency problems of moral hazard and adverse selection within enterprises, by complexity and bounded rationality at the top of any hierarchy, and by communications decay in between. VGMKs in Hungary have been developed, since 1981, in an attempt to strengthen the element of clan and market in an industrial system that can still be described as a CPE. Almost three per cent of the total workforce, or some 121,000, were organised in about 11,000 partnerships by 1984, and numbers had perhaps doubled by 1987.

VGMKs are partnerships of up to thirty members, formed from the existing workforces within State firms, but State managers are excluded from them by law. Up to five partnerships can combine to create co-operatives with a maximum of 150 members. By agreement with the State enterprise, partnerships may convert State materials into partnership sales using State plant and machinery without charge.

The kind of work that has been carried out by VGMKs reflects the CPE's problems of motivation and complexity, discussed above. Broadly speaking, partnerships have been considered necessary for the areas of activity with a very high non-routine content. First, unscheduled jobs of a 'one-off' nature are often not susceptible to the sequencing and planning of a CPE. So, for example, the author has witnessed VGMKs which add the final, 'customising' finish to a coach in the buyer's own livery, and teams that construct wooden pallets for the delivery of an unexpected export order to the West. Second, where specialist knowledge and the *quality* of service is important, monitoring is often easier and more effective when it occurs in the course of a separate market transaction. Thus, VGMKs have been contracted to maintain those State buildings for which VGMK members, as State employees, were responsible for designing and constructing.

As shown below, VGMKs have the potential to contribute to the solution of the CPE's standard problems of individual motivation and central complexity. Individual motivation is weakened by the presence of adverse selection and moral hazard in any rigid vertical hierarchy: for example, above-average workers may find it difficult to demonstrate and enjoy the fruits of their ability and efforts (adverse selection results from uniform pay), and yet VGMKs create the opportunity to link individual effort and reward more closely. For the State firm, payments to VGMK members make it easier to retain good workers and to reduce labour turnover; partnerships may also succeed in reducing moral hazard, since members sharing partnership profits will have less incentive to shirk and more reason to monitor others horizontally. The non-completion of planned tasks and the 'storming' of output at the end of the planning period, which is characteristic of CPEs, can be rectified relatively easily by transferring unfinished work to the VGMKs.

The complexity of central decisions can also be reduced by the formation of VGMKs. For example, Stark (1985, p. 264) reports how the installation of heavy machinery in a Hungarian State (or any large) firm involves formal planning and sequencing in a number of separate departments, while the VGMK, composed of employees from each department, can eliminate paperwork and organise the installation on a cheap, informal basis. Vertical monitoring can be expensive and complex, but Révész (1984), p. 345) points out that the individual motivation and horizontal monitoring within VGMKs will lead to levels of labour productivity that are about 20–30 per cent higher than in the State firm itself.

Taken together, these potential benefits of VGMKs provide a possible solution to some of the basic problems of the CPE. Although they represent a mixture of plan, clan and market, they can have the effect of *strengthening* the CPE by reducing complexity at the centre and by removing bottlenecks in the attainment of planned levels of output. Individual workers have also had reason to support VGMKs, since they have often raised their incomes by more than two-thirds (Révész 1984, p. 339).

Nevertheless, VGMKs and similar market reforms can constitute a *threat* to the CPE, and act as an obstacle to the attainment of planned levels of output. They lead inevitably to the growth of income differentials and personal jealousies, since only the best workers are invited to join, but this could be considered to be an acceptable price to pay for greater efficiency through reductions in complexity, adverse selection and moral hazard. Work partnerships do, however, create a serious threat to the CPE in a number of other ways.

First, the different sets of prices prevailing within the State firm, within the VGMK and on the black markets provide an obvious opportunity for arbitrage operations of an entrepreneurial nature that amount to moral hazard. The free use of machines and materials by the VGMK can obviously be abused, and Stark (1985, p. 262) reports 'that members of the VGMK are hiding spare parts, raw materials, and machine fittings that are in short supply to use during their work for the partnerships'. In addition, State managers are acutely concerned (see Révész 1984, p. 352) with the possibility that regular working time will be characterised by shirking which is designed to raise the demand for VGMK production. Workers may also enjoy what Oliver Williamson calls 'information impactedness', and Stark (1985, p. 259) writes of ' . . . numerous cases in which workers used their tacit knowledge of enterprises to bargain for better rates for their partnerships.' In this way, resources may be diverted from the central plan, thus threatening the achievement of planned outputs.

Second, work partnerships may be strangled at a local level by the very complexity which gave rise to their birth. Thus, local managers may thwart the reforming intentions of the central authorities. For example, the free use of State machinery and materials at weekends, by VGMKs, does not ensure that the premises will be lit and heated, that the power for the machines will be turned on, or even that the factory gates will be unlocked—these complementary services are complex and difficult to include in any contract. Therefore, they provide an opportunity for local managers to keep VGMK prices low, but also to frustrate the decentralising intentions of the central authorities.

So, in practice, VGMKs may bolster or threaten central plans. Above all, however, the author's experience suggests the general conclusion that reform in any economic system is likely to be 'corrupted' by the economic regime that dominates the environment. In the case of work partnerships in Hungary, the convenors have often turned out to be those shop-floor Communist Party secretaries who, in turn, have such a great influence over the formal system of economic management in State firms. Although State managers themselves are expressly forbidden from joining VGMKs, they can still dominate them. Révész (1984, p. 358) recognises the possibility that management may organise VGMK work and Falus-Szikra (1985, p. 17) claims that: 'The leasing of shops and the contractual running of shops, specialised groups of co-operatives or economic work teams are practically built into the inner mechanisms of big enterprises'. Bureaucratic favouritism now becomes a clear possibility and VGMKs may end up with budget constraints that are as soft as those in the vertical hierarchies they purport to replace.

VGMKs may therefore reinforce a major *weakness* of the CPE: a bureaucratic inflexibility which is generated, usually, at local levels rather than at the centre. Work partnerships have had their most liberating effect in Hungary when they provide local management with an opportunity to evade central wages controls. In turn, however, the VGMKs may become part of the local status quo and new State employees can be attracted by incomes which include VGMK payments amounting to overtime, controlled and guaranteed by local managements. There are obvious pressures which prevent the clan and market elements inherent in the Hungarian VGMK from surviving as an island in a sea of central planning. This conclusion has clear implications for any economic reform proposed from the centre of a CPE.

Reform and Self-Management

The characteristics of clans, or self-managed enterprises, were reviewed in the previous section. They have potential strengths in the areas of members' identification with the firm, motivation and horizontal monitoring; but horizontal monitoring becomes more difficult as firm size increases. In addition, self-managed firms may not grow as fast as their capitalist equivalents because of attitudes to risk, an unwillingness to invest in one's workplace, or because few industries require a significant degree of entrepreneurial activity at all levels. Without subsidisation or further organisational adaptation, self-management is likely to be restricted to small firms, usually in service industries.

One attempt to reconcile self-management with large-scale manufacturing has been made in Northern Spain, in a development—the Mondragon group of co-operatives—which involves many tiers of self-management, with a co-operative bank at the top. Mondragon, however, has already attracted a great deal of academic debate (see, for example, Thomas and Logan 1982), and so the rest of this section is concerned with self-management in Yugoslavia in relation to a reform which features prominently in the literature on transactions costs, (and in other chapters of this book): divisionalisation.

It was noted, in the previous section, that the clan element in profit-sharing has faced a hard struggle in the context of an environment dominated by capitalism. In Yugoslavia, too, a country wracked by nationalistic divisions, clannishness has had to struggle against the forces of a CPE—especially the power of central authorities, local authorities, trade unions and the League of Communists. Despite a series of decentralising reforms, Yugoslavia's industry is still highly concentrated, and in 1981 the 130 largest firms accounted for 75 per cent of total industrial sales (Sacks 1983, p. 33). Industrial firms are not subject to an overt central plan, but factories find it impossible to function without social infrastructure—in the form of housing, public transport, energy, etc. The authorities control the provision of these services to suit their priorities (Pienkos 1986) and bank finance is available on political, and not just straight commercial, grounds.

The 1974 Yugoslav constitution was designed to break down the power of the external authorities and of the enterprise director and departmental heads within the enterprise. Each section within the enterprise to which revenues and costs could be attributed was to become a profit centre or Basic Organisation of Associated Labour (BOAL). BOALs were supposed to compete with others, both inside and beyond the original enterprise's boundaries; alternatively, they could co-operate with other BOALs through 'self-management' agreements. In either case, BOAL decisions were to be made by mandated delegates from each BOAL department at a workers' council.

Just as M-form corporations in the West have had to recognise that scale economies make the decentralisation of *all* functions to divisional profit centres impracticable, so in Yugoslavia central routine and strategic functions were considered necessary. Routine personnel, marketing, accounting, legal and secretarial functions were to be hired, in the form of work communities (RZs), and specialists in these departments were simply supposed to serve different BOALs on a contract basis, without participating in their decisions. Non-routine, strategic decisions involve the largest-scale economies. On the face of it, independent strategic decisions within each BOAL would involve at best wasteful duplication and at worst contradictions. Collective strategies for Yugoslav BOALs were to be produced by 'self-management agreements' between otherwise independent BOALs, or by the voluntary association of BOALs in an enterprise or, more strictly, a work organisation (RO) with strategy determined by a workers' council of BOAL representatives.

In practice, however, this attempt to marry clannishness with large-scale production has been corrupted in a number of ways. Stephen (1984, pp. 106–115) reports that RZs have been given the rights of BOALs in some cases, and that ROs may be nothing more than the old, pre-1974 monopolistic corporations. Together with the possibility of politically-determined transfer prices for inter-BOAL trade, these developments have facilitated the continued bureaucratisation of Yugoslav industry.

The essence of divisionalisation is competition, or at least quasi-competition, between divisional profit centres, which are responsible and answerable for their profit out-turns. With self-management in Yugoslavia, however, BOAL members are not usually involved in the initial decision to create a BOAL, which is made by local authorities, State banks and the Party, among others. This means that profitability is largely determined by the quality of investment, location and product-mix decisions made outside the allegedly self-managed BOAL. Sirc (1979, p. 155) claims that the League of Communists 'guides' or even 'meddles' with most subsequent BOAL decisions, and the 'unlimited solidarity' (Stephen 1984, p. 115) embodied in many self-management contracts between BOALs means that profits (and losses) are pooled. In any case, State banks can be relied upon to subsidise loss-making BOALs, even if associated BOALs are not. Sirc showed (1979, p. 155) that in 1976 at least 34 per cent of all BOALs incurred losses but survived; and, on behalf of the World Bank, Knight (1984, p. 16) showed for 1981 that 1,277 BOALs with 4.5 per cent of workers in the social sector made losses, and that subsidised 'rehabilitation credits' from the Banks financed two-thirds of these losses and permitted loss-making BOALs to expand rather than reduce their investment levels (p. 18). The World Bank has subsequently insisted that industrial credits should be made available at realistic rates of interest, i.e. at one per cent above the current rate of inflation, or a discount rate of 81 per cent in April 1987 (*Financial Times* 1987, supplement, 10 June, p. 2).

It is hard to disagree with Stephen (1984, p. 115) who concluded, ' . . . that the decentralisation into BOALs with seemingly market relations is a chimera . . . '. Some competition between divisions exists, but (Sacks 1983, p. 6), 'in a peculiar reversal of the traditional problem in the United States, the Yugoslav situation seems, at least in some cases, to be one of competition persisting despite government efforts to suppress it.'

Of course the Yugoslav authorities have had to cope with serious internal divisions, but the consequence is a system of so-called self-management in which workforces feel frustrated and alienated (Sirc 1979, p. 176). The 1974 Yugoslav Constitution was a brave attempt to encourage clannishness in large-scale industry that probably deserves a less divisive environment. In any case, any new experiment would need to legislate for the demand in a market economy for nimble-footed arbitrage operations of an entrepreneurial nature, which are difficult to reconcile with self-management in large firms; this is especially true where arbitrage means the contraction or closure of divisions or firms.

6.4   Conclusion

It is tempting to conclude that technology and the nature of products and services together define particular mixtures of plan, clan and market, which represent the optimal governance structures for particular industries. For example, separate market transactions or self-management can reduce costs in industries where adverse selection and moral hazard constitute serious problems. Central planning may be considered appropriate where the *ex-post* costs of market adjustment are high, and clans are useful where a significant amount of entrepreneurial activity is demanded by each member of the workforce. Such a conclusion implies Tinbergen's (1967) 'optimal economic order', and the convergence of the world's economic systems on an optimal mixed economy.

The second section of this chapter has demonstrated that the participants and authorities in all three types of economic system are only too aware of some of the weaknesses of their particular systems. This awareness is reflected in the variety of reforms being tried around the world. Economic institutions are potentially very adaptable: consider, for example, the unique blend of market and hierarchy represented by the sub-contracting in Japanese car manufacture, compared with the same technology elsewhere in the West.

'Optimal orders' are unlikely, however, for two reasons. First, Kornai's (1985, p. 137) 'supermarket fallacy' must apply. Economic systems cannot be assembled piecemeal, off-the-shelf. If the attempt is made to eliminate the shortcomings of the dominant system by grafting on elements of another, this can result in new shortcomings inherent in the graft itself, and possibly a reduction in the vitality of the dominant system. Furthermore, each of our three case studies suggests that there are powerful forces within each variety of economic system which lead to the rejection of 'alien tissue'. Second, there is no unanimity on the desirable characteristics of an economic system, even if systems were infinitely flexible. For example, different authorities place different weights on features like unemployment and productive efficiency. The situation is complicated further when these features are recognised as being interdependent.

7

Organisational Forms and Multinational Companies

PETER J. BUCKLEY*

7.1 Introduction

This chapter synthesises several strands of theory which centre on the internal organisation of multinational enterprises. We begin by providing the conceptual framework for this discussion by concentrating on the internalisation approach and the relevance of transaction cost economics for the organisation of multinational firms. After an examination of the literature on the organisation of multinational firms in the light of the transactions cost framework, we then introduce the related, but distinct, internationalisation and globalisation views of the dynamics of the growth of multinational firms. Finally, the interplay of market forces and organisational structure is assessed, and the role of cultural and national influences is analysed, before the various threads in the body of the chapter are drawn together in the conclusion.

7.2 The Internalisation Approach and Transaction Cost Economics

Several theories of the multinational firm may be identified (Buckley, Chapter 1, in Buckley and Casson 1985; Casson 1986a). The ideas of Coase (1937) have been extensively applied to the multinational firm by McManus (1972), Buckley and Casson (1976, 1985), Rugman (1980), and Hennart (1986), in what has become known as the internalisation approach. In addition, Dunning's 'eclectic theory' of the multinational firm (Dunning, 1981), combines ownership, internalisation and location-specific advantages in a synthesis of the literature on foreign direct investments. Third, Teece (1983) has extended Williamson's (1975) markets and hierarchies approach explicitly to the multinational firm. These approaches attach fundamental importance to the role of transactions costs in the development of multinational firms, and hence distinguish themselves from the work of Hymer (1976) who did not separate market structure problems from those relating to transactions costs.

There has been considerable debate in the literature as to the comparative contributions of these various approaches to the under-standing of why firms engage in activities in more than one country. For example, Dunning and Rugman (1985), have examined the extent of Hymer's contribution in terms of the internalisation approach, and Parry (1985) and Rugman (1985) have debated whether internalisation provides a general theory of foreign direct investment. The internalisation and markets and hierarchies approaches have developed their own vocabu-laries in analysing the multinational firm, but there are close similarities once terminological differences are removed (Williamson 1981, 1985; Casson 1987). However, there are some differences which it is worthwhile highlighting in what follows.

Internalisation

The basic approach of internalisation theorists is marginalist: by carefully specifying the transactional benefits and costs of internalisation which face firms in particular economic circumstances, predictions can be made on the division between internally organised and externally organised markets. A firm will grow by internalising imperfect external markets until it is bounded by markets for which the transactions costs of further internalisation outweigh the transactions cost savings to the firm. The motive for internalisation is profit. Internalisation may be particularly important to gain the benefits of international transfer pricing in order to reduce the firm's overall tax bill, to obtain improved quality control, and to gain vertical integration benefits.[1]

The incidence of transactions costs in internal and external markets can be used to derive propositions on the speed and direction of growth of the firm, (Buckley and Casson 1985, Chapter 5; Buckley 1983; Casson 1981).

The purist internalisation view taken by Buckley and Casson (1976, 1985) is that the internal organisation of the multinational firm is an approximation to a perfect market whereby the firm's internal processes are designed to transmit shadow prices to the key decision makers, which optimise the firm's overall profit. Thus, decentralised profit centres transmit shadow price signals to other decision makers in cost or profit centres (Buckley 1983). The multinational enterprise is thus a device for reducing transaction costs by buying or creating complementary assets in different nations and integrating their operations within a single unit of control. This is the internal market for intermediate goods and services. In this way, individual managers within the firm have decentralised decision-making powers such that control over the intermediate product actually changes hands as the product moves between plants, although ownership of the product does not (Casson 1981).

Hennart (1986) has drawn parallels between this view and views of economic planning (e.g. Heal 1973). Each decision maker within the firm maximises his profits, given these internal prices; the firm includes in these prices an optimal tax, leaving members with an income which is just enough to keep them in their present employment (Hennart drawing on Hirschleifer 1956). Thus the approach implies not only a decentralised organisation, but decentralised decision making based on central determination of goals and distribution of rewards. The organisation necessary to achieve this result is not made explicit, nor does it imply a black and white decentralised or centralised ruling principle. Consequently, an appraisal of the literature with this in mind is timely.

The internalisation approach has strong links with resource dependence approaches to organisational design (see especially Pfeffer and Salancik 1978). The role of management is seen, to a large degree, as reducing or loosening dependencies, deemed as the extent to which the organisation depends upon an external source for a large proportion of its output or input. This is a strong indicator of the direction of growth of a firm towards reducing those dependencies by internalisation of the market in the input (or output) which is crucial to its survival (Buckley and Casson 1976).

Internalisation versus Markets and Hierarchies

The original objective of the approach adopted by Buckley and Casson (1976) was to use the concept of internalisation of markets to develop a model of the growth of the firm. This has often been abandoned by more recent writers who take technological capability and/or marketing skills and/or management skills as given and, therefore, fixed (Buckley 1983). The most general statement of internalisation is tautologous: firms exist where they minimise transactions costs, and this has led to it being described as 'a concept in search of a theory' (Buckley 1983, p. 42). However, it is the wide applicability of internalisation as an explicator of growth which gives the theory its generality, and thus poses dangers. It is therefore necessary to place restrictions on the general theory to give rise to a number of 'special theories' which have empirical content and can be tested (Buckley 1988). By specifying different types of cost which can arise in internal and external markets, these testable propositions can be derived. As a result, it is possible to see a convergence between the internalisation approach and the markets and hierarchies approach of Oliver Williamson and others (Williamson 1985, 1975). The markets-and-hierarchies approach to the internal organisation of firms envisages the organisation as a substitute for policing the settlement of disputes: as a privatised (or internalised) legal system. Thus the 'firm as production function needs to make way for the view of the *firm as governance structure* if the ramifications of internal organisation are to be accurately assessed' (Williamson 1981, p. 1539). This notion has been developed by Williamson (1979), and Teece (1983), into 'governance costs' which occur because of incomplete contracting, arising because formal contracts cannot capture tacit knowledge. These problems are resolved by integration of the contractors (internalisation). This enables 'better disclosure, easier agreement, better governance and more efficient transfer' (Teece 1983, p. 55).

The markets-and-hierarchies approach is founded on the twin behavioural assumptions of 'bounded rationality' and 'opportunism'. The former refers to the limited capability of human beings to hold a wide variety of options to complex problem-solving situations. Only a restricted number of options can ever be fully considered and even these cannot be implemented by preparing a completely specified set of contracts in advance. The second recognises that individuals may act in their own interest rather than the organisation's, and this gives rise to potential costs of monitoring and enforcing agreements and contracts (see the Introduction to Francis, Turk and Willman 1983).

These behavioural assumptions—placed in a world where uncertainty and complexity dominate the environment—are subject to the constraint that many assets (including human assets) are specific and difficult to translate across tasks. The constraints of 'asset specificity' are well documented, possibly because this is the simplest concept, in the Williamsonian tool-box, to operationalise. Hierarchy thus becomes the best, though not the only, means of resolving governance costs, given this set of assumptions.

The internalisation approach emphasises an alternative to hierarchy as the means of resolving the problems of monitoring individuals within the organisation and reducing governance costs. Foreign subsidiary managers may have better knowledge of local conditions and thus it may be difficult to use hierarchical direction to remove discretion in decision making. The same result may be achieved at less cost by altering the incentives to individuals through the imposition of a decentralised shadow pricing system. This involves the managers of subsidiaries (or units within the firm) acting as profit centres and responding to the internal prices set by top managers to achieve the firm's overall objectives (Buckley 1983;

Hennart 1986). Hennart suggests that the incentives given by the internal market are more powerful and less costly than hierarchical control, which will only be used when price signals are inappropriate. This has important implications for the centralisation of activities within the multinational firm, as will be seen below.

However, the markets-and-hierarchies and internalisation framework are complementary in two important ways: first, they share the view that organisations economise on transactions costs; second, they require the use of supporting assumptions to give empirical content. Much of the empirical content derives from the incidence of transactions costs in internal and external markets. Contributions by Casson (1985), Teece (1983), Buckley (1987), Nicholas (1986) and others have shown that the incidence of transactions costs is particularly high in vertically integrated process industries, knowledge-intensive industries, quality-assurance dependent products and communication-intensive industries. What is crucial is the relative ability of the two approaches to predict *changes* in operational mode (market or firm)—both approaches need to be more fully operationalised (see Teece 1986). But major problems arise in the definition and measurement of transactions costs: the magnitude of transactions costs in relation to transport costs, production costs, marketing and distribution costs must be specified as well as the spatial configuration of their incidence. Causal empiricism suggests that transactions costs are high, but estimates are essential if the theories are to move beyond heuristic models to concrete propositions about market configurations (Buckley 1988). The dynamic considerations must also be drawn out—mirroring an early preoccupation of Williamson (1964).

7.3 The Organisation of Multinational Enterprises

The previous section has examined the basic tools of analysis of the internalisation approach to multinational enterprises (and to firms in general). This section examines the literature on the organisation of (multinational) firms, tracing its development through the pioneering work of Alfred Chandler and the strategy–structure framework, which attempts to plot the correlation between the objectives of the firm and the internal mechanisms necessary to achieve the firm's goals, to the evolutionary framework of organisational development and the tension between centralising and decentralising pressures. This section ends with a brief examination of principal–agent problems as they apply to the organisation of multinational firms.

The empirical literature on multinational enterprise has developed from the seminal work of Alfred Chandler (1962, 1977) and the ensuing strategy–structure approach. From this, the organisational form of multinationals has been examined in a number of countries and contexts. There is also an intertwined literature on the degree of centralisation in multinationals. This, in turn, is linked with the notion of governance structures. In this discussion, an attempt is made to link these concepts by examining them within the structure introduced in the previous section.

Chandler and the Strategy–Structure Debate

Alfred Chandler's review of the changes in organisation form through multifunction operation to divisionalisation (1962), and the growth and effect of managerial hierarchies (1977), spawned a group of studies of the organisation of multinational firms of different origins: Pavan (1972) on Italy, Rumelt (1974) on the United States, Channon (1973) on the UK, Dyas and Thanheiser (1976) on France and Germany and Wrigley (1976) on Canada. In addition, the painstaking historical work of Mira Wilkins (1970, 1974) on American business abroad has illuminated these processes.

The crude exhortations on organisational design that 'structure should follow strategy' belie the richness of the approach, as a perusal of Chandler's eight basic propositions as to why management (internal) control of economic activity has replaced the market will show (the *Visible Hand* 1977). However, the specification of the relationship between strategy and structure has not always been clear. To some degree, the internalisation framework can help. The direction of growth of the firm, and thus of managerial control, can (to some extent) be predicted if the markets surrounding the firm, and in particular the nature of market imperfections, are understood. Moreover, Chandler's propositions can be given more rigour and predictive content by an injection of the economics of internalisation. Unwise extrapolations of Chandler's analysis can result from excessive attention being given to the firm without adequate consideration of the industrial context in which it is placed and the macroeconomic framework surrounding it.

Organisational Forms of Multinational Enterprises

An immediate distinction must be made, in the analysis of the organisational form of multinationals, between the statutory or legal organisation and the managerial organisation. It is the latter which will be discussed here.

It is conventional to discuss the organisation of multinationals in terms of a framework which is, implicitly at least, evolutionary. The conventional stages approach has suggested an autonomous subsidiary stage, followed by an international division approach, then an international organisational structure and finally a global matrix approach. While such a rigid evolutionary typology is now a thing of the past, the international development of the firm is clearly one major influence on organisational form.

The problems of organising a multinational firm have been considered in the context of various tensions in the firm and external pressures on it. One issue is whether the company should be divided into domestic and international divisions; a second is the direction of managerial line responsibility—should it be subdivided according to major function (marketing, finance, R & D), product lines or geographical areas? Arising out of this dilemma is how best to provide for co-ordination with the other two variables, when one of the three key parameters (function, geographical area, product) is chosen as the predominant organisational principle (see *inter alia* Stopford and Wells 1972, Brooke and Remmers 1978).

This literature is equivalent to the M-form debate concerning unitary organisation (U-form) based on product divisions. The work of Chandler (1962, 1977) is usually used as a touchstone. From divisionalisation within a formal administrative structure, traced from the US railroads to the organisational innovations of Pierre S. du Pont and Alfred P. Sloan, the M-form is held to aid (1) strategic planning and (2) monitoring and control of activities through management hierarchies (Williamson 1981). This leads to the view that a global strategy—whereby strategic planning and major policy decisions are taken centrally and implemented worldwide—could only be accomplished through a multi-divisional framework (Stopford and Wells 1972, p. 25). Such an approach remains unnecessarily rigid, and, in an approach allowing greater flexibility, Brooke (1986) interprets an organisation in terms of four main objectives:

(1) enabling decisions to be taken effectively and at the right time,
(2) providing a channel within which to exercise authority,
(3) providing a system for reporting and communication, and
(4) providing a career structure.

Although retaining a basic evolutionary approach, Brooke allows for options at each stage, and for informal pressures as well as formal structures to influence developments. Crucially, he also makes the point that organisational structure at any moment of time is a snapshot of a dynamic process.

Centralisation and Decentralisation

The issue of the degree of centralisation of multinational firms has so far been explicitly avoided, even though it is implicitly ever-present. Brooke

(1984) sees the organisation as the result, at a point in time, of continuing conflicts to which the firm seeks a resolution. This leads to a dynamic view of organisation structure as an evolving, interim solution. At a moment in time there will be pressures on head office towards greater centralisation and towards greater autonomy for the subsidiary; similarly, these conflicting pressures will operate on the subsidiary (Brooke 1986). Consequently, external pressures will be moderated, directed and influenced by power struggles within the firm. Amongst the most important pressures are, for *centralisation*: (1) the need to direct scarce resources on the basis of worldwide information, (2) the need to pursue the interests of the firm as a whole, even where this conflicts with those of one or more individual subsidiaries (rationalisation is an excellent example), (3) a career structure militating for head office interests; and for *decentralisation*: (1) cost reduction by devolving decision making, (2) problems of communication, (3) the view that more rapid decision making results from autonomy, (4) the fact that subsidiary management is more likely to be in tune with local economic conditions, (5) incentive effects arising from freedom in decision making, (6) external political influences requiring devolved decisions.

The resolution of these pressures depends upon the particular situation of the firm. Of great importance are:

(i)   industry-specific factors such as standardised products, the nature of integration and the nature of the external markets which the firm faces;
(ii)   region-specific factors, including the geographical and social distance between the centre and the subsidiaries (these of course influence communication costs)
(iii) nation-specific factors, particularly political and fiscal relations between the countries spanned by the firm;
(iv)   factors specific to the firm itself, including the availability of skills and cost of management in each location (these will influence the degree of centralisation) (Buckley and Casson 1976, Brooke 1986).

It is no surprise that the factors which determine the degree of centralisation are also determinants of internalisation, but the two should not be too closely equated. It has been argued, that internalisation is undertaken in order to impose centralisation. For instance, Rugman has argued, 'resource allocation processes that are internalised are those carried out in a centralised manner' and 'unless R & D is centralised in the parent there is no firm specific advantage at risk through licensing, yet we know that MNEs prefer to control the rate of use of their knowledge advantage by direct foreign investment, thus they must be afraid of dissipation' (Rugman 1981, pp. 29, 105). As pointed out above, it is possible to envisage a situation which represents the opposite of 'internalisation for centralisation'. By transmitting a set of shadow price signals to decision makers in subsidiaries acting as cost or profit centres, the firm operates as closely as possible to a perfect internal market: this enables the plans of each decision maker to be meshed and optimum co-ordination to be achieved (Buckley 1983).

Principal–Agent Problems

Whose objectives are paramount in the multinational corporation? Top decision makers in the multinational firm face a classic principal–agent problem. The issue is how best to ensure that managers of foreign subsidiaries respond effectively to the commands or directives of the parent company. Further, how far are parent company managers responsible to *their* principals; the corporate shareholders? This is not the place to review the literature on ownership and control but the parent–subsidiary relationship is capable of being analysed as a principal–agent problem. Problems of monitoring costs (governance costs) loom large in widely dispersed multinational firms, and the firm, as a network of relationships, must respond to these demands. It is an outgrowth of the Coasian approach to see the firm as a set of contractual relationships between individuals (Jensen and Meckling 1976), and a minimisation of costs of contracting and maintaining these contracts is a driving force of organisational design.

The multinational firm can thus be seen to be analogous to a decentralised socialist economy (following Arrow 1987, pp. 39–40). Knowledge of (potential) productivity of each (foreign) subsidiary cannot be centralised and so individual units have information about the possibilities of production not available to the 'central planning unit'. The subsidiaries may have incentives not to reveal their full potential because it will be easier to operate under a less rigorous regime. The problem becomes one of tapping the subsidiary's information. This is known as incentive compatibility.

Summary

To summarise, this section has analysed a variety of approaches to the organisation of multinational firms: the strategy–structure view, the organisational form literature, analyses of centralisation and the internal organisation of the firm as a principal–agent problem. A synoptic view, based on the internalisation framework, has been taken. It is clear that there has been a coalescence of views: the feasibility of central management control is a core issue as is the means by which this control can effectively be exercised; the role of asymmetric information is crucial; both the monitoring and measurement of performance present an underlying difficulty to organisational design; and costs of communication and reward structures have an important role to play. Consequently, there is broad agreement on the key variables which play a role in determining internal organisation. However, the weighting given to the variables differs markedly in the separate approaches. The remainder of this chapter attempts to shed further light on dynamics, the role of market forces and cultural and national factors as they affect organisational structures.

7.4 Internationalisation and Globalisation Models of Organisational Change in Multinational Firms

The literature examined in the last section rather begs the questions relating to the process of internationalisation of the firm, its timing and direction. This section examines two parallel, but distinct, models of the development of multinational firms: the 'internationalisation' model, developed largely in Scandinavia and used in European-based studies,[2] and the 'globalisation' model, developed largely in US business schools and used in models of international business strategy.[3]

The internationalisation model, as a generic type, suggests an incremental approach to development: 'deepening involvement' with foreign markets is suggested, a process of 'creeping incrementalism' as the firm grows in international stature. This contrasts with the more grandiose planned globalisation of Porter-type models.

The cautious evolutionary model has been widely applied to small- and medium-sized companies—often those investing abroad for the first time (Buckley, Newbould and Thurwell 1987, Buckley, Berkova and Newbould 1983, Luostarinen 1980). The reaction to risk and uncertainty is a primary determinant of this caution. Firms react to this uncertainty by collecting the appropriate information and learning about foreign conditions by incremental learning and slow organisational development. (Such a process was well described by Aharoni 1966.) This information gathering and the 'biased search', applied by Aharoni and others, have a cost implication: the costs of managerial time are a major problem in the planning processes of smaller firms and are an effective constraint on internationalisation and organisational development. The difficulties of recruiting and absorbing an adequate cadre of managers has long been recognised as crucial for organisational change (Penrose 1959).

The applicability and relevance of the internationalisation model must be limited in scope. Young (1987) suggeests that it does not apply to 'rapidly changing high technology sectors' (p. 39) because the time scale involved in moving from domestic to foreign manufacture is so short. The phenomenon of shortening product cycles was noted by Giddy (1978) ten years ago. Industries with rapid competitor reaction are also an exception, as are industries which are dominated by firms capable of global scanning. It is important to make a distinction between small firms in 'small firm industries' where the average size of firm is low and the representative firm is not widely different from the industry average, where such strategies may be optimal, and small firms in industries dominated by large ones where the long-run future of smaller competitors is bleak. Firms practising 'niche strategies' may be able to pursue caution, but the increasing pace of change in many industries may render this strategy less than widely applicable.

However, the same issue arises with the globalisation thesis[4]—what is the industrial range of its application? In its pure form—the implication of a global product, standardised marketing techniques and centralised planning and control—the answer is that probably not many sectors, industries or product divisions conform to a homogeneous worldwide strategy. Perhaps the model is an idealised view of the organisation of firms at the opposite end of the size spectrum from the internationally naive first-time foreign investors? National markets in many areas remain firmly idiosyncratic. The focus of most analysts on successful multinationals leads us to ignore the many failed attempts to impose a foreign (international or global) product on an unwilling national market. Moreover, the existence of market niches leaves global marketeers vulnerable to competitors from non-standardised products.

Consequently, a more cautious version of the globalisation model is now the norm. Porter's recent work (1986b) suggests that there is not a single global strategy (Young 1987): rather, a strategy is constrained by the value chain (i.e. vertical integration imperatives), configuration (location costs of interrelated activities internalised within the firm) and co-ordination issues. This leads to a typology of global strategies. A related categorisation by White and Poynter (1984) distinguishes the types of integration amongst networks of foreign affiliates (miniature replica, marketing satellites, rationalised manufacture, product specialist and strategic independent). This has much in common with Casson's typology arising from a recent study of multinationals and world trade which relies on an extended version of the product cycle to analyse changes in the international division of labour. Casson provides a typology of industries: new product industries, mature product industries, rationalised product industries, resource-based industries and trading and non-tradeable service industries in which intra-firm trade (and therefore the organisation of the firm) can be studied (Casson (ed.) 1986a).

Consequently, from a rather disparate literature on the international development of the firm, several key points can be distilled. First, both the size of the firm and its history influence organisation. Second, the nature of the industry and its relationship to, and influence on, individual firms is of great importance. Third, a complex interaction between changes in the international division of labour (through intra-firm trade to organisational development) is at work, and these elements must be studied in an interactive framework to enable a full comprehension of the processes at work. The following section analyses the interaction between firm and market in order to elucidate these issues.

7.5   Market Forces and Organisational Structure

How far are organisational structures under the control of management? How much of organisational design is actually determined by external market pressures? Economists, including those advocating internalisation as a major influence on the growth of firms, see the market as paramount. Organisational theorists and management writers often appear to believe that management can decide upon and impose not only a strategy but also a structure on the world economy. Clearly there is an interaction: the greater the degree of market power, the greater the degree of management discretion. The contestability of markets will be a major constraint on organisational form.

Many writers view organisations in an implicitly social Darwinist framework. Those which fail to achieve survival levels of profit will be killed off either by failure (bankruptcy) or absorption of predators (takeovers). Whilst there is no doubt that the pressures of the market and of the takeover threat constrain organisations towards efficient organisational modes, the degree of observed organisational diversity suggests that inertia is strong in many areas.

Part of this diversity is perhaps explicable by reference to the 'dualism' in the nature of the multinational firm, pointed out initially by Hymer (1976): one element is the market power possessed by most large multinational firms, typically operating in an oligopolistic world market; the second is the multinational firm's transaction costs minimising role emphasised in internalisation approaches. Whilst market power, or the possession of firm specific advantages is not a defining characteristic of multinational firms, nor a necessary condition for their existence (Casson 1987), there is no doubt that market power is often associated with large multinationals. Again, the importance of linking the firm to the industry is apparent in the analysis of organisation. The existence of organisational slack or X-inefficiency is directly linked to non-competitive situations.

Attempts to extend market power by takeovers of competitors, joint ventures, implicit or explicit cartels and the response to antitrust or anti-monopoly legislation obviously further influence organisational form.

A Third Principle

The distinction between firm and market as major principles of organisation is analytically precise but has been challenged as inadequate. The role of co-operation between firms can be traced back to G. B. Richardson's 1972 article 'The Organisation of Industry' which points to a 'dense network of cooperation and affiliation by which firms are interrelated' (p. 833).[5] Subcontracting, supplier relationships in manufacturing and marketing and the pooling or transfer of technology are given as examples of planned co-ordination across firm boundaries. This 'third principle' of organisation has been seized upon by Kojima and Ozawa (1984b) to explain the group investment activities of Sogo Shosha (Japanese general trading companies).

Parallel to Richardson's discovery, a paper by Brown (1984) shows that, as well as the widely acknowledged market-like behaviour in firms, there also exists firm-like behaviour in markets through administered marketing channels arising from non-pecuniary influences of one channel partner on another.

A further development is the work of Imai and Itami (1984) who distinguish 'area' and 'principle' in resource allocation mechanisms. They divide the competing principles of allocation (1) by the type of decision-making transaction, and (2) by membership of participants and their mutual relationships ('arena') to arrive at a classification of resource allocation mechanisms (see Figure 7.1). They then compare US allocation systems with Japanese systems, finding that their conceptualisation explains stylised differences between the two economies.

A further attempt to integrate co-operative ventures into the theory has been made by Buckley and Casson (1987) as 'coordination effected through mutual forbearance', identifying co-operation as a special type of co-ordination. They analyse the conditions under which co-operation leads to an increase in efficiency, and they define the meaning of forbearance.

Forbearance arises when one party refrains from cheating another party. Transactions-cost economics recognises that all parties in a venture have a potential for self-interested opportunism. Thus aggression can arise when one party perpetrates an act which damages another party's interests; a weaker form of cheating is to refrain from an act which would benefit someone else—this is termed neutrality. Consequently, actions can be classified as: taking advantage of another party (strong cheating), refraining from either taking advantage of them or helping them (weak

Decision-making principal \ Membership of participants and their mutual relationship 'Arena'	M_2	$M_2 + O_2$	O_2
M_1	Pure market	Organisation-like market	
$M_1 + O_1$	Organisation-like market	Intermediate organisation	Market-like organisation
O_1		Market-like organisation	Pure organisation

Source: After Imai and Itami (1984) especially p. 289.
Notes: M_1 = free private interest maximisation in which price, or some other equivalent signal, is used as a major medium of information
M_2 = free entry and exit
O_1 = direction based on authority, for common interest maximisation
O_2 = fixed and continual relationship

Figure 7.1 Interpenetration of Organisation and Market

cheating) or assisting them (forbearance). Forbearance is a useful concept in the analysis of the negotiations leading up to a joint venture and its continuation. The analysis is confined to the single, but crucial, case of 50:50 joint ventures between independent firms. Joint ventures are explained in terms of a combination of economies of internalisation, indivisibilities and obstacles to merger. It is possible to analyse joint ventures using conventional economic analysis because they are shown to compromise contractual arrangements which minimise transactions costs under certain environmental constraints. However, the analysis contains not only the concept of forbearance but also those of trust, reputation and commitment—concepts not normally encountered in economic analysis. Joint ventures are found to be, in certain circumstances, devices by which the parties can demonstrate mutual forbearance and thus build up trust; and trust is shown to be both an input and an output of joint ventures. Dynamic considerations can be built in by the analysis of reputation effects, which are the result of repeated instances of forbearance. However, it is also the case that joint ventures are often devices for enhancing collusion and for luring 'partners' into unfavourable deals. Development of this type of analysis would seem to promise benefits in the understanding of organisational problems.

This analysis brings in an element of altruism—or, at least, the sacrifice of short-term opportunistic gains for longer-term aims—which the Williamson framework lacks (Francis, Turk and Willman 1983, p. 6). It may well prove fruitful, for instance, in the analysis of Japanese multinationals for precisely this reason. However, Williamson acknowledges the importance of 'both institutional and personal trust relations' (Williamson and Ouchi 1983, p. 19). In outlining the future research agenda of the markets and hierarchies programme, further emphasis is placed on the frequency and uncertainty of transactions, which accords well with the evolving dynamic elements of the internalisation programme (Buckley 1983) as well as transaction-specific investment (Williamson and Ouchi 1983, p. 33).

The importance of influences which are not conventionally 'market' or 'firm' (neither are they easily resolved into these two components) is thus acknowledged in the literature. In examining the detailed issues of the allocation of resources and rights, a simple dichotomy—firm and market—often will not convey the richness of organisational design. However, it is important not to forget that the purpose of a theory is to explain as wide a variety of observed phenomena as possible with a parsimonious set of axioms, otherwise, there is a danger that theory will slip into simple description or an arid taxonomy. In order to be explanatory and predictive, the analysis must explain the mechanism by which one organisational principle changes into another, and the conditions which precipitate that change. The incidence of the costs and benefits of the co-operative firm must be specified as well as the shift from firm to market, and vice versa, otherwise its introduction allows the analysis to decline into description. In other words, Richardson's framework requires further operationalising in the way that Coase's 1937 article has been operationalised by Buckley and Casson (1976) and others.

7.6 Cultural and National Influences on Organisational Form

It is undeniable that national and cultural differences influence the organisation of multinational firms originating from different backgrounds. The review of the empirical literature in Chapter 2 suggests that the multidivisional form (M-form) of organisation has developed at different rates in different countries—more specifically, less in Japan than in the USA,

Britain and West Germany (Steer and Cable 1978, Cable and Dirrheimer 1983, Cable and Yasuki 1985). Japan's relative slowness in adopting the M-form organisation may be attributed to the macro-environment; most notably the membership of business groups by Japanese firms. Pinpointing the similarities and differences in firms of different nationalities is the stock in trade of cross-cultural studies. The imperatives of international competition notwithstanding, strong differences arising from country of origin still persist. As an example, the market-servicing strategies of firms of different nationalities persist within the same industry, even after allowing for the effects of size (Buckley and Pearce 1979, 1981, 1984).

One important influence is that of domestic economic structure (Buckley 1985)—an obvious example of this is the imperative of resource-poor nations to spawn multinationals in order to control key (foreign located) inputs. Other aspects likely to affect the organisation of multinational firms include: the significant influence of home government policies on multinationals' control regulation or encouragement; the influence of the parent company's configuration on the form of outward investment; the attraction of offshore production (designed to benefit from low-cost labour) when domestic labour is expensive or troublesome; and the appeal of tax havens to multinationals from high tax countries.

In the case of radically different organisational forms, such as the general trading companies of Japan (Sogo Shosha), it has been suggested that a different explanation from the internalisation approach is required (Kojima 1973, 1978, 1982 and Kojima and Ozawa 1984a, 1984b, 1985). The use of specific information in a confidential manner within Sogo Shosha has a direct parallel with the development of international merchant banks in other advanced economies. The relatively under-developed nature of the pure capital market in Japan is a major reason for this development. Thus, the use of internal capital markets within Sogo Shosha is a response to the institutions of the home country.

In contrast, such services in the UK and USA have developed within specialised banks operating in the external market for capital. As Yannopoulos (1983) has pointed out, there are differences among countries in the availability of information inputs characterised by high communication costs; the performance of services requiring these inputs necessitates a local physical presence. These facts contain the explanatory 'germ' of the development of transnational banks and the international expansion of Sogo Shosha.

7.7 Conclusion

It is immediately apparent that many of the issues, problems and conceptual difficulties in the analysis of the organisational form of multinational enterprises are common to the analysis of any organisation. This should not be a surprise. The multinational firm is a special case of commercial organisation—a polar extreme, not a different category. However, it holds more interest for the organisational specialist because it encompasses cultural, national and regional differences.

This chapter has shown that a coherent framework for the analysis of the organisation of multinationals as a generic type does exist: the use of the internalisation framework gives a set of central concepts with great analytical power. The scope of the firm has, until recently, been the main dependent variable which the framework has been used to explain rather than its organisation. However, in drawing together literature on the organisation of multinational firms—on strategy and structure, centralisation and decentralisation, internationalisation and globalisation, market and firm and the role of cultural and national differences—the internalisation approach provides a bonding element which is capable of leading to synthesis.

It is essential to realise that any synthesis of literature on the organisation of multinationals must cope with dynamics. As international competition evolves so too does organisational design. Multinationals are adaptive and innovative organisations whose very competitive strength depends upon response to changing environments. Any modelling which assumes a static framework is doomed. Consequently, a successful analysis must be able to deal with change. In this respect, the underlying framework given here must commend itself for its simplicity and predictive power.

Notes

* The author is grateful for comments on a previous draft to the editors, Michael Brooke, Richard Butler, Mark Casson and Jean-François Hennart.

1. The benefits of international internalisation frequently arise from the opportunities to reduce the firm's overall tax liability. As much government intervention depends on (amongst other things) the valuation of traded intermediate goods, internal markets provide an ideal opportunity to reduce tax liabilities and other forms of government intervention. Imputed prices of intermediate goods in internal markets can include a tax limiting factor, particularly in markets for knowledge (or knowledge-intensive goods), the valuation of which is notoriously difficult. Multinational firms may impute mark-ups in the lowest tax countries and may alter their location strategy in order to include a low intervention 'tax haven'. Evidence on transfer pricing is provided in Lall (1973, 1978) and Rugman and Eden (1985) and a classificatory scheme is given by Plasschaert (1981). Evidence on the nature and

amount of intra-company trade is given by Buckley and Pearce (1979, 1981, 1984).

2. A selection of references is: Carlson (1975), Johanson and Vahlne (1977), Luostarinen (1978), Welch and Wiedersheim-Paul (1980,a,b), Wiedersheim-Paul (1972), Cavusgil (1972), Juul and Walters (1987).

3. References are available in Porter (1986b).

4. Models of globalisation owe a great deal in conception to the earlier generation of product cycle models deriving from Vernon's (1966) path-breaking article.

5. See also Thompson (1967).

8

Organisational Form and the Control of Labour

PAUL MARGINSON

8.1 Introduction

The benefits of innovations in the internal organisational structure of firms have been seen largely in efficiency terms, and the discussion so far has essentially taken this perspective, although Chapter 5 referred to the importance of power issues with respect to the design and operation of control systems. Thus the multi-divisional form of internal organisation has been viewed in terms of facilitating growth through diversification (Chandler 1962) or of curbing managerialism (Williamson 1970). One neglected aspect of a firm's internal organisation structure has been its power, or control, properties. This chapter demonstrates why power is particularly important when looking at the labour aspects of the firm's internal organisation. The issue is addressed by considering the labour control implications of adopting the multi-divisional form of organisation. Workers' responses, in the form of innovations in union organisation, are also investigated. Given that the great majority of large firms in the UK are now M-form (Hill and Pickering 1986a), the discussion differentiates between different structural arrangements amongst M-forms, according to whether the principal driving force of diversification has been into horizontally related, vertically related, or unrelated activities (Hill and Hoskisson 1987). In considering the implications for labour relations, particular attention is paid to the key issues of collective bargaining over pay, and to multi-plant trade-union, or combine, organisation.

The chapter begins with an elaboration of the distinction between control and efficiency attributes of organisations and seeks to show how managements' attempts to improve control will influence organisational change and the way in which labour organises itself in trade unions. The second half of the chapter addresses, firstly in conceptual terms and then by presenting empirical evidence, the implications of the M-form for the control of labour.

8.2   Control versus Efficiency

The pioneering work of Chandler (1962, 1977), and Williamson's subsequent reformulation (1970, 1975) within a framework to minimise transactions costs, has demonstrated the importance of the internal organisation structure of firms to their economic performance. Chapter 2 reviews the empirical evidence on the relationship between internal organisation and performance. Profitability Π may be viewed as some function, g, of the internal organisation structure of firms, OF, and a vector of other variables, X:

$$\Pi = g\ (OF,\ X) \tag{8.1}$$

X could include other influences on profitability such as capital intensity, the state of demand and market structure.

The benefits of innovations in organisational form have been seen as stemming largely from efficiency improvements. Thus, Williamson (1970) argues that the expansion of functionally organised (U-form) firms generates internal inefficiencies, in terms of cumulative control loss as the hierarchy is extended and top decision-makers become overloaded. Beyond a certain size, and in particular environments, the firm may be more appropriately reorganised into a multi-divisional structure, with operating decisions being delegated to a number of quasi-autonomous operating divisions. Cumulative control loss is curbed by this separation, and by the institution of an internal control apparatus between corporate office and the divisions. Top management is freed from overload, by delegating operating decisions, to concentrate on decisions of a strategic nature. These efficiency improvements are supposed to enhance profitability. Likewise, empirical studies have attributed the superior profitability associated with M-form adoption to efficiency effects, such as those deriving from its internal capital allocation mechanism (Steer and Cable 1978). Under this view, organisational form is comprised of a vector of efficiency attributes E:

$$OF = h\ (E) \tag{8.2}$$

That the internal organisation structure of firms is likely to have power, or control, implications, as well as efficiency ones, has been largely neglected. Given the dominance of efficiency considerations in the analysis of the firm, some reasons why labour aspects of firm organisation should also be viewed in power terms are outlined below—followed by the setting out of a control model of the firm.

Efficiency theorists have tried to demonstrate the irrelevance of power considerations. If forms of internal organisation which vest more power in the managers of firms, through strengthened hierarchy, can also be shown to be more efficient, then, it is claimed, considerations of power can be set aside (Williamson 1980). We outline, and then question, two such justifications: first, Williamson's contention that, historically, less efficient modes of employing labour have been succeeded by more efficient modes; second, that unions developed for efficiency reasons, and not as a means through which workers exercise countervailing power.

Williamson (1980) contends that the historical evolution of the firm can be best explained in efficiency terms. Holding technology constant, the transactions cost properties of alternative modes of organising work are compared. The starting point is the putting-out system associated with domestic industry in the early phase of the industrial revolution; Williamson argues that embezzlement and cheating were endemic to putting-out, which also required large inventories to be held. Eventually, putting-out was supplanted by modes of work organisation which possessed superior efficiency properties, in terms of transactions costs: the first step was inside contracting, followed by the hierarchical capitalist firm, where labour is directly employed. However, the direct employment of workers is itself associated with transactions costs arising out of asset specificity—workers with firm-specific skills in small numbers exchange relations have the ability to act opportunistically (Williamson, Wachter and Harris 1975). Such problems, it is argued, can be overcome by the creation of a collective organisation, involving both employers and workers, aimed at generating an atmosphere of trust, a common frame of reference and goal congruence between management and workers. The bureaucratic mode of employment relation in contemporary large corporations—characterised by a structured internal labour market with low ports of entry, internal job ladders, on-the-job training, associated promotion opportunities and deferred compensation—is cited as exhibiting the requisite properties to overcome problems of asset specificity when workers are directly employed. In this way, the evolution of the modern firm is seen to be the result of a search for ever more efficient forms of employment organisation.

The basis of this claim can be questioned on a number of grounds (Marginson 1986), but we will focus on one central objection. Williamson includes two forms of co-operative organisation in his comparative exercise. Although it scores well in transactions cost terms, the second form—communal ownership and communal reward—fares badly in terms of leadership and monitoring properties. But its poor rating in these two areas is a direct result of Williamson's definition of 'co-operative', requiring rotation of tasks, including leadership and monitoring tasks. In practice this is not the case in functioning co-operatives: producer co-operatives are observed to have a permanent division of tasks, including monitoring (Putterman 1986). Moreover, Williamson's low rating of its leadership and monitoring properties notwithstanding, the communal ownership/communal reward form of co-operative organisation compares favourably in efficiency terms with the bureaucratic hierarchical mode, characteristic of the contemporary large firm. If this is the case, why do we observe the latter to be so widespread, whilst co-operatives are relatively rare? A dimension of analysis is missing, explaining why one form of efficient organisation should develop and not another.

This dimension is the extent to which alternative modes of employing labour enhance or encumber managerial control. Marglin (1974), for example, argues that the evolution of the capitalist hierarchical mode of employing labour is best understood from a perspective which emphasises the managers' aim of securing control over labour. If employers seek forms of organisation that enable them to dominate workers most effectively, then it is necessary to consider the organisation of the firm in terms of its power, as well as its efficiency properties. Two examples will help to illustrate the point. First, workers have not passively accepted the transition of the employment relationship from putting-out through to the internal labour market: at times they have resisted. Montgomery (1979), for example, demonstrates how, at the turn of the century in the USA, an upsurge in worker agitation for co-operative ideals coincided with the attempts of large firms to impose new systems of direct control and supervision in place of delegated systems akin to inside contracting. And Lazonick (1979) shows how the persistence of inside contracting in the UK cotton industry, long after its US counterpart had adopted direct systems of control, was related to the organised strength of key operatives in production. Second, technology is not a neutral force enhancing output for new configurations of given inputs, or maintaining given output with fewer inputs: employers choose technologies which facilitate dominance over labour. Bowles (1985) cites machine pacing as an example of a technology with desirable control properties. Ozanne (1967) shows how, in the 1880s, new, untested and untried machines were brought into a plant specifically to break the power of a group of workers who controlled a crucial production operation.

These examples raise a more general issue, namely the nature of union organisation, and introduce a second line of argument by which efficiency theorists attempt to demonstrate the irrelevance of power considerations. The discussion above implicitly views union organisation as a form of countervailing power exercised by workers in the face of employer dominance. Williamson (1984), by contrast, views unions solely in terms of their efficiency role, arguing that the growth of union organisation can be subsumed within a more general analysis of the development of the firm as a continuing employment relation. Williamson's argument runs as follows: unions find it difficult to organise and sustain their existence unless their members have scarce, and difficult-to-replace, skills. The more firm-specific skills become, the greater interest both workers and employers have in a continuing employment relation; this, in turn, facilitates union organisation. Drawing on Hirschman's (1970) exit-voice model, Williamson (1984) argues that workers are likely to develop a collective voice through a union in preference to individualised means of expressing dissatisfaction, such as quitting, only when they have a strong interest in a continuing employment relationship. Hence, workers *and* employers in firms characterised by a high degree of firm-specific skills, such as the modern bureaucratic corporation, have a mutual interest in collective organisation. As a result, Williamson predicts that, historically, unions will form early in the life of industries with a high degree of firm-specific skills (e.g. railways) and later on in those industries where skills are undifferentiated (e.g. farm labouring).

Thus, in Williamson's view, workers' bargaining power derives solely from their possession of firm-specific skills, and the union is a means by which this power is exercised collectively (in the common good) rather than individually (for sectional or opportunistic gain). Aoki (1984) similarly sees workers' bargaining power as deriving from firm-specific skills, although in his case the social dimension of these skills is emphasised. Firm-specific skills are treated as collective goods, not individually appropriable, resting on work customs which are transferred through social processes.

Williamson's argument, however, is flawed by its omission of other bases of workers' bargaining power, and therefore trade-union organisation. Once these are taken into account, it becomes impossible to subsume the reasons for, and history of, trade-union organisation into the transactions cost approach to the firm. Crucially, an important category of skills is overlooked by writers such as Williamson and Aoki: namely market skills. These are skills which are transferable across markets. Enderwick (1984) distinguishes between bargaining power deriving from market skills, and workplace bargaining power. Although the acquisiton of firm-specific skills may enhance workplace bargaining power, this is contingent on trade-union organisation which is by no means an automatic consequence. Market bargaining power may diminish as equivalent employment opportunities outside the firm disappear. But it does not follow that workers with market bargaining power have no trade-union organisation—the long history of craft unionism testifies to that (Hyman 1975)—or that workers with firm-specific skills will have no market bargaining power, or even that workers with no firm-specific skills will have no bargaining power. Further, union organisation was a *precondition* for the ending of the casual labour system in certain industries in the UK (such as printing and the docks), and not the consequence of the evolution of a continuing employment relationship. In short, neither bargaining power nor union organisation rest on the possession of firm-specific skills, and hence the development of a continuing employment relation.

Instead, trade-union organisation can be viewed as a means by which workers exercise countervailing bargaining power within an employment relationship, characterised by employer dominance. In Williamson's (1984) model, workers act opportunistically whilst managers act in the interests of the organisation as a whole. As Willman (1983) notes, these behavioural assumptions are arbitrary. If managers, too, behave opportunistically, then workers are likely to form trade-union organisations as a countervailing mechanism against such behaviour. An approach along these lines is proposed by Fitzroy and Kraft (1985, 1987). Where workers possess firm-specific skills, their mobility in the labour market is impeded. As a result, they are susceptible to 'managerial pressure' aimed at eliciting additional effort. In the face of such 'managerial pressure', workers will resort to union organisation as a means of exercising countervailing power against attempts to raise effort to excessive levels. Fitzroy and Kraft emphasise that the effects of countervailing organisation will not necessarily offset exactly the increased managerial pressure. An efficient outcome cannot be presumed.

Once trade unions are seen as exercising countervailing power within the employment relationship a further possibility arises: employers may be concerned to shape trade-union organisation into forms that minimise the threat to their dominance. Indeed, employers may go further and attempt to eliminate trade-union organisation altogether, as is currently the case in the United States (Kochan, Katz and McKersie 1986). In the UK, for example, Brown (1981) has suggested that in some circumstances employers have promoted facilities for shop stewards, including time-off for trade-union duties, preferring to deal with a trade-union organisation that is internally (or firm) based, rather than the externally based union organisation. More recently, a number of incoming employers to the UK, such as Nissan, have demonstrated a clear preference for a particular type of unionism: single union and 'no strike'. In short, the shape of trade-union organisation itself is a product of conflicts between employers and workers.

Control models of the firm, such as those proposed by Marglin (1974) or Edwards (1979), start from the premise that there is an inherent conflict of interest in the employment relation. Workers are motivated by the need to attain an adequate standard of living, and to exert control over the pace and content of their work. Employers are motivated by the acquisition of profit which necessitates cost minimisation and control over the work process, including workers' effort. Employers do not purchase a specified quantity of performed labour through a precise contract, rather they exert control over the workers' capacity to produce through an incomplete contract. Scope for conflict thus exists both over the terms of the incomplete contract, and over the precise labour which the worker is subsequently required to perform. Employer control can be secured through the institution of hierarchy.

Bowles (1985) has formalised a model along these lines, focusing on the conflict of interest over the intensity of the workers' effort. His method is to add a third term to the traditional production function, representing worker effort. Thus a distinction is made between the capacity to labour purchased, and the actual labour input. It is assumed that employers are able to compel workers to act in ways that they would not themselves choose, but that the exercise of this power is costly. This cost takes two forms: the use of supervision and the payment of a wage premium above the market rate—assuming decreasing returns to both these elements generates a unique profit maximising point, which is at a lower level of output, incidentally, than if no such costs arose. Thus, Bowles is also able to demonstrate that the form of internal organisation preferred by capitalist employers will not be socially efficient.

By looking at the historical evolution of firms' internal organisation, and at the role of union organisation, we have shown the importance of considering the power (as well as efficiency) aspects of the employment relation. Whereas, under the efficiency approach, hierarchy is seen as being in the mutual interests of both employers and workers (Williamson, Wachter and Harris 1975), under a power approach the role of hierarchy is to facilitate the dominance of employer goals over workers' goals. Thus, in contrast to Williamson *et al.*, Edwards (1979) sees the structured internal labour markets which characterise the large bureaucratic firm as fragmenting the workforce, enabling managers to employ a divide-and-rule strategy. Internal organisational form can be seen as having control as well as efficiency attributes. These can be represented by a vector of control variables, C, and equation (8.2) can be modified to give:

$$OF = h' (E, C) \qquad\qquad (8.3)$$

The main points from this section can be drawn together in four propositions:

(i)   the internal organisation structure of firms has control as well as efficiency attributes;
(ii) following from (i), securing an improvement in control can be one amongst a number of factors precipitating organisational change;
(iii) union organisation develops as a form of countervailing power against management control;
(iv) management will try to shape the form of union organisation so as to minimise the threat to its control.

In the rest of the chapter, we look at the labour control implications of the dominant form of internal organisation amongst contemporary large UK enterprises, the multi-divisional form.

8.3   The Multi-Divisional Form

The Nature of the M-Form

Whilst the M-form embodies a single set of organising principles, precise internal arrangements within the firm can vary. Hill and Pickering (1986a) found a wide variety of internal arrangements amongst their divisionalised companies. The basis of divisionalisation appeared to vary according to the degree of product diversity within the enterprise. Diversified enterprises were likely to divisionalise along product lines, whilst undiversified companies divisionalised along geographic lines. Whereas divisions in less diversified enterprises tended to be functionally organised, in more diversified businesses they were more complex organisations, embracing a number of quasi-autonomous operating subsidiaries. Moreover, Hill and Pickering found evidence of fundamental organisational change within some companies that were already divisionalised. This was in the direction of both further decentralisation and centralisation:

> Several companies had moved away from a structure where the divisionalised tier mattered as a managerial unit . . . and towards one where the divisional tier had only a very minor role. This downgrading of the divisional tier was accompanied by a further decentralisation of short-run decision-making power to subsidiaries within divisions (such as marketing functions), while long-term strategic functions and financial control functions were centralised at the head office. (p. 35)

The result would appear to be a transformation of the M-form structure into a larger number of 'strategic business units' subject to primarily financial, rather than administered, control from corporate head office. Hill and Hoskisson (1987) view the principal benefits of M-form organisation in such firms as 'financial economies', achieved through the superior allocative properties of the internal, as compared to the external, capital market. These enterprises are likely to diversify into unrelated activities. In contrast, the benefits of M-form organisation for enterprises diversifying into related activities lie either in synergistic economies— where, say, a common technique is used to produce a range of products—or in vertical economies associated with vertical integration. Hill and Hoskisson go on to identify three variants of M-form structure corresponding to these sources of economies, with administrative co-ordination being much greater where economies are vertical in nature than when they are, in turn, synergistic or financial. To these three variants of M-form a fourth may be added: undiversified enterprises, where the benefits of divisionalisation are in economies of scale, performing the same set of specialised tasks in many different locations.

Administrative co-ordination is expected to be prominent in this fourth variant.

M-form: Labour Control Attributes

The labour control attributes of the multi-divisional structure can be usefully assessed in the context of those of the 'loose' holding company structure which preceded M-form in many large UK companies. Arguably, an H-form structure was congruent with the multi-employer framework of collective bargaining which, for many years, characterised the formal structure of industrial relations in many industries. A corporate framework, where grievance resolution and the determination of pay and conditions are subject to corporate-based procedures and structures, requires the presence of a strong, centralised management capability. But this was, by definition, absent in the loosely structured H-form.

Sisson (1987) argues that a multi-employer framework can have distinct advantages in securing labour control, through its potential to remove industrial conflict from the workplace. The establishment of district and national dispute procedures in the engineering and chemicals industries, for example, sought to remove grievance resolution from the workplace. Determination of substantive issues, such as pay and conditions, also became the subject of district and national agreements in these and other industries. The scope for union activity in the workplace was thereby minimised. Moreover, employers were able to vary local terms and conditions. H-form firms were frequently federal in character, each constituent part having different family, traditions and modes of operation (Hannah 1983). Individual subsidiaries, or establishments, registered as separate organisations with employer federations and were party to their own district agreements. This enabled them not only to take advantage of the prevailing circumstances in their own local labour market, but in so doing to make each workplace different. The interests of labour were thereby fragmented across workplaces as employers attempted to divide and rule.

By the 1960s, this two-pronged strategy for controlling labour— minimising industrial conflict and union activity in the workplace, and sustaining differences in terms and conditions between workplaces—was being seriously undermined. First, the developing shop-steward organisation had spawned an upsurge of informal bargaining and conflict in the workplace in, for example, the engineering industry (Royal Commission on Trade Unions and Employers' Associations 1968). Such informal bargaining—so called because it occurred outside the formal agreements between unions and employers—was a primary cause of 'wage drift', the process by which actual earnings diverge from formally agreed basic rates. In turn, wage drift led to payments structures that were increasingly out of managerial control (Brown 1973). Second, in the engineering industry, at least, shop stewards were becoming involved in cross-plant trade-union organisation, with consequent comparability claims (Lerner and Marquand 1963; Lerner and Bescoby 1966).

In these circumstances, the adoption of M-form organisation provides two specific advantages for management in securing control over labour. First, the emergence of a strategic corporate planning function and associated systems of internal audit and financial control has direct implications for the control of labour, in so far as labour costs are integrated into the wider context of financial performance. Moreover, these controls are aimed at inducing profit maximising behaviour on the part of managers in the divisions and operating units (Williamson 1970), and this is likely to instil a greater efficiency drive into these managers. Reduction of costs is likely to receive attention as a means of enhancing overall performance, and control over labour costs can be enhanced through such means as the use of job evaluation; the reform of payments systems aimed at linking pay with performance; and productivity bargaining.

Second, the creation of a centralised strategic management capability opens up the possibility of developing a corporate framework (to displace the increasingly ineffective multi-employer one) for the control and co-ordination of labour relations in the divisions and operating units. In particular, management can seek to conduct pay bargaining within, rather than outside, the enterprise. In the face of the growth of unregulated, informal, workplace bargaining, management was faced with two options. One was to formalise bargaining within the workplace and to achieve corporate control and co-ordination of payment levels and structures behind the scenes—in this way the benefits from making each workplace different could still be attained. The second was to shift bargaining away from the workplace, to divisional level, in order to circumvent strong plant-based trade-union organisation. Management's decision can be considered to be contingent on the nature of each firm's internal arrangement: whether its activities are vertically integrated, and the extent, if any, of diversification.

In so far as management control over labour is enhanced, following the adoption of a multi-divisional structure, we would anticipate a subsequent response by workers. A particular response to the adoption of a corporate framework for the control and co-ordination of labour relations by management would be the development of multi-plant trade-union organisations, known as combine committees. Combine organisation need not be contingent on the bargaining level being shifted to divisional level. Trade unions may act to counter managerial co-ordination at corporate and divisional levels, even where bargaining remains at establishment level. In turn, we might expect management to attempt to shape such multi-plant trade-union organisation, or to resist it altogether. We would expect management's approach to vary according to the firm's internal arrangements. Where the same products or services are produced in several establishments, or divisions, there might be advantages, for management, in reaching common arrangements across establishments, and therefore in dealing with a multi-site trade-union organisation. Alternatively, where establishments produce very different products and services, management may be hostile to the development of contacts between trade-union representatives from different sites.

Above, we have derived three propositions concerning: the control attributes of the multi-divisional form, the development of combine organisation as a countervailing response by workers to the adoption of a corporate framework by management for the control and co-ordination of labour relations, and management's attempts to shape such combine organisation. These correspond to the first, third and fourth propositions outlined on page 151, and empirical evidence on these is discussed in the next section. The remaining proposition suggested that control considerations could, in principle, be amongst the factors which precipitate a change in internal organisation structure.

Whether or not the adoption of M-form was in part precipitated by a 'crisis of labour control' is difficult to demonstrate. Thompson (1981) found that many H-form companies underwent severe profitability crises during the 1960s, immediately prior to adopting a multi-divisional structure. But the source of these profitability crises is far from clear, as is the origin of the profitability gains attributed to M-form (Steer and Cable 1978). At present, empirical evidence to test this proposition is not available, and the question of control considerations precipitating the adoption of M-form is not pursued in the remainder of the chapter.

8.4 The M-Form and Labour Control: Evidence

The evidence presented here is drawn from a series of industrial relations surveys. The focus is largely on two aspects of industrial relations: collective bargaining over pay and multi-plant (or combine) trade-union organisation. Collective bargaining between management and workers (through their trade unions) can take place at a number of different levels, over different issues, involving different groups of workers or bargaining units. Bargaining units range from the shop or department to the establishment, division or company, and beyond that to the industry (see Brown 1981). Within any one company, issues such as staffing or overtime allocation may be bargained over at one level, whilst pay is determined at a different level. A central characteristic of companies' bargaining structure, however, is the level at which pay is negotiated: hence our focus.

Control Attributes of M-form

The first broad control attribute of M-form identified above was the ability to integrate labour costs into the wider context of financial performance. It was suggested that this would result in the adoption of more formal mechanisms aimed at categorising and measuring labour's contribution to performance. The Warwick Workplace Survey, conducted amongst manufacturing establishments in 1977–8, found that uses of job evaluation and work study techniques, symbolising more formal control over work processes, had increased markedly over the five-year period since 1972, a period when the effects of M-form adoption by many large UK manufacturers on labour control were beginning to be felt. On job evaluation, Brown (1981) comments that 'it is safe to conclude that the number of establishments using it increased by a half (to 43 per cent) between 1972 and 1977' (p. 111). Three years later, the 1980 Workplace Industrial Relations Survey found no further increase in the use of job evaluation in manufacturing (Daniel and Millward 1983, p. 207) since 1977, giving some confidence that the increase observed in the Warwick Workplace Survey might be attributed to some discrete shift in managerial control.

Secondly, it was suggested that M-form facilitates the development of a corporate framework for the control and co-ordination of labour. Dramatic evidence of this comes in the shape of the demise of the multi-employer framework of collective bargaining, still characteristic of much of British industry in the 1960s, by the later 1970s. Thus, summing up the findings of the Warwick Workplace Survey, Brown (1981) comments:

> Ten years before our survey, industrial relations in manufacturing industry was dominated by multi-employer agreements. They might have become ramshackle and inadequate, but they were the foundation of the formal bargaining structure. By 1978 that had been transformed. For two-thirds of manual and three-quarters of non-manual employees, the formal structure of bargaining has become one of single-employer agreements covering one or more factories in a company. (p. 118)

In terms of establishments, 68 per cent reported that single employer bargaining was the most important, in terms of determining manual workers' pay increases, including 47 per cent reporting the establishment level to be most important. Only 27 per cent reported a multi-employer agreement to be most important in terms of manual workers' pay (Brown 1981, Table 2.1). The evidence of the 1980 and 1984 Workplace Industrial Relations Surveys shows that this trend has continued, albeit at a decelerating rate.

The decline of the multi-employer framework for conducting pay bargaining is further illustrated by the collapse of some agreements covering whole industrial sectors, as companies have signed company, division or establishment agreements. The Soap, Candle and Edible Fats Joint Industrial Council—covering such giants as Unilever and Bibby—wound itself up in 1984. Elsewhere, the major companies have pulled out of the Food Industry JIC; in engineering, BL, GEC and Phillips have all withdrawn from the industry agreement. Neither is the trend confined to the manufacturing sectors: in 1987, the remaining members of the Federation of Clearing Banks pulled out of industry negotiations, in favour of pursuing their own corporate agreements; and more recently, Tesco withdrew from the retail distribution trade's industry agreement.

It was suggested above that managers in multi-divisional companies would opt for one of two forms of corporate framework: to bargain formally above the establishment level as a means of circumventing strong plant-based trade-union organisation; or to formalise bargaining at establishment level, exercising managerial control from division and corporate levels behind the scenes. The level preferred by management might be contingent on the nature of the company.

Thus, we would expect corporate bargaining to occur where there were considerable interdependencies between divisions, either in that the same good or service was produced across the different (geographical) divisions of the enterprise, or that the enterprise was vertically integrated. In the first case, there may well be economies to be gained for management in standardising pay structures and bargaining across divisions. Moreover, under decentralised bargaining arrangements, the scope for union negotiators to push comparability claims across divisions with similar working methods and conditions would be considerable. A policy of making each workplace different becomes relatively more difficult to operate. Standardisation (through centralised pay bargaining) would eliminate the union's ability to push up pay levels and labour costs through leapfrogging. Examples of such companies are the large retailers, building societies and the high street clearing banks.

In the case of vertically integrated companies, the linkages between different parts of the company create the potential for industrial action in one part to have major repercussions elsewhere. This might lead corporate management into centralising decisions on key industrial relations matters, including pay—an example of this type of company would be a major vehicle producer, such as Ford. Similar considerations apply to divisional bargaining, which we might expect to occur where the operating establishments within a division all produce the same good or service, or where there are vertical links between them.

Where operating establishments produce a diverse range of goods and services, including within divisions, and where consequent interdependencies between establishments are low or non-existent, we would expect management to prefer establishment bargaining. Localised procedures and structures enable, for example, pay to be linked to the performance of individual businesses. This by no means implies that the establishment is autonomous in its pay negotiations. On the contrary, internal controls are more likely to be financial rather than administrative in character and we would expect local management's conduct of pay bargaining to be integrated into the wider framework of corporate planning and financial control. This could be achieved through the use of advice and guidelines, budgetary processes and close monitoring of labour costs.

Marginson (1985) has investigated the first option outlined above, that M-form companies may seek to relocate bargaining over pay at divisional level, using data from the 1978 Warwick Workplace Survey (Brown 1981) and Steer's classification of the organisational form of large companies (Steer and Cable 1978). The Warwick Workplace Survey interviewed managers responsible for industrial relations in 970 manufacturing plants. One question asked about the most important level of pay bargaining for manual workers. Using these data, establishments were categorised according to whether the establishment, division or company was the most important bargaining level, and whether their parent company was organised along M-form lines.

Regression estimates were encouraging: bargaining at divisional level was positively and significantly associated with M-form organisation.[1] The elasticity of the probability of divisional bargaining with respect to M-form was in the region of 0.5. In other words, for each additional firm adopting M-form, it had an equal probability of bargaining at divisional level. In addition, union strength at establishment level, measured by the presence of a regularly functioning shop-steward organisation, was negatively associated with divisional bargaining, but not significantly so. This may suggest that management was more succcessful at shifting bargaining away from establishment level where union organisation was weaker.

A recent survey of industrial relations in large enterprises (Marginson, Edwards, Purcell and Sisson 1988) provides evidence on both the options outlined above. Managers responsible for personnel and industrial relations at head office, division and establishment levels were questioned about industrial relations matters (including the conduct and level of pay bargaining) within 143 large companies. The companies each owned establishments in one of six industrial sectors: four in manufacturing and two in services. In addition to industrial relations matters, data were obtained about the structure, ownership and environment of the enterprises. In particular, managers were asked about four aspects of companies' organisational form: whether or not there was a divisional tier in the company, and the basis of divisions; whether profit responsibility was devolved to divisions or establishments, through designating these levels as profit centres, and whether these profit centres were able to retain a portion of funds generated for investment purposes; the extent to which the company diversified its activities across different sectors and, if not, whether the same goods and services were produced across different divisions and establishments; the existence of any vertical linkages between different divisions and establishments. Following Hill and Hoskisson (1987) these data enabled the study to look at the differing configurations amongst multi-divisionalised companies and their implications for, amongst other things, pay bargaining.

First, the levels at which pay is negotiated are examined. Managers in the establishments interviewed were asked whether they recognised trade unions for the purposes of collective bargaining, and if so at which levels negotiations occurred that resulted in increases in pay for manual and non-manual workers. If more than one level was mentioned, and this was so in about 10 per cent of cases, then managers were further asked what was the 'most important level of bargaining' in terms of the subsequent increase. (The effect of this last question was to slightly reduce the proportion reporting bargaining on a multi-employer basis, and to slightly decrease the proportion of single employer bargainers reporting negotiations at corporate and divisional levels). Findings, for both manual and non-manual workers, are shown in Table 8.1.

Amongst this sample of establishments belonging to large enterprises, a single employer bargaining level was the most important for

Table 8.1 The Most Important Level of Pay Bargaining (%)

	Manuals	*Non-Manuals*
National/Industrywide multi-employer	25	15
Single-employer, covering *all* establishments	20	24
Single-employer, covering *some* establishments	11	11
Single-employer, individual establishments	41	45
Other/not classifiable	5	6

Notes: (1) Base: Establishments recognising unions for bargaining purposes.
(2) Sample sizes are 133 (manuals) and 89 (non-manuals).

determining manual workers' pay in almost three-quarters of cases. In 31 per cent of cases this was the corporate or divisional level, and in the remaining 41 per cent the establishment was the most important level of pay bargaining. The study found that both size and industry were important influences on bargaining level. In particular, smaller establishments were more likely to be covered by divisional or corporate bargaining, and enterprises and divisions with greater numbers of establishments were more likely to bargain at corporate or divisional levels. The service sectors were strongly associated with divisional and corporate bargaining, particularly financial services, and—with the exception of textiles, clothing and footwear—the manufacturing sectors were associated with establishment bargaining. (Multi-employer bargaining was most prevalent in textiles, clothing and footwear.) These differences also reflect broad differences in unionisation (Price and Bain 1983). Corporate and divisional bargaining were much more likely in those sectors where unionisation was lower. As suggested above, bargaining at divisional (or corporate) level may occur where union organisation at establishment level is weak. For management in these organisations the benefits of minimising union activity in the workplace may outweigh those of making each workplace different. Otherwise, where plant-level union organisation is strong, management may prefer a policy of establishment bargaining, which enables them to minimise the potential for inter-establishment comparisons, and union organisation.

But it was argued that management's choice between divisional or corporate bargaining and establishment bargaining will also be constrained by the precise form that multi-divisionalisation takes within companies. Here, the evidence from the study pointed to a strong connection between product diversification and bargaining structures. Where the good or service produced in the establishment was also produced in other establishments in the division, or across other divisions of the company, then the most important level of pay bargaining was significantly more likely to be at divisional, or corporate, level. In contrast, where the establishment was producing a specific good or service, the most important level of bargaining was significantly more likely to be the establishment. Thus, where there is standardisation of output across establishments in the same division, or across divisions within the company then pay is negotiated on a standardised basis as well. Further, the study found that the more diversified the company was across industrial sectors, the more likely it was that the establishment was the most important level of bargaining.

In contrast, the existence of vertical linkages appeared to have little influence on pay bargaining structures. Indeed, neither the existence of divisions nor their basis, nor the extent to which profit responsibility was devolved, nor the existence of vertical linkages had an independent influence on pay bargaining structure once product standardisation and the degree of diversification had been taken into account. Thus, companies' product structure appeared to be the principal influence on management's decision to bargain at establishment, division or corporate level.

The study notes the correspondence of pay bargaining structures with other industrial relations structures, and thus enables more general inferences to be drawn about the implications of organisational form for the management of labour. Thus, union recognition across all establishments within the enterprise was associated with divisional or corporate pay bargaining, whilst recognition in some establishments only was associated with establishment level bargaining. The existence of common job grading or evaluation schemes across establishments was also significantly associated with divisional and corporate bargaining. So, too, was the existence of division or company joint consultative arrangements. In short, there appears to be some considerable consistency between pay bargaining structures, other industrial relations structures and one aspect of organisational form: product structure.

It has been shown that certain types of company have formal bargaining arrangements at the establishment level. But it has yet to be demonstrated that these establishment negotiations are tied into the broader framework of planning and control at divisional and corporate levels, as the above hypothesis suggests. It could be the case, equally, that management negotiators in these establishments have complete autonomy to conduct negotiations, as might be the case in a loosely structured holding company.

Fifty-four establishments reported that the establishment was the most important level of bargaining for manual workers' pay (40 for non-manual workers) and the managers in these establishments were asked a number of follow-up questions aimed at establishing the extent of any intervention from divisional and corporate levels. (For the purposes of these questions, the different levels above the establishment were not differentiated, being referred to as 'higher levels'.) The questions, and the responses, are shown in Table 8.2.

Intervention 'behind the scenes' from managers at division and corporate levels was widespread, but not universal. Two-thirds of the establishments reported that higher levels of the company had a policy on pay settlements, or issued pay guidelines; this applied equally to negotiations for manual and non-manual workers. A similar proportion indicated that there were consultations with management at a higher level before the start of negotiations over pay for either group within the workforce. Fifty per cent of the establishments reported *both* a higher level policy and prior consultations, leaving just 17 per cent of establishments reporting neither. The figures were identical for manuals and non-manuals.

Table 8.2 Higher Level Intervention in Establishment Bargaining (%)

	Manuals	*Non-Manuals*
Higher level has policy on pay or issues guidelines	65	65
Consultations with a higher level before the start of negotiations	67	68
Initial offer decided at a higher level	37	43
Final offer decided at a higher level	19	23
Direct participation of higher level management in negotiations	17	23

Notes: (1) Base: Establishments reporting that the establishment is the most important level of bargaining.
(2) Sample sizes are 54 (manuals) and 40 (non-manuals).

The study further attempted to uncover the extent of higher level intervention in the particulars (as distinct from the broad shape) of negotiations. As can be seen, such involvement was less widespread. With one exception, wherever a final offer was decided at a higher level, so too was the initial offer. Equally, direct participation of higher level managers in actual negotiations was strongly associated with cases where the initial offer was determined at a higher level. Thus, the last two forms of intervention were contained within the cases where the initial offer was determined at a higher level. In turn, these establishments were contained within the larger group of establishments reporting either that higher levels had a policy or that there were prior consultations, or both. In short, managers from divisional and corporate levels were involved in the particulars of the negotiations in roughly one-half (slightly less for manuals, slightly more for non-manuals) of the establishments where they intervened at all.

Although no major differences in organisational form were found between establishments where higher levels intervened in the particulars of negotiations and those where they intervened to broadly shape negotiations, there *were* significant differences between establishments where there was one or other of these two forms of intervention, and those where there was none. Specifically, establishments where there was none were significantly more likely to be designated profit centres and to be able to retain a portion of funds generated for investment purposes. They also belonged to diversified enterprises, producing goods or services specific to that establishment.

We could infer from their being able to retain a portion of profits for capital purposes, that these establishments were part of companies that were organised along H-form lines. (In M-forms, all profits are supposedly turned over to corporate office.) This would be consistent with the absence of a divisional or corporate management framework within which local managers negotiate. Further support for this conclusion comes from the study's finding that monitoring of financial, product and labour relations in these companies was patchy. Again, this is characteristic of H-form, rather than M-form, organisation.

Coverage of Combine Organisation

We argued, above, that workers will respond to managerial initiatives in order to enhance control, arising from the adoption of the M-form. In particular, it was suggested that workers will respond to the development of a corporate framework for the conduct of labour relations, including pay bargaining, by establishing multi-establishment trade-union, or combine, organisation. We would expect to find combine committees where bargaining was shifted to divisional or corporate level, but also to some extent, where managers were co-ordinating establishment bargaining 'behind the scenes'. This is because the effects of such co-ordination may well become apparent to union negotiators.

Where bargaining is at divisional or corporate levels, it does not necessarily follow that cross-plant union organisation will exist. It is common, for example, for companies bargaining at divisional or corporate levels to negotiate with the full-time officials of unions, rather than with the lay representatives drawn from the different plants. It is, therefore, valid to view cross-plant trade-union organisation in the form of a committee of shop stewards from different plants, as an independent response by workers in the company to a managerial preference to bargain on a cross-plant basis. Frequently, such committees are viewed with hostility within official trade-union structures (Wainwright and Elliott 1982), as well as from management. In other cases, management may prefer to deal with union representatives from within the company, rather than from outside (Brown 1983), and they may offer various forms of support to such organisations. This issue is considered in the following section.

Marginson (1985) considered the influences of bargaining structure, union organisation at plant level and parent companies' organisational form on combine organisation.[2] The existence of a multi-establishment committee of trade-union representatives was, as expected, positively and significantly associated with pay bargaining at divisional or corporate, as opposed to establishment, levels. The organisation of the parent company along M-form lines also had a positive and significant independent effect on the existence of a combine committee: this provides support for the argument that to adopt a corporate framework for the conduct of labour relations would generate counter organisation by workers—whether or not bargaining shifted to divisional or corporate level. Plant-based union organisation, in the form of a regularly functioning shop stewards organisation, was a further positive and significant influence on the existence of a combine committee. This is not altogether surprising: effective plant-based union organisation is likely to be a precondition of any multi-establishment trade-union organisation.

The survey of the management of industrial relations in large enterprises (Marginson *et al.* 1988) asked managers at divisional and enterprise levels whether there were 'any meetings' between 'stewards or union representatives from different establishments' within the division or company, respectively. Findings are shown in Table 8.3.

At divisional—and more so at corporate—level, cross-plant union organisation appeared to be reasonably widespread amongst the companies surveyed.

The study also found both pay bargaining structure and organisational form to be significant influences on the existence of a cross-plant committee of shop stewards. Committees were much less common where bargaining occurred at establishment level, and much more common where bargaining was at division or corporate level. In the case of non-manual workers, for example, 83 per cent of head office managers, who reported that bargaining took place at corporate level, claimed that there was a cross-plant committee of union representatives at that level. Where bargaining occurred at establishment level, cross-plant trade-union

Table 8.3 The Existence of Cross-Plant Trade-Union Organisation Within Divisions and Enterprises (%)

	Divisions		*Enterprises*	
	Manuals	*Non-Manuals*	*Manuals*	*Non-Manuals*
Meetings between union representatives from different establishments	48	41	60	54
No meetings	42	51	33	34
Not classified	10	8	7	16

Notes: (1) Base: Divisions/enterprises where unions recognised for bargaining purposes in at least some establishments.
(2) Sample sizes are 79 (manuals, divisions), 69 (non-manuals, divisions), 92 (manuals, enterprises) and 79 (non-manuals, enterprises).

organisation on a company basis was reported in only 36 per cent of cases.

In terms of organisational form, company-based committees were more common where there was no divisional tier in the organisation, and therefore no basis for divisional committees—this explains the relatively higher incidence of enterprise committees reported in Table 8.3. Beyond this, product structure was, once more, the dominant aspect of organisational form which influenced whether or not there was a committee. This occurred because both manuals and non-manuals cross-plant committees were significantly more common in less-diversified, or undiversified, companies than they were in firms which diversified their business activities across two or more broad industrial sectors. Commonalities across establishments may well have facilitated cross-plant union organisation, but, in addition, management may be less resistant to such organisation in these enterprises: a point we return to below.

Company size and industry were also important influences, with larger companies being more likely to have committees—this might be explained in terms of the greater resources which union organisations have in larger enterprises—and committees being less common in the service sectors and in electrical engineering. This might be explained in terms of weaker plant-based union organisation within these sectors, given that electrical engineering also covers the newly established electronics sector.

Management Policy and Combine Organisation

It has been argued that management will try to shape the form that trade-union organisation takes. In the case of combine committees, one might expect companies to adopt a hostile attitude where bargaining is decentralised to establishments, and management policy is to emphasise differences between establishments. Such hostility may effectively undermine trade-union efforts to establish a multi-establishment organisation. Where there are commonalities across establishments, and divisions, and where pay bargaining is conducted at divisional or corporate level, managerial policy may be to encourage multi-plant trade-union organisation. This would be the case where companies prefer to deal with internal union representatives rather than external union officials.

The study of the management of industrial relations in large companies throws some light on this issue. Divisional and head-office managers reporting the existence of cross-plant trade-union organisation were questioned about the managerial support, if any, received by such organisations. Specifically, they were asked: 'Do these meetings constitute a

Table 8.4 Managerial Support for Cross-Plant Trade-Union Organisation (%)

	Divisions		Enterprises	
	Manuals	*Non-Manuals*	*Manuals*	*Non-Manuals*
Meetings in company time	92	89	87	87
Committee recognised	81	89	65	72

Notes: (1) Base: Enterprise and divisions reporting cross-plant trade-union committees.
(2) Sample sizes are 38 (manuals, divisions), 28 (non-manuals, divisions), 55 (manuals, enterprises) and 43 (non-manuals, enterprises).

committee recognised by management?' Findings are reported in Table 8.4.

In fact, as the table shows, the overwhelming majority of committees met in company time, indicating a degree of managerial acceptance. In addition, more than eight out of every ten are recognised by management, taking divisional responses, and more than six out of ten for manuals (seven for non-manuals) taking head-office responses. Recognition enables these committees to bargain effectively at divisional and corporate levels with management.

However, recognition was not strongly associated with the conduct of pay bargaining at divisional or corporate levels. One-third of the companies bargaining at corporate or divisional level, and reporting that a committee existed, did not recognise that committee. This clearly illustrates that recognition of these committees is only one option open to management, and that bargaining can proceed perfectly well (for example, with external officials of the union) at divisional or corporate level without recognising a committee of union representatives, drawn from the various plants.

Given that the overwhelming majority of committees received some form of managerial support, it might be concluded that committees are only able to sustain their existence in exceptional circumstances in the face of management hostility. A degree of management support is essential to their continuation. Committees are most likely to exist, and therefore to receive such managerial support, in a particular type of company—namely, one which is relatively undiversified, and where the same good or service is produced in several establishments or divisions. In more diversified companies, managerial policy is hostile to combine committees, which, in turn, exist in only a handful of cases.

8.5 Conclusion

Organisational form has been shown to have control as well as efficiency attributes. Hierarchy is not so much an efficient form of organisation, as a means by which managers ensure that their objectives dominate the goals of those who work in the organisation. Consequently, a strengthening of hierarchy cannot be taken as having unambiguous welfare consequences, as Williamson (1980) has argued. Employers will select forms of internal organisation that enable them more effectively to control workers. In this respect, we argued that the M-form offered large UK companies two sets of attributes: the integration of labour costs into financial planning and control mechanisms, leading to a greater emphasis on the measurement and reduction of costs; and the adoption of a corporate framework for the co-ordination and regulation of labour relations. Workers, in turn, will try to exercise countervailing power through trade-union organisation. We considered particularly the extent to which combine organisation has emerged as a counter to the M-form. But there is no reason to suppose that such countervailing power will offset exactly the effects of strengthened hierarchy: again an efficient outcome cannot be presumed.

Notes

1. The following equation reports the results of regressing, whether pay bargaining was at divisional (as distinct from plant) level, on variables measuring organisational form and union strength (Marginson 1985):

   Divisional Bargaining $= 1.23MF^* - 0.48TR - 0.26SSM$
   or not $\quad\quad\quad\quad (2.92) \quad\quad (1.17) \quad\quad (0.72)$

   -2 log likelihood ratio $= 9.6^*$
   * denotes significance at 95 per cent level
   MF is a dummy variable, indicating whether the parent company was M-form or not.
   TR is a dummy variable, indicating whether the parent was in transition to M-form.
   SSM is a dummy variable, indicating whether the plant had a regularly functioning shop-steward organisation.

2. The following equation reports the results of regressing whether plants were part of a multi-establishment trade-union (or combine) committee, on variables measuring bargaining structure, organisational form and plant-based union organisation:

   Combine Ctte $= 2.80CM^* + 1.22^*DV = 0.99MF^* + 0.75SSM^*$
   or not $\quad\quad\quad (2.58) \quad\quad (3.17) \quad\quad (2.74) \quad\quad (2.10)$

−2 log likelihood ratio = 29.9*

* denotes significance at the 95% level

CM, DV are, respectively, dummy variables, representing whether bargaining was at company or divisional level.

MF is a dummy variable indicating whether the parent company was M-form.

SSM is a dummy variable indicating whether there was a regularly functioning shop stewards organisation.

9

Internal Organisation and Investment

FRANK STEPHEN AND STEVE THOMPSON

9.1 Introduction

This chapter explores the implications of the internal organisation of firms for the efficiency of investment in the corporate economy. In particular, it examines Oliver Williamson's contention that an internal capital market operating within a multi-divisional form firm (see Chapters 1 and 2 above) possesses superior efficiency properties to *either* external capital market allocation or alternative internal arrangements. The M-form hypothesis (Williamson 1971a, 1975, 1981) attributes this superiority to two features. First, it argues that the internal allocation of investment funds economises on the transaction costs associated with using external capital markets. Second, it suggests that the separation of divisional and corporate staff responsibilities, within an M-form structure, reduces any tendencies for management to take investment decisions which conflict with the maximisation of shareholder welfare. Both parts of the argument are examined below.

We begin by outlining the conventional role ascribed to the capital market in restraining the exercise of managerial discretion: it is suggested that informational problems impose severe limitations on the capital market's ability to fulfil this function. Next, we examine the M-form as an internal system for allocating funds and we suggest that for the M-form to get optimal use of the information available within itself requires complex interactions between its parts. There follows a review of a number of recent empirical studies on the internal organisation of large firms. This literature confirms the suggestion of Williamson and Bhargava (1972) that many divisionalised firms fail to achieve the separation of responsibilities and the system of controls which characterise true M-forms. Specifically, the evidence suggests that the arrangements for making investment decisions do not necessarily conform to the model of the competitive internal market. We close with the question of whether, in the M-form firm, funds are allocated in the best interests of both its own shareholders and efficiency within the wider economy.

9.2   The Capital Market and Managerial Discretion

The traditional neoclassical view in economics is that reliance on unrestricted product and factor markets will ensure *ceteris paribus*[1] that resources are efficiently allocated and thus social welfare maximised. As long as these markets are competitive, decentralised decision-making will generate efficiency. However, where product markets are imperfect there will be reduced pressure on firms to operate in a productively efficient manner. Thus the ability to earn super-normal profits 'cushions' the firm— and its managers—against the consequences of internal inefficiency.

If managers could be relied upon always to behave in the interests of shareholders (and so maximise profits) the relaxation of the product market constraint would not matter. A body of literature has developed, however, which suggests that managers will not inevitably behave in this way (Berle and Means 1932, Baumol 1959, Marris 1964, Williamson 1967, etc.). Furthermore, shareholders are unable to police managerial behaviour directly because, in effect the transactions costs of doing so are too high.[2] Consequently, the property rights of shareholders are attenuated. (Furubotn and Pejovich 1972). All is not lost, however, in the case for the efficiency of decentralised capitalism if the relevant factor markets can curtail the exercise of managerial discretion. For example, the market for managerial talent (Fama 1980, Fama and Jensen 1983a) may ensure that executive remuneration reflects firm performance, if only *ex post*. (This argument is examined in Chapter 4.) Of particular relevance to this chapter is the disciplinary role played by the capital market. This may constrain the exercise of managerial discretion in two ways: first, via its function as a market for corporate control; and second, through its role as a source of finance for new investment. These possibilities are considered in turn.

The market-place for takeovers and mergers allows one set of managers to bid for assets currently operated by another set. Where financial returns are not being maximised, therefore, there is the potential scope for acquisition, followed by the displacement of underperforming managers and the realisation of any gains made possible by greater resource productivity. Where the potential target is a quoted public company the influence of the market for corporate control should be at its greatest. The share price may function as a continuous indicator of performance, whilst the very marketability of the shares facilitates any takeover approach. Outside acquisition also affects unquoted companies, wholly-owned subsidiaries and divisions and associate companies, but in these cases external bidders may be hampered by a lack of suitable information.[3]

The effectiveness of the market for corporate control depends critically on the transactions costs (including information and displacement costs) of the acquisitions process. As a device to police inefficiency it also requires that those acting as bidders are motivated by profits and not merely a desire to pursue their own managerial goals. These issues are addressed in detail elsewhere in this volume by Mueller (Chapter 3) and Thompson (Chapter 4).

The capital market may also restrain managerial behaviour in so far as firms have to use it as a source of new funds (both debt and equity). If managerial performance is considered unsatisfactory, the suppliers of funds may require a higher risk premium and so will raise the cost of new capital to the firm. Thus the scope for further expansion may depend on a management's reputation with the financial institutions.

The capital market's ability to constrain managerial discretion is contingent on the extent to which firms actually rely on it. Company formation is highly likely to necessitate share issues and/or the issue of debt. (It is unlikely that individuals are in a position to use their own wealth to form a company of more than the smallest size.) However, existing large companies with some degree of market power (i.e. those on which this chapter focuses) may be able to finance most of their capital investment and expansion from retained earnings. They are unlikely to raise substantial proportions of their investment funds from share issues. Mueller (1984, p. 166) demonstrates that in the 1970s US manufacturing and non-manufacturing business issued new-shares to only 10 per cent of the value of its expenditure on plant and equipment (i.e. physical investment). In the UK the ratio of capital issues to fixed asset formation for the years 1973–83 averaged 30 per cent.[4] The issue of ordinary shares by UK companies in the period 1971–83 represented only 4.5 per cent of their total sources of funds whilst internal funds represented, on average, 58.5 per cent of sources.[5] A more recent study covering the behaviour of large UK companies for the years 1969–84 concludes that 'around 25 per cent of the extra funds needed to finance new fixed capital expenditure was met by new debt issues . . . ' (Bank of England Quarterly Bulletin May 1987, p. 263). These figures suggest that the capital market's ability to exercise direct constraints on the investment decisions of most companies is restricted.[6]

9.3   The M-Form Firm and Investment

Managerial discretion could manifest itself in a number of ways within the firm: These might include tolerance of inefficient production arrangements (Leibenstein 1966), above-optimal levels of staff expenditures (Williamson 1964) or simply low effort levels and the pursuit of a 'quiet life' (Hicks 1946). With specific respect to the investment decision there are at least three reasons why managers might not choose those projects which maximise shareholder well-being:

(1)   Management may not select projects according to their risk/return criteria but may, instead, choose 'pet' schemes which further objectives such as 'empire building' or the pursuit of political influence.

(2)   Growth-conscious managers may retain earnings within the firm and re-invest them rationally but in projects yielding less than the external cost of capital. (This possibility is discussed by Mueller in Chapter 3.) The dispersal of the funds as shareholders' dividends would allow a profitable reallocation of resources within the economy.

(3)   The managers' own specific investments in the firm (including pension rights and human capital as well as any equity involvement) may lead them to adopt more risk averse attitudes than those of owners holding shares within a balanced portfolio. Risk aversion may induce a preference for income smoothing via conglomerate diversification (Amihud and Lev 1982).

The M-form hypothesis suggests that at least the first two of these distortions may be checked by the separation of the strategic and operating levels of the firm. Within the M-form, at least as described by Williamson (1975, 1981), major investment decisions are not made by the managers who propose them or from whose division they emanate. Instead they are approved by the 'general office' staff who might be expected to have little vested interest in expenditures elsewhere in the organisation. The pooling of surpluses from divisions and their allocation to projects chosen with a strategic, corporation view in mind ensure that surpluses are not dissipated in investment projects in areas of the company which are currently profitable but have no long-run future. This wider, strategic view in the M-form may suggest investment in new areas of activity which in a U-form firm would have no advocates and might indeed be seen as threatening vested interests within the firm.

Williamson (1975) suggests that the internal reporting mechanisms within an M-form corporation have lower costs than those which the outside market must incur in trying to police managers. The 'general office' is thus in a better position to monitor the performance of the various parts of the corporation. Not only will it receive detailed reports but it is able to carry out internal audits to verify the claims of divisional management. The quality and quantity of information available to the general office will be greater, therefore, than that available to the capital market in general and shareholders in particular. 'Insiders' can be treated more frankly: providing them with information does not breach commercial secrecy, whereas keeping the capital market informed might.

Internalising transactions within the firm sometimes has the effect of suppressing market mediation and locking the parties to a supply relationship into a bilateral monopoly—or at least 'small numbers'— bargaining problem (Williamson 1975). There are clear attendant dangers of high haggling costs and reduced pressures for productive efficiency. However, in the *multi-divisional* firm's internal capital market there remains inter-divisional competition for investment funds. Provided that these are distributed along rational lines, the M-form may combine the internalisation of information flows with some of the benefits of competitive allocation.

Detailed investigation of the operation of internal capital markets have been carried out in surveys and case studies by management accountants and business policy specialists. This work (e.g. Scapens and Sale 1981, Pike 1983a, 1983b for the UK; and Schall *et al.* 1978 for the USA) confirms that most divisionalised companies require all substantial investment expenditures to be approved by top management. Furthermore, most projects are defined and developed at the divisional level (King 1974, Pike 1983a). However, the relationship between senior and divisional management is more subtle than that implied by a simple bifurcation of responsibilities. Bower (1970, pp. 320–32), after a detailed study of investment decisions, commented:

> . . . the most striking aspect of the process of resource allocation . . . is the extent to which it is more complex than most managers seem to believe. It bears little resemblance to the simple portfolio management problem described in traditional finance theory. Moreover, the systems created to control the process sometimes appeared irrelevant to the task. They were based on the fallacious belief that top management made important choices in the finance committee when it approved capital investment proposals. In contrast we have found capital investment to be a process of study, bargaining, persuasion and choice spread over many levels of the organization and over long periods of time.

Surveys suggest that the general office approval of proposed projects is very largely a formality. Pike (1983a, b), for example, found a 10 per cent rejection rate amongst very large firms (annual investment > £100m) but much lower rates still in smaller companies. Scapens and Sale (1981) reported that very few projects were rejected at the formal stage. On the few occasions where a new investment was not sanctioned, they found that it was referred back for more information. Bower (1970) indicates a similar position for US companies. Yet it is not divisional autonomy which is responsible for generally high levels of project approval: the explanation appears to lie in the prior involvement of senior management in shaping the developing investment proposal.

King's (1974) detailed study of the process of investment decision making led him to identify a sequence of distinct necessary stages leading up to the formal approval level. This stylised progression is shown in Figure 9.1. Each of King's stages has one or more separate functions in the overall process of decision making; furthermore, different organisational influences are brought to bear at each stage. King's description gives senior management a substantial input, particularly at the early stages of *triggering*, *screening* and *definition* of a new project. Indeed, the strategic perspectives of senior executives appear to be important in locating new directions for investment. King concluded (p. 25):

> . . . particularly for new ventures, top management can carry out the triggering and screening stage themselves. Consideration of the strengths and weaknesses of their company may be used as a means of identifying potential areas for capital which merit further investigation.

The detailed proposals for any scheme remain a divisional responsibility; furthermore, since that division will be responsible for overseeing any approved project, the sanctioning decision is also equivalent to endorsing the competence of the division's managers. Indeed, the intra-organisational competition for funds within the M-form overlaps with the operation of the internal market for managerial labour services. Information generated in the former may be used to make promotion or firing decisions within the latter.[7]

To summarise, the M-form internal capital market can reduce transactions costs in two ways: by reducing the problems of opportunism and by improving the efficiency of the transmission of information. Both methods utilise the reduction in informational asymmetry made possible by the internal separation of middle management and those sanctioning the investment decision. The internal capital market features of the M-form can be viewed as introducing a competitive element in the allocation of investment resources within the firm and as such reducing a 'small numbers' problem which might otherwise exist. The corporation has not only alternatives but also, because of the permanent relationship between the divisions and the general office, experience of a division's ability to deliver what it is proposing, i.e. recurring transactions restrain opportunism.

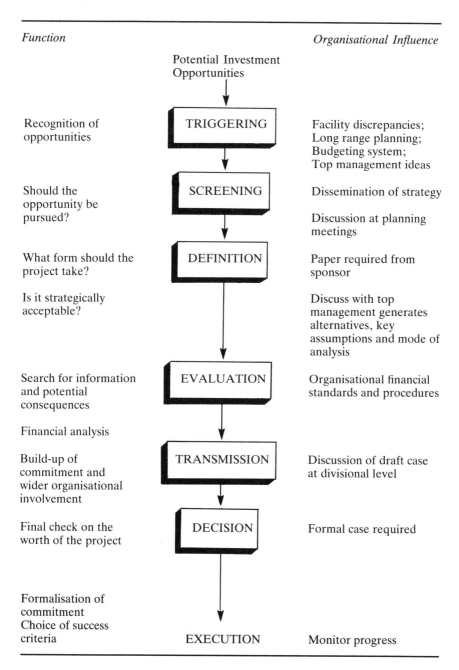

Function   *Organisational Influence*

Potential Investment
Opportunities

Recognition of   **TRIGGERING**   Facility discrepancies;
opportunities   Long range planning;
                                                    Budgeting system;
                                                    Top management ideas

Should the   **SCREENING**   Dissemination of strategy
opportunity be
pursued?   Discussion at planning
                                                    meetings

What form should the   **DEFINITION**   Paper required from
project take?   sponsor

Is it strategically   Discuss with top
acceptable?   management generates
                                                    alternatives, key
                                                    assumptions and mode of
                                                    analysis

Search for information   **EVALUATION**   Organisational financial
and potential   standards and procedures
consequences

Financial analysis

Build-up of   **TRANSMISSION**   Discussion of draft case
commitment and   at divisional level
wider organisational
involvement

Final check on the   **DECISION**   Formal case required
worth of the project

Formalisation of
commitment
Choice of success
criteria   **EXECUTION**   Monitor progress

Source: King (1974) p. 26

Figure 9.1   The Process of Decision Making: Proposed Procedures for
Major Projects

9.4   Divisionalised Firms or M-Forms?

Most empirical work on the M-form hypothesis has been concerned to identify the overall performance effect of *either* the possession of an M-form structure *or* the reorganisation towards one. This literature—which is reviewed in detail by John Cable in Chapter 2—tends to suggest that the suitability of the M-form type depends critically upon the institutional environment of the country concerned. In the USA and UK, countries with relatively well-developed equity markets, a number of studies report an association between M-form and superior performance (Armour and Teece 1978, Teece 1981, Steer and Cable 1978, Thompson 1981, Hill 1985a, 1985b, etc.). In those countries where bank financing appears to be more important, including Japan (Cable and Yasuki 1985) and Germany (Cable and Dirrheimer 1983, Cable 1985a) no such performance effect has been identified.

The above literature has concerned itself with the overall performance of M-forms and not merely the internal capital market argument. Conversely, there have been a number of empirical studies (reviewed by Dennis Mueller in Chapter 3) which have examined the return on earnings retained within the corporation and compared it—generally unfavourably—with the current return on outside assets. However, as far as we are aware, there have been no attempts to control for organisational form in this work. A rigorous test of the effectiveness of the M-form as a miniature capital market would involve a comparison of the marginal returns on retained earnings under different internal structures.

One difficulty, which hampers all quantitative testing of the M-form hypothesis, concerns the variety of divisionalised structures encountered by researchers. In part, this is because different firms' activities are not equally decomposable and, in consequence, different degrees of decentralisation may be required.[8] *Ceteris paribus*, the greater the extent of shared facilities or the level of inter-divisional trading—as in, say, a vertically integrated firm—the higher the degree of general office control. However, even apparently decomposable divisionalised firms also exhibit considerable differences in the extent to which they achieve the separation of responsibility which characterises Williamson's true M-form. Williamson and Bhargava (1972) recognised this very quickly and identified sub-optimal types in which head office control was totally inadequate (H-form), underdeveloped (M'-form) or overdeveloped (M̄-form). Unfortunately, the assignment of actual firms to these categories is a partially subjective task based on necessarily incomplete information.

Hill (1985a) presents a comparison of the distribution of firms by organisational form between his own study and that of Steer and Cable (1978)—both studies are concerned with UK companies but relate to different time periods and slightly different populations. Hill (1985a) argues that, since the earlier study relied only on published information on firm organisation, it overestimated the extent to which the M-form had been adopted; but his estimate will be more accurate because it is based on a postal questionnaire completed by officers of the firms themselves. Hill finds that only 19.7 per cent of firms satisfied the M-form definition in 1982 whilst Steer and Cable (1978) allocated 32.1 per cent of firms to that category for the 1970–2 period. He allocated 23.5 per cent to the M̄ or corrupted M-form category as compared with only 6.4 per cent by Steer and Cable. M̄-forms are identified as multi-divisional firms where the separation of operational and strategic decision making is not clearly established. Similarly, Hill identifies 30.3 per cent of firms as holding companies whilst Steer and Cable find only 12.8 per cent in this category. Conversely, Hill identifies only 1.8 per cent as U-form whilst Steer and Cable allocate 8.3 per cent to this category. This last result is, perhaps, a valid reflection of company growth and diversification in the decade between the studies. The significant finding of this comparison is that, in Hill's view, only a minority of firms with a formal divisionalised structure satisfy all the requirements for them to be classified as M-form.

The evidence reported by Hill (1985a, 1985b) emphasises that there are crucial differences between a *pure M-form* firm and a *divisionalised* firm. These differences really hinge on the role of the 'general office' in the M-form compared with corporate (as opposed to divisional) management in a divisionalised firm. Williamson (1985, p. 284) summarises the 'general office' in an M-form firm as engaging in the following activities:

(i)   identifying separable economic activities within the firm;
(ii)   according quasi-autonomous standing to each;
(iii)   monitoring the efficiency performance of each;
(iv)   awarding incentives;
(v)   allocating cash flows to high-yield uses;
(vi)   performing strategic planning (diversification, acquisition, divestiture and related activities).

The creation of a divisionalised structure is implied by (i) but it is clear that much more is involved. Two recent major studies of divisionalised companies in the UK which do not distinguish pure M-form firms from other divisionalised companies show that divisionalisation *per se* does not generate the benefits which would appear, from the evidence quoted above, to derive from establishing a pure M-form firm. These studies are by Grinyer, Yasai-Ardekani and Al-Bazzaz (1980), which was based on data collected from 48 large UK companies and by Hill and Pickering (1986a), which used the same data as Hill (1985a) but with a somewhat different structural classification. No evidence was found that divisionalised companies outperformed others on the various measures of profitability (Grinyer *et al.* 1980, p. 210; Hill and Pickering, 1986a, p. 43). Indeed, there were indications that divisionalised companies were outperformed by others: Hill and Pickering found that in one year the return on sales of holding companies was significantly greater than that for other organisational firms; Grinyer, *et al.* found that growth in the return on invested capital and net profits was *negatively* correlated with diversification. These results contrast with Hill's (1985a) finding that M-form firms significantly outperform others.

Hill and Pickering (1986a, pp. 37, 45) did not find that the reallocation of profits between divisions or the centralising of investment decisions by themselves affected profitability. Indeed, the same study (p. 40) found that 43 per cent of firms reallocated profits to 'troubled, cash-needy businesses'. However, 71 per cent also said that they reinvested profits in 'those' businesses which offered the highest return. Yet the formal *locus* of the investment decision did not influence profitability (Hill and Pickering 1986a, pp. 37, 45). It was found that companies which allowed a stronger head office involvement in operating decisions tended to be less profitable, as was the case for those companies where divisional head offices were involved in operating decisions (Hill and Pickering 1986a, p. 47). Thus firms which separate operational and strategic decisions (e.g., activity (v)) do appear to perform better.

These results confirm that it is not divisionalisation *per se* that generates the superior performance of M-form firms but its combination with the other attributes of M-form. However, attaining the pure M-form would appear to be more difficult than hitherto appreciated, given the evidence from Hill (1985a, b) and Hill and Pickering (1986a). The appropriate balance between divisional autonomy and the general office's monitoring and strategic roles may be quite difficult to obtain, and it is here, perhaps, that the M-form has the greatest potential for corruption: if the balance tips too far towards divisional autonomy the strategic role of the general office may be impaired; if it tips too far towards 'general office' dominance operational and strategic roles may be compounded.

This is borne out by subsequent research from Hill and Pickering (1986b) which reports a detailed investigation of the internal capital markets operated by 12 highly diversified UK multi-divisionals. The authors describe three broad types of observed control systems, only one of which resembles that necessary for a pure M-form. While further investigation is needed to determine the generality of their results, the authors' categories may be described briefly:

Type 1: Competitive Internal Capital Markets
This one operates along the lines of a Williamson M-form. The allocation of funds and the assessment of performance are determined

by anticipated and actual profitability, respectively. The role of top officers is limited to major strategic initiatives.[9]

Type 2: Planned Internal Capital Markets
In this one, the strategic role of top management is more pronounced and the firm is run as a portfolio of business, each of which is given different objectives. The designation of particular activities as cash generators, growth businesses, etc. overrides inter-divisional competition and leads to the performance of the firm relying more on the goals of top management.[10]

Type 3: Latent Internal Capital Markets
Here, there is no rational reallocation of cash flow among competing claimants: typically, divisions retain and reinvest their own profits. In consequence, the potential benefits of internal allocation cannot be realised.[11]

It was noted earlier that whilst the formal investment decision is normally made centrally, there is usually an informal system of discussions between levels of the organisation such that very few formal proposals are rejected. It can now be seen that the investment approval procedure will be shaped by the precision with which 'head office' sets strategy. In Hill and Pickering's (1986b) *Type 2: Planned Markets* the scope for divisional-level initiators is very limited. Scapens and Sale (1981) cite instances of this type of curtailment: in such cases investment appraisal is largely a cost controlling exercise.

These considerations also suggest that the internal capital markets operated by multi-divisional firms may be highly constrained ones. A high net present value or internal rate of return[12] may be a necessary but insufficient condition for project adoption. Only those projects which are compatible with general office corporate strategy will reach the organisation's agenda. Indeed, in the Scapens–Sale (1981, Table 7) survey, quite small proportions of US and UK firms said that capital expenditure ceilings arose because of a shortage of funds, more said they resulted from corporate management's desire to control areas of activity and a mix of products.

The discussion thus far, of the management of internal investment, has largely focused on *ex-ante* control. However, the monitoring role, which Williamson ascribes to the 'general office' in the M-form presumably implies *ex-post* monitoring of, *inter alia*, investment projects. The Scapens–Sale (1981) surveys suggest there may be substantial national variations in the emphasis placed on this function. In their US sample, 84.2 per cent of firms carried out post-completion audits to determine whether projected benefits did, in fact, accrue. In their UK sample, the proportion was only 36.3 per cent. To some extent this disparity may be the result of a lag in adoption of management accounting techniques: a similar survey by Pike (1983a, b), shortly afterwards, found 48 per cent of respondents using post-completion audits and indicated rapid change in the control procedures being employed.

The use of post-completion audits, even on a random basis, signals that investment appraisal is being treated seriously and that opportunistic misrepresentation at the project approval stage will be detected. Respondents to the Pike study reported that audits provided valuable feedback on biased estimates. Pike (1983a) quotes a reply: 'we have found a significant improvement in the quality of feasibility studies submitted since we started auditing the performance of major projects' (p. 205).

9.5   Corporate Strategy: But in Whose Interests?

The potential benefits of the internal capital market in the M-form were emphasised earlier in this chapter. This was followed by a suggestion that the strategic role of the general office also creates a particular constraint in that internal market: namely, that all projects must fit within the defined corporate strategy. This in turn raises the question, 'Whose interests is the strategy designed to serve?' It is plausible that the separation of head office and divisional managements will curb managerial discretion at the operating level. However, this does not necessarily imply that the corporate staff will choose a strategy to maximise shareholder welfare.

Williamson (1981) acknowledges that even an ideally organised M-form does not end the conflict of manager and shareholder preferences, although he suggests that it has done more than any regulatory or external reforms to relieve it. The harmonisation of senior executive behaviour and shareholder interest would still appear to depend upon the establishment of a suitable incentive system. Without this, those running the corporation would appear to have a vested interest in any strategy which emphasised its continuance and growth, even at the expense of profits. Chandler (1977, p. 10), a leading historian of the rise of the M-form is in no doubt that its founding managers put growth and stability before dividends:

> . . . in making administrative decisions, career managers preferred policies that favoured the long-term stability and growth of their enterprises to those that maximised current profits. For salaried managers the continuing existence of their enterprises was essential to their lifetime careers. Their primary goal was to assure continuing use of and therefore continuing flow of material to their facilities. They were far more willing than were the owners (stockholders)

to reduce or even forgo current dividends in order to maintain the long-term viability of their organisations. . . . If profits were high, they preferred to reinvest them in the enterprise rather than pay out in dividends . . .

Thus, any managerial pursuit of stability and growth through diversification would be facilitated by divisionalisation. Indeed, a logical step for U-form managers with this motivation might be to adopt the structure of a divisional form *prior* to pursuing the strategy of diversification. This could well improve resource allocation within the firm but still represent an inefficient use of funds across the economy as a whole. In the previous section it was noted that empirical work on divisionalised firms suggests that a significant proportion of them fail to achieve a complete M-form structure. In particular, it was seen that many did not evolve a competitive internal capital market. The existence of these 'sub-optimal' M-form structures is compatible with the view that divisionalisation can further corporate goals other than profit.

9.6 Conclusion

There has been a good deal of recent empirical work—particularly in the agency cost literature (see Chapter 4)—which examines the relationship between managerial compensation and firm behaviour. In the present context this includes studies of diversification and executive shareholding. Amihud and Lev (1982), for example, report that managerial share-holdings exercise a negative effect on a firm's propensity to engage in conglomerate mergers. Agrawal and Mandelker (1987) found that executive equity holdings (including stock options) influence the market's response to firm investment decisions in a manner consistent with the hypothesis that they curb managerial discretion. What are needed now, are studies which relate relevant aspects of firm behaviour to executive remuneration *and* organisational form.

A recurrent theme of this chapter has been the need for more precise empirical work on the internal capital market idea. One obvious omission concerns the lack of information on the efficiency of the reinvestment of retained earnings. Another gap in the literature relates to the interaction of organisational form and managerial compensation as determinants of corporate strategy. The evidence reviewed here does suggest that the M-form appears to increase the efficiency of the complex corporation. What is not clear, however, is how far M-form investment decisions are made in the interests of shareholders or, more importantly, from an economic standpoint, whether they promote a wider efficiency of resource allocation.

Notes

1. That is in the absence of any of the traditional sources of 'market failure' (i.e. externalities, public goods, natural monopolies, etc.) which prevent the generalised equivalence of marginal rates of substitution and transformation. Rowley and Peacock (1974).
2. If the investor holds shares in a balanced portfolio, his individual stake in any one firm is likely to be small. However, if he is to police the management of that company he must expend resources in acquiring information and subsequently acting upon it. Since the investor only recoups a very small fraction of any resulting gains (in proportion to his total holding), monitoring managers becomes a public good problem with corresponding incentives to free-ride.
3. In countries such as the UK there is a large volume of inter-firm trade in divested companies. (Coyne and Wright 1986)—a substantial proportion of this involves horizontal acquisitions (Wright and Thompson 1986). This is not surprising as the company's competitors may be better informed about its potential profitability than other outsiders. The importance of management buyouts on divestment reflects the informational advantages of managers (Wright and Coyne 1985).
4. Bank of England Quarterly Bulletin, September 1984, p. 365.
5. Ibid. p. 372.
6. However, Stiglitz (1985) points out that borrowing from banks introduces monitoring by another set of financial institutions.
7. Pike (1983a, p. 203) comments: 'It also becomes clear that the sponsor is appraised every bit as much as the proposal'. He quotes one respondent: 'Obviously if we think Joe [divisional sponsor] has performed wonderfully well in the past it will have an important bearing on how we evaluate doubtful projects. We would normally back his judgement . . . but eventually it comes down to whether Joe is the right person to be running the business'.
8. Thompson (1967, pp. 54–70) analyses the interaction of heterogeneity and environmental stability in determining the optimal degree of decentralisation.
9. Hill and Pickering (1986b, p. 69).
10. Hill and Pickering (1986b, pp. 69–71) point out that a 'planned internal market', in which profit criteria are overridden by other strategic factors, facilitates the pursuit of multiple and non-profit goals at corporate level. For example, corporate capital could be allocated to maximise the firm's long-term survival and growth.
11. Hill and Pickering's (1986b, pp. 70–71) *Latent Capital Market* type corresponds with Williamson and Bhargava's (1972) 'H-form'.
12. Pike (1983a) reports that net present value, internal and average rates of return and pay back periods were all widely used criteria for appraising divisional projects. However, net present value and internal rate of return techniques were gaining popularity.

10

Redrawing the Boundaries of the Firm

MIKE WRIGHT

10.1 Introduction

The preceding chapters have had as their focus the problem of the effective internal organisation of a firm with a given set of activities. Recent research has emphasised that organisational choice is not limited to a distinction between internalising within the firm or transacting on impersonal spot markets. As such, the firm's spread of interests need not be regarded as fixed.

This chapter is concerned with the boundary of the firm and the determination of whether activities are carried on inside or outside the firm and the form they take. The approach builds on the notion of governance structures developed by Williamson (1979), and seeks to provide a specific and dynamic view about inter-organisational relationships. Emphasis is placed on the externalisation of activities previously undertaken internally. Schematically, the relationships can be categorised as shown in Figure 10.1. On the one dimension, a conglomerate or various forms of trading relationship may exist. As alternatives to internal organisation, a firm may choose to switch to trading with a newly created firm or divest itself of its ownership interests wholly or in part whilst still continuing to trade. Where conglomerate interdependence exists, ownership may also be severed. The rationale for these changes and the form they may take are developed in what follows.

The chapter is divided into six main sections. The first examines the internal control problems which may lead to a change from pure internalisation. Drawing on the discussion in previous chapters these are identified as relating to the operation of internal markets, the role of monitors and management motivation, and various contingent factors.

The second section considers intermediate transactional forms between markets and internal hierarchies. These relationships may concern research,

	TRADING RELATION			CONGLOMERATE
	INPUT contract out	DISTRIBUTION franchise	JOINT VENTURE research link	
INTERNAL ORGANISATION				
NEW FIRM				
IN-HOUSE TEAM				
BUY-OUT				
SPIN-OFF				
SELL-OFF				
ASSET-SWAP				

Figure 10.1 Matrix of Types of Relationships and Their Organisational Form

marketing, distribution as well as straightforward production processes and may involve franchising, contracting-out and joint ventures. A firm may simply cease to produce a good or service itself and may begin trading with an entirely new firm. Alternatively, it can offer provision of the service or input to tender so that either another firm provides it or supply is continued by existing employees with a changed remuneration package (see the cases of local authority and health services in Chapter 11).

The forms that ownership change might take, either to effect these intermediate transactional relationships or to deconglomerise, (where unrelated activities are externalised) are several. They may involve the separation of a firm into two or more parts, the spinning-off of an entity where the vendor retains an equity interest, sale to another group, sale to incumbent managers and employees or an exchange by barter for part of another firm's activities. The rationale for each of these firms is discussed in section three. There follows a review of a number of empirical studies on the effects of different kinds of ownership transfer on the performance of vendor and purchaser.

In a dynamic environment, the process of internalisation and externalisation may be a continuing feature of the development of organisations. Organisations may acquire and divest as part of their search for an appropriate configuration of activities. Search activity may be prompted by the kind of problems addressed in earlier sections of the chapter. The fifth section discusses the extent of search activity amongst organisations. The sixth section presents some conclusions.

10.2 Internal Control Problems

Earlier chapters have addressed various approaches to internal organisation. The review of empirical studies presented in Chapter 2 indicated broad support for the view that performance was better for firms having achieved a multi-divisionalised structure than for other organisational forms. However, subsequent discussion suggested that the form of internal organisation may not be fixed over time and that the appropriate structure may depend heavily on various contextual factors. Corrupted, mixed and incomplete divisionalised forms may persist.

Chapters 3, 4 and 5 offered insights into internal organisation from the perspectives of the principal–agent theory, the life-cycle theory and the contingency theory. These approaches are drawn upon in this section to examine the conditions under which control problems may arise and lead to consideration of divestment. The issues essentially relate to difficulties in the functioning of internal markets, the role of monitors, and the problems posed by various contingent factors.

Internal Markets

Internal Labour Markets

An internal labour market is a hierarchy characterised by low-level entry and subsequent internal promotions supplemented by limited competition from the external market at ports of entry. Such an arrangement, according to Williamson (1975, 1980) has a number of potential advantages over the external supply of labour:

(1) It allows better-informed recruitment to senior positions than would be feasible for outside hirings.
(2) The possibilities of internal promotion may encourage employee commitment to the organisation—particularly where the selection criteria correspond with the employee's own norms.
(3) Employees in large organisations may experience an improved risk–return trade-off with increased job security and better advancement opportunities (Edwards 1975).
(4) Internal labour markets capture the returns from job-specific skills (Fitzroy and Mueller 1979).

However, the potential benefits of internally organised labour supply are not necessarily captured by either or both parties to an employment relationship. As Willman (1982) points out, opportunism does not end upon entering a labour contract: either one or both parties may seek to exploit the specific circumstances to their advantage. The hypothesised benefits of internal organisation—whether informational or the attitudinal or 'atmospheric' gains from increased commitment—may disappear in the face of sufficient bilateral opportunism. Increased job security may give way to decreased responsibility and free-riding.

Moreover, the development of multi-product and multi-plant firms creates a potential control problem where unions press for wage parity across different product or geographical markets. These factors overlie the difficulties posed by workplace custom and practice which may limit the flexibility of the internal labour supply in the face of incomplete employment contracts. The M-form may have been a device to thwart shop-floor control by trade unions (see Chapter 8), but it is doubtful whether it has prevented the spread of remuneration systems across divisions which are based on notions of parity rather than marginal productivity or profit (Frank 1984).

Internal Capital Markets

The superiority of the internal over the external capital market is a key element of the markets-and-hierarchies hypothesis. In the pure M-form, divisions compete for capital allocation, with the general office being responsible for overseeing this process. However, as discussed in Chapter 9, major problems may exist in the operation of such a system. Even amongst those firms which achieve a basic M-form structure, divisions may not be subject to capital reallocation by corporate management. The persistence of established codes and practices (see below) may mean that the nature of power relations between divisions heavily influences the allocation of investment funds. Moreover, strategic planning may be used to override divisional competition for resources (Hill 1984). The solution may be exacerbated by capital rationing imposed by profit crises or by the external market's problems in identifying the characteristics of the organisation as a whole. With capital rationing, some units may be designated as 'cash cows' and deliberately starved of investment funds whilst being milked to finance priority developments elsewhere (Govindarajan and Gupta 1985). This treatment is likely to impair the efficiency of the division concerned. The company's very survival may be threatened in extreme cases—either by bankruptcy or an unwelcome takeover. As a result, the kind of crisis conditions which have been shown to stimulate a move to the M-form, may also indicate that it should subsequently be amended.

Interdependencies between activities pose particularly important problems. Great care is required in deciding which activities are related since there may be important spill-over benefits from one part to another which may not be immediately obvious (Spicer and Ballew 1983). One solution may be to reorganise the structure of the firm so that interdependent activities fall within the same division (Kilman 1983). However asymmetries of interdependence (Pfeffer and Salancik 1978) and the varying managerial styles which may be required to control different activities may mean that the problem is not resolved but becomes less transparent.

Beyond these factors the functioning of an internal capital market may be hindered by the need to monitor an increasing number and diversity of operating divisions. This may become an important issue where the sub-divisionalisation of the divisions is introduced as an attempt to resolve the control problems involved in coordinating larger units (Hill 1984). As this process continues corporate staff become less able, because of information processing problems, to make use of specific knowledge in monitoring the divisions. As a result, increasing reliance may have to be placed upon standardised performance targets and, moreover, where performance targets are not met, central office resources may not be available to intervene directly to raise divisional performance.

The Role of Monitors and Management Motivation

Incomplete employee contracts give rise to the need for a monitoring function. But monitors themselves must be satisfactorily motivated, or they may divert gains away from shareholders to themselves (Dugger 1983). In the classical owner-managed firm the residual claimant status of the proprietor provides this motivation (Alchian and Demsetz 1972). However, in large complex organisations with diffuse ownership, a divorce between ownership and control may exist so that goals other than those of shareholders may be pursued.

In such conditions, central management has incentives to develop the firm beyond the optimal size, measured in profit terms, because of the rewards which will accrue to itself (Jensen 1986). Such a preference may be motivated by a desire for safety which is believed to come from diversified earnings or by size (which should be a deterrent to hostile takeover bids) (Armihud and Lev 1982). Weak pressures in the product, factor and corporate control markets may excaberate growth tendencies. Hence the separation of responsibilities in the M-form, which ought to reduce the scope for central management to indulge in 'preferred expenses' (Williamson 1964), may not have the desired impact. Moreover, the role of the M-form in accommodating managerial sub-goal pursuit may be called into question. Sub-goal pursuit ought to be contained, as central headquarters has a limited budget whilst the operating divisions are profit-accountable and run by executives whose remuneration depends upon performance.

However, neither corporate nor divisional level management may be highly profit-oriented. In the UK, at least until recently, divisional management included, primarily, salaried employees. Residual claimant status is being increased progressively with the introduction of stock-option schemes; in addition, there is an increasing use of profit-related remuneration packages. However, these approaches, which deal with the monitoring problems inherent in decentralisation, contain serious difficulties. First, there is an issue as to the proportion of the total remuneration package that needs to be performance related in order to motivate management. Second, there are problems in specifying contracts which are tight enough to provide incentives and reward individual performance. The difficulties to be overcome include free-riding, the lack of observability of effort and individual performance, the lack of goal congruence between central and divisional management, the existence of asymmetric information (to the advantage of divisional management), and the danger in encouraging short-term performance to the detriment of the firm's longer term prospects.

Recent developments in the principal–agent literature have attempted to deal with these patterns, and have been discussed more fully in

Chapter 4. However, many of the difficulties remain in practice as the inability to write water-tight contracts allows management to engage in opportunism and shirking, whilst the parent continues to act as 'lender of last resort' (Klein 1983).

Contingent Factors

Contingent factors were shown in Chapter 5 to affect both the structure of organisations and the processes through which they operated and changed. Certain contingent factors are particularly relevant to the control problems which may give rise to a desire to redraw the boundaries of the firm. These factors are analysed in more detail below.

Strategy and Environment

It might be expected that the strategy of a firm responds intuitively to changes in the environment, which in turn produces adaptations in the organisational structure. However, as seen in Chapters 2 and 5, the relationships between these factors are not quite so straightforward, particularly under conditions of uncertainty. Increasing size and diversity in a stable environment may be absorbed by an existing organisational control system, and poor performers in steadily declining markets may be removed (Harrigan 1980).

In turbulent and uncertain conditions a quantum change in the organisational structure may be required (Miller 1982). Inertia in the firm may mean that it is only under such crisis conditions that an overdue shift will occur. Internal control mechanisms may need to be changed so that information is aggregated in ways that recognise the true boundaries of interdependent activities. Moreover, decisions may need to be taken at levels which make fullest use of locally available information which it is not possible to transmit to the general office of the group (Chenhall and Morris 1986).

A changing environment, however, may break down the traditional affinities between product areas so that the original benefits of synergy from integration or conglomerate risk-spreading no longer apply (Rumelt 1982). Hence, simply redrawing the divisional boundaries of existing activities may not be a sufficient response. Integration in different markets may now be required, or different markets may need to be entered. Problems arise where it is not possible to put specific capital to other uses, so that ownership mobility is required to allow unwanted parts to be sold and the proceeds invested in other activities.

Fit and Search

Part of the review of activities which may be undertaken in stable conditions and intensified during a period of rapid change involves the need to identify activities that fit the firm's strategy. Fit is defined in terms of an entity's contribution towards achieving the parent firm's overall objectives. Poor fit does not necessarily mean poor performance *per se*: it may refer to past 'mistakes' in internal development or acquisition activity which, under conditions of uncertainty and imperfect information, are likely to occur. In such circumstances, a prospective entrant to a sector is unsure of either the market conditions or the potential economies of scope to be had from exploiting interdependencies, so that the search procedure engaged upon to find the most satisfactory configuration of assets is likely to produce disappointments (Cable 1977). However this does not mean that search activity ought to be abandoned, rather the control system needs to be flexible enough to allow for it as a normal part of the development and implementation of strategy. The relative fit of a subsidiary may be positively correlated with size (Duhaime and Baird 1987). For smaller subsidiaries, the costs of control and of effecting turnarounds may outweigh the returns to be gained, and vice versa for large divisions.

The degree of fit will also be influenced by internal control and technological change. Moreover, the life-cycle of the product and the firm may be influential though not usually the general economic cycle (Duhaime and Grant 1984). The work of Harrigan (1980) has shown the importance of divesting product areas in a declining phase of their life-cycle. Stigler (1951) argued that vertical disintegration might be expected during a market's expansionary phase through the spinning-off of decreasing cost activities, to allow maximum scale economies to be gained (and vice versa in the mature phase). The limited evidence available does not, however, support this view about the nature of vertical disintegration (Wright and Thompson 1986).[1]

The nature of fit also has implications for acquisitions. A group may be purchased because the acquirer perceives that one particular part fits with existing activities. Sale of the other parts can help recoup some of the initial outlay and avoid future control problems. However, as noted above, where a divorce exists between ownership and control, corporate management may have the incentive to force the growth of the firm beyond its optimal size because of the rewards which will accrue to itself (Jensen 1986), and so sell-offs may be resisted where they are perceived as an erosion of empire. But we should not overlook the basis for greater growth which is provided by divestment. Moreover, corporate management may increasingly wish to trade-off the benefits of empire building against the problems of controlling larger organisations.

Extending this point, it may be expected that activities to which corporate management have a particularly strong attachment—perhaps because they initially helped to develop the activity, or because of the status it conveys—may be retained even when profitability and other criteria suggest they ought to be removed. Where senior management changes, such activities may become vulnerable (Gilmour 1973), although there may come a point at which profitability crises override attachment issues (Duhaime and Grant 1984).

Technology

As seen in Chapter 5, contingency approaches to management control suggest that different organisational forms are appropriate for different types of technology, and changing technologies may call for a different type of organisational structure. However technical change may call into question the whole nature of the firm: first, it may erode natural monopoly-type arguments for economies of scale; second, it may also remove the benefits of joint production of goods and services of either a vertical or horizontal nature (Chiplin 1986). In the first instance it may be more efficient to produce via two or more separate entities; in the second either separate firms or joint ventures between firms may improve efficiency. Developments in information technology (IT) may help increase the codification of information and the speed at which it can be diffused. Moreover, IT developments are also making it easier to transmit non-codified information (Child 1987). Together with quantum reductions in costs, these improvements may argue for a move away from hierarchies and make managing markets easier.

Internal Organisational Processes

The inherited characteristics of established organisations may have an important impact on the functioning of an organisational structure. Organisations are governed by a specific set of codes which may prove difficult to change even when personalities change (Arrow 1974). The ways in which organisations are able to change may also be heavily influenced by inherited learning systems (Srivastava 1983). These problems may be exacerbated by the difficulties posed by an informal distribution of organisational power which does not correspond to the formal organisation chart. For example, an intended M-form may be dominated by a ruling coalition whose activities interfere with the rational allocation of resources. In a seminal study, Jones (1985) has demonstrated that the assimilation of new acquisitions may be prevented where the corporate culture of the acquirer is incompatible with that in the acquired firm even though a divisionalised structure ought to make integration easier. Attempts may be made during the process of negotiation to deal with such issues and identify matching characteristics, but the nature of incompatibilities may become apparent only when the deal is consummated. A recent survey of acquirers in the UK showed that half considered their acquisitions to be failures, primarily because of the problems in integrating activities and personnel following the transfer of ownership (Hunt 1988).

10.3   Intermediate Transactional Relationships

The above internal control problems indicate that conditions may exist for the externalisation of a transaction to another entity, but that retention of some form of co-ordination may be required. The three main types of co-ordination of intermediate relationships between markets or hierarchies are examined in this section and involve, in turn, franchising, contracting out and joint ventures.

Franchising

Two specific forms of franchising are traditionally distinguished. The first form is associated with products such as fast-food, automobile retailing, fashion retailing, etc., and may be defined as:

> . . . a business form essentially consisting of an organisation (the franchisor) with a market-tested business package centred on a product or service, entering into a continuing contractual relationship with franchisees, typically self-financed and independently owner-managed small firms, operating under the franchisor's trade name to produce and/or market goods or services according to a format specified by the franchisor. (Curran and Stanworth 1983)

The second form applies to circumstances where an exclusive right to produce a particular product or service for a given period is auctioned: one of the prime examples of this type of franchising is the auctioning by government of the right to provide television services in particular areas. This section focuses on the first form, the second being addressed in the next chapter.

The management of the transactional relationship between franchisee and franchisor usually involves a close specification by the latter of how the service or product will be offered. Close monitoring of standards is required in order to protect the value of the good name of the franchisor.

One of the key conditions under which this form of franchising may be used in preference to internal or market arrangements is the existence of divergent scale economies between, say, production and distribution. In some franchise operations there may be economies from centralised production of the product and decentralised distribution (e.g. automobiles). In others, centralisation of image-creation may be combined with decentralised production (e.g. fast-food outlets) (Caves and Murphy 1976, Rubin 1978). By themselves, these factors may not be sufficient to justify separation of transactions into two legal entities, and yet the existence of significant control costs may warrant such separation. The vertical separation provided by franchising can make commitment to a transaction more observable and harder to reverse than may be the case with internal incentives and organisation (Bonanno and Vickers 1988).

Where the specific characteristics of individual transactions are important, salaried employees may not have the incentive to negotiate the most advantageous terms; but where the specific characteristics of individual transactions are of less importance (e.g. petrol or fast-foods), then ensuring that local distribution outlets conform to the image provided centrally by the franchisor may be best obtained through a detailed contract. Under the terms of such a contract the franchisor is likely to have the bargaining power to determine the specific conditions of operation, and the franchisee has the residual claimant status incentive to achieve them. This power may be reinforced by the right to terminate the contract being vested in the franchisor. Additionally, the franchisor often maintains some key decision rights as to the way the product will be presented. Franchising may be appropriate where the 'distribution' outlet is geographically distinct from the 'manufacturer' and where repeat sales to customers are high—in the former, internalisation may raise monitoring costs; in the latter a franchisee will have less incentive to supply a lower quality of service. Where repeat business is low, an individual franchisee can free-ride as the costs of poor quality service are borne by other units and the franchisor who lose further business.

For franchising to be a viable alternative to internalised transactions it is necessary to deal with certain potential problems. First, it is necessary for the franchise contract to be clearly specified and complete. In uncertain conditions it may be necessary to include conditional clauses to take account of contingent events or have regular renegotiation. Second, franchise contracts must give the franchisee the incentive to perform. Making the provider of the service a residual claimant on a separate legal entity and allowing a substantial share of the profits from activities under his/her control to accrue to him/her is the generally accepted solution to this kind of problem. Third, it is important to avoid the problem of inefficient risk-bearing which might occur where a franchisee has a large proportion of his/her wealth tied up in an undiversified investment portfolio. As such, franchising may be more appropriate for cases of low investment risk.

Even though monitoring is required to ensure that the contract is adhered to, the residual claimant status of the franchisee reduces the coverage of such monitoring and usually ensures that a single supervisor can oversee a large number of outlets than would be possible under conventional hierarchical ownership and control.

A key issue concerns the extent to which franchises remain in the hands of franchisees or are bought back by franchisors. Evidence suggests a life-cycle effect, particularly with respect to services where the characteristics of individual transactions (e.g. fast food) are less important (Lillis *et al.* 1976, Caves and Murphy 1976). Franchising may be important in the early stages to establish rapid low-cost entry, but a return to vertical integration occurs in the mature phase of the cycle. Moreover, there may be control economies where there are several franchisees in a relatively small geographical area, which is more likely to be in the case of the mature phase. However, the problem of monitoring the manager who oversees the franchisee remains. (See also Rubin 1978 and Matthewson and Winter 1985). Brickley and Dark (1987) argued that common ownership and operation of production units would compel the parent company to monitor both quality standards and cost minimisation at many dispersed production points. If, alternatively, the product technology is leased to independent producers, cost control is no longer relevant but quality maintenance is. Each local producer—particularly when selling to a transient market—would have the incentive to reduce quality and free-ride on the reputation of the others. The franchise solution checks this problem by giving the franchisor the right of termination where quality is deficient, whilst bonding the franchisee by causing him to make specific investments which must be sold on termination.

Brickley and Dark show, using a sample of US firms which make use of both franchising and owned retail outlets, that the decision whether or not to franchise is related to the level of monitoring costs. It was found that the company-owned outlets were located closer to company monitoring headquarters and in areas of higher population, with franchised units being farther away in more rural areas. Additionally, the proportion of units franchised was found to be larger where repeat customer business was prevalent, as might be expected. Similarly, an examination of franchising in restaurants, refreshment places and motels, using aggregate data, by Norton (1988) found it to be positively and significantly related to principal–agent incentives such as physically dispersed operations, increasing labour–output ratios and establishment size, and also information incentives concerning the value of brand name capital and managerial screening.

The organisational decision whether to employ independent sales representatives or a direct sales force has parallels with the franchising decision. Anderson and Schmittlein's (1984) and Anderson's (1988) analysis of the electronic component company's decision in this respect uses a discrete choice model and finds that employees tend to be preferred to independent agents where highly specific assets are involved and where there is a difficulty in evaluating performance.

Contracting Out

The key features of contracting out are that an agent or set of agents provide a product or service to a prime producer or principal on a recurring basis over a number of years. Since the services provided by the agents are inputs into the principal's activities, an important role is assigned to co-ordination of the transactions. Various terms may be assigned to the type of relationships embraced by contracting out, including 'quasi-vertical integration' (e.g. Blois 1972; Monteverde and Teece 1982b); 'managed markets' (e.g. Butler and Carney 1983) and 'Just-In-Time (JIT) purchasing' (e.g. Schonberger and Gilbert 1983). 'Networking' (Thorelli 1986) encompasses these relationships between markets and hierarchies.

The original transactions-cost model posits that transactions should be internalised when a lack of trust exists, especially under conditions of complexity in the transaction. Lack of trust may arise because of informational asymmetries and provide the basis for opportunism. These problems may be removed and goal congruence restored through the re-placement of market control by internal hierarchical control (Williamson 1975). However, the contracting out of transactions to a specialist may provide an intermediate approach where the firm can achieve economies of scope and scale, flexibility, and avoid transactions cost problems.

Williamson (1979) has shown that the appropriate governance structure for dealing with contractual relations depends heavily upon the frequency with which transactions occur, and the degree of asset-specificity (idiosyncracy). At one extreme, the market is most appropriate for transactions of a non-specific nature—irrespective of the frequency with which they take place—whilst at the other, recurrent transactions involving a high degree of asset-specificity are preferably handled through internalisation.

Occasional transactions involving at least some degree of specificity lend themselves to trilateral governance structures, whereby third parties (arbitration) may be used to resolve disputes between the main parties. Bilateral governance (obligational contracting) deals with instances of frequent transactions involving only some degree of specificity. In this mode, the two parties to the transaction have the incentive of adhering to formal arrangements in order to adopt contracts in the light of various changes where they perceive that the long-run maintenance of the relationship overrides gains from opportunistic behaviour (see also Teece 1980b). These last two structures have parallels with the work of Thompson (1967), Pfeffer and Salancik (1978) and Butler and Carney (1983), who argue that where firms are interdependent they may seek ways of reducing that dependence and may increase their discretionary ability to act, not by acquisition but through a co-operative strategy under managed market conditions.

The key feature of a managed market, noted above, of recurring transactions over a long period provides the basis for the establishment of trust in relationships, for the development of routine procedures and for mutual adjustment. A potential problem arises where outputs are difficult to define in detail in advance, and setting contracts in terms of inputs raises monitoring difficulties. Opportunism may be contained by the use of contingent contracts and formalised rules about the nature of contracting in particular industries. Recurrent short-term contracting may give undue benefit to incumbent providers as other bidders are disadvantaged.

Mutual adjustment procedures may involve arbitration machinery and management committees to deal with unforeseen issues. However, an important element in the relationship is the extent to which an asymmetry of dependence exists between the purchaser and the supplier. Let us assume that a purchaser has the choice between obtaining supplies internally or by contracting out: the power of the purchaser may be increased where it is a large customer of the supplier, where alternative suppliers exist and where the supplier's product is market specific. Under these circumstances, the purchaser has a credible threat to withdraw orders and can impose special requirements. As a result, the supplier's managerial independence may be severely curtailed, producing what Blois (1972) has termed vertical quasi-integration. This kind of approach is seen in several industries, such as the provision of inputs to large retailing chains or components to the automobile industry. Multi-sourcing and just-in-time purchasing are features of this transactional mode.

Where a supplier is in the relatively more powerful position, initially, its room for manoeuvre may be constrained by the purchaser's threats not to renew contracts, to withdraw from the market or to reintroduce backward integration—such threats have credibility where low entry barriers to other suppliers exist. The dominant position of the supplier may result only from the barrier to entry provided by common ownership and it may be removed by contracting out. Contracting out also provides an important signal that the purchaser is no longer responsible, as lender of last resort, should the supplier get into financial difficulties. These factors should encourage the supplier to act efficiently.[2] In addition, where contracting out gives former employees a residual claimant status which was previously absent, the incentive to efficient performance may also be increased.

As a general principle, the greater the dependence of one of the parties to the transaction upon the other, the greater will be the incentive in the longer run to reduce the level of vulnerability. So long as low barriers to entry exist, there is every possibility that over time substitutability will increase, so reducing the need for the closely managed relationships between purchaser and supplier.

Joint Ventures

Joint venture, or co-contracting, involves such things as the production or distribution of a good or service and the carrying out of research by two or more separate firms. Often the joint venture may be organised at arm's length through a jointly owned company.

Joint ventures in production or distribution may be attractive where a recurring relationship exists between otherwise independent firms and where high asset specificity, high economies of scale, scarcity of resources and small markets (too small for each producer) may make it inefficient for each firm to act separately. Where the firms are located in different countries, cultural factors and considerations of national strategic interest may prevent merger from occurring. Hence joint venture may be necessary frequently to satisfy local legal and cultural requirements.

In the personal financial services sector, joint ventures are common. Bank payment services rely upon correspondent arrangements and interbank co-operation through the clearing house. More recently, joint ventures have been established to develop ATM (Automatic Teller Machine) networks, and joint ventures have been used by building societies and smaller banks in the UK, particularly prior to recent legislative changes. These links, together with others, have enabled groups to offer transactions services in competition with the clearing banks. (Merger may be prohibited because of legal restrictions, and may also be unattractive where different managerial styles are required to handle different kinds of transactions.)

Such relationships in the personal financial services sector widen the ability of smaller firms to diversify. Additionally, joint ventures have introduced a separation between suppliers of intermediate products and final producers which is common in other industries, such as retailing, but was previously unusual in this sector (Chiplin 1986). Alternatively, such transactions may take the form of contracting out where a joint entity is not established to effect the transaction. (For example, the separation of the stages involved in the origination, financing and servicing of housing loans afforded by the introduction of a secondary mortgage market) (Wright 1986c).

Aside from production and distribution, joint ventures also allow the sharing of costs and risks of Research and Development and for the pooling of expertise. Research joint ventures may help deal with the problems involved in the transfer of knowledge between firms—preferable to licensing arrangements where moral hazard and opportunism can be avoided. In addition, much technological know-how may be tacit, uncodified and closely related to particular employees. However, joint ventures are not unproblematical and such problems contribute to an explanation of the creation of larger firms, including multi-nationals (see Chapter 7). Where joint ventures are not designed to handle the joint production of new products created from the research, some means must be found of apportioning benefits back to individual firms. On a wider level joint research may reduce innovation through reductions in competition between firms, and from a lack of diversity which would stem from firms pursuing independent lines of research. But, joint ventures may help firms avoid developing rigidities in their approach to research and may provide access to a wider range of ideas and technological knowledge. Moreover, where joint production, marketing and distribution develop from joint research, firms may obtain easier access to newer markets. (For a more detailed review of these issues, see Kogut 1988.)

10.4   Externalisation: Types of Ownership Transfer

Externalisation of an activity may be to either a spot market or an intermediate market transactional relationship, or it may involve deconglomerisation where no trading relationship exists. Previous sections have examined the conditions whereby satisfactory internal organisation may break down and lead the firm to consider the externalisation of some of its activities; they have also discussed the nature of intermediate market forms where transactional relationships exist. This section deals with the forms of ownership transfer which may be used to effect externalisation. Essentially three main forms may be identified. In the first case, severence is complete with the divested subsidiary becoming part of another group or independently owned by its managers and/or employees. In the second case the vendor retains at least a partial ownership stake. The third possibility is where the divestment of one set of assets to another company occurs simultaneously with the acquisition of a bundle of that company's assets of the same value. The conditions under which each occur are examined in turn.

Sell-Offs and Management Buy-Outs

A sell-off involves the sale of a subsidiary or division of a group to a new parent. A management buy-out involves the purchase of a subsidiary or division by the incumbent managers who, using a mixture of outside debt and equity funds, usually obtain effective executive control, though not necessarily a majority of the ordinary shares (Wright and Coyne 1985). In both cases, trading relationships may or may not exist between parent and subsidiary. Where there are trading relationships, care may need to be taken in selling a subsidiary to a competitor for fear of being subjected subsequently to some degree of monopoly exploitation, even though there may initially be attractive benefits from reductions in control costs and from the economies of scale and scope to be had from a specialist producer. For a sale to take place, the purchaser must value the subsidiary more than the vendor: in other words, the purchaser considers that he can make the firm perform better than could the former parent. A decision to sell has important behavioural implications for incumbent managers.

Obtaining full divisional management co-operation in the divestment of all or part of its division may be problematical. A change of ownership will increase the insecurity of managers and may provoke intense resentment if the division was not a relative under-performer. Emmanuel and Otley (1985) argue that such decisions are best taken on the basis of interaction between group and divisional managements. Unfortunately, however, constraints of time and the confidentiality of negotiations with outsiders may limit this process. Moreover, where the future of a division is in doubt, divisional management has to assess its own prospects. Traditionally, the choice may have presented itself as either a transfer to another division or owner, or redundancy. Hence, management may have preferred to act in the parent's interests. The option to buy-out, however, allows subsidiary management to weigh their risk–reward preferences which, with the ability to turn informational asymmetries to their advantage, may cause their behaviour to diverge from that which is in the parent's interest. The problem is further exacerbated where a significant element of the value of the subsidiary derives from the specific contribution of employees, so that a 'management walk-out' is a credible threat. Hence corporate management may increasingly need to consider pre-emptive action to prevent a buy-out attempt taking place in key divisions.

In qualitative terms, incumbent management may be in a relatively stronger position than an outside buyer for a number of reasons: the former may possess important inside information not available to the external party; a significant local parental reputation may exist which could be damaged by sale to a third party; the vendor may wish a speedy, no-fuss sale; the management may be an important part of the value of the company; and local management may be have significant control over the flow of information within the subsidiary. The position of a potential external purchaser may also be affected by the existence of a serious bid from management. Should the external buyer succeed, it may be necessary to deal with problems of loyalty and to incur the costs of replacing managers who leave or have to be removed. Moreover, should managers possess specific non-transferable skills which contribute greatly to the value of the subsidiary, the threat of a walk-out may deter a prospective buyer: managers may be able to use such skills in establishing or joining a rival firm. Even if managers are apparently locked in by highly idiosyncratic (Williamson 1986, pp. 106–7) firm-specific skills, an implicit threat of mutually damaging exit may still be credible to a possible buyer, because of the importance of non-pecuniary motives in human behaviour. Where the incumbent management team are perhaps not strong enough to find financial support for a buy-out an alternative possibility is for an outside manager with institutional backing (and possibly including some internal managers) to purchase the unwanted subsidiary (see, for example, Crawford 1987; Wright, Coyne and Robbie 1987a; Clinch 1987). In this way the range of options open to the vendor is extended without the danger of selling to a competitor.

In management buy-outs, a key issue is what happens after the transfer of ownership has taken place. Once committed to the buy-out, with a personal investment in an equity stake, management ought to have a powerful incentive to perform effectively. Pressure to perform well may be further strengthened by the bonding of the management to the financiers through conditions attached to quasi-equity and debt, such as ratchet mechanisms, whereby the future size of management's equity stake varies according to their performance (see Chapter 4 for further discussion of debt bonding).

Deviation from financial targets could result in the removal of management on disadvantageous terms. Moreover, the possibility of failure restores the bankruptcy sanction, which is arguably absent where a corporate headquarters acts as 'lender of last resort' as noted earlier (Thompson and Wright 1986). However, the strength of this threat may be reduced where management have used their possession of asymmetric information to effect a transaction on very favourable terms. The role of finance and financiers in buy-outs can be of crucial importance to their success. An over-leveraged financial package may bond management, but it may leave insufficient funds for investment. Ratchet mechanisms may have undesirable effects such as encouraging short-term behaviour or manipulation of accounting information (De Angelo 1986).

Financiers with their typically close relationship with buy-out teams and their detailed access to financial information, may be seen essentially to replace a failing internal control system with quasi-internal monitoring (Thompson and Wright 1987). This is similar to the relationships between the banks and firms in West Germany which largely replace the capital allocation functions of the M-form's corporate staff.

More directly related to trading activities, post buy-out action may be heavily dependent upon the nature of interdependencies as discussed earlier. The greater is the dependence upon the former parent, so managers of the bought-out subsidiary will have the incentive to seek alternative trading partners.

Spin-Offs and Demergers

For expositional purposes it is useful to make the distinction between a spin-off, where a small, perhaps newly developed, part of a group is separated-out into a new legal entity in which the incumbent management have a significant equity stake together with a continued interest by the parent, and a demerger (where a group as a whole separates into two or more entities). In the case of a demerger, existing shareholders usually obtain *pro-rata* new shares in the new entities.

A spin-off may be attractive where a new product is developed which is peripheral to the main interests of the parent, but which may have longer-term attractions. By spinning-off, a parent can remove the problems of control yet retain the possibility for greater return in the future (Garvin 1983). What is more, it may also overcome motivational problems that may otherwise occur where those who have developed the product are frustrated in their desire to extend its application. Whilst such experience is widespread in the USA, there has until very recently been more resistance to such an approach in the UK. However, perhaps with the growth of management buy-outs, spin-offs in the UK are becoming more of a reality (Mills 1987).

Demerger may be conceptualised as the final solution to attempts to develop a coherent strategy within one entity (Wright 1985). In a large complex organisation, where there are two or more key products and/or geographical areas, problems of cultural conflicts and capital allocation can develop to the point where separation is the only feasible option. Sell-off may be problematical because of the decision as to which half is to be sold and how the proceeds are to be reinvested. Capital allocation problems may arise when both parts are viable but the time-scales for investments and returns are very different. Hence, for example, the need to invest heavily over a long period of time in one area may preclude others from investing to obtain faster returns. The problems may be compounded where the external capital market is unwilling to provide further funds as it is unable to identify satisfactorily the nature of the enterprise (see, for example, Wright 1986a).

In its extreme form the splitting implied by demerger may. involve selling all assets, using the proceeds to pay off creditors and disbursing the residual funds to shareholders for investment in another portfolio of assets.

Asset-Swaps or Strategic Trades

In an asset-swap, or strategic trade, the transfer of ownership is effected by exchanging a bundle of one firm's assets for assets of equivalent value in another firm. As with barter, the process requires a coincidence of wants before trade can occur. In its purest form: Firm A must wish to enter Industry X and divest activities in Industry Y, at the same time as Firm B wishes to enter Industry Y and divest activities in Industry X. Firm A must value the assets of Firm B more highly than does Firm B, and vice versa. Moreover, the value of the assets to be received in a trade must exceed the cash proceeds to be expected from an outright sale. Additionally, the timing of the decision processes of A and B must coincide.

10.5   Externalisation: Empirical Evidence

Previous sections have examined the conditions under which it may be appropriate to divest part of an organisation, and the various forms of ownership transfer which may be appropriate. This section reviews the evidence on the extent to which various forms occur, and the impact of such changes in ownership on both the vendor and the acquirer. The studies presented cover divestment both where trading relationships exist between the seller and the subsidiary disposed of, and where the relationship is a conglomerate one. Only voluntary divestments are examined here. Divestments, which are the result of government privatisation or antitrust policy, are dealt with in the next chapter. The main recent studies under each category of voluntary divestment are summarised in Table 10.1.

Sell-offs

Voluntary sell-offs, or indeed spin-offs, might be expected to produce an upward movement in the share price of the seller, since the sale should

Table 10.1   Recent Studies of the Effects of Divestment, 1987

Voluntary sell-offs	Alexander *et al.* 1984
	Rosenfeld 1984
	Jain 1985
	Wright and Thompson 1986
	Montgomery *et al.* 1984
	Duhaime and Grant 1984
	Harrigan 1980
	Hite *et al.* 1987
	Hearth and Zaima 1986
	Klein 1986
	Casson 1986b
	Duhaime and Baird 1987
	Denning 1988b
	Sicherman and Pettway 1987
Voluntary spin-offs and demergers	Boudreaux 1975
	Miles and Rosenfeld 1983
	Schipper and Smith 1983
	Hite and Owers 1983
	Garvin 1983
	Hakansson 1982
	Galai and Masulis 1976
	Wright 1986a
	Denning 1988
Voluntary divestment buy-outs	Wright and Coyne 1985
	Wright 1986b
	Thompson and Wright 1987
	Hanney 1986
	Scherer 1984
	Wright, Robbie and Coyne 1987
	Wright *et al.* 1984
	Jones 1988
Voluntary asset swaps/ strategic trades	Davis, 1986a, 1986b

have an expected positive net present value in comparison with retaining the divested entity. These results may be expected given the evidence that divested entities are often poor performers and peripheral to core interests and hence, perhaps, more difficult to control, (Harrigan 1980, Duhaime and Grant 1984, Davis 1986b). Such findings are consistent with the view that the sale of divisions/subsidiaries can ease control problems (by reducing complexity) and that divestment represents a plausible response to financial difficulties. The available evidence to date shows no support for the Stigler (1951) life-cycle hypothesis that vertical divestments were associated with industry growth rates (Wright and Thompson 1986).

Jain (1985) found that gains to buyers were smaller than those to sellers: although the buyer must expect to be able to manage the acquired entity better than the vendor, there is an element of asymmetric information which affects the buyer's perception of how much better he can do and which the market is taking account of. Whilst Montgomery *et al.* (1984) found positive effects for divestments with a clear strategic rationale, negative announcement effects were observed where this was absent. A study by Hearth and Zaima (1986) also supports this view that the effects of sell-offs are closely linked with the firm-specific reasons for sale. Interestingly, analysis by Sicherman and Pettway (1987) found positive announcement effects for acquirers of divested assets which had product-line relatedness and negative effects for the acquisition of unrelated divested assets. In addition, this latter group of firms had smaller proportions of inside equity ownership than firms acquiring related divested assets, suggesting that an economically significant agency conflict exists in decisions to purchase unrelated oriented assets. See also the analysis by Denning (1988). Evidence also suggests that relatively larger divestments have positive announcement effects (Klein 1986).

When assessing the internal organisational impact of sell-offs it is also necessary to separate out the informational and synergistic effects of an announcement to divest. Information effects may arise where the market, previously faced with imperfect information about a subsidiary, is able to reassess the position once a sell-off is announced; synergistic effects may arise from the productivity gains that can be achieved only by transfer of the assets to a new owner. These effects may be identified on the initial announcement of a sell-off decision (information effect) and the completion of the sale (synergistic effect). An analysis by Hite *et al.* (1987) shows positive benefits for both sellers and buyers when transactions are completed. When decisions were abandoned, however, all the announcement gains were found to disappear, suggesting that the market had not previously valued the subsidiary incorrectly, due to lack of information, and had recognised the loss accruing from the inability to obtain synergistic benefits consequent upon the transaction not being completed.

These results are generally consistent with those found for acquisitions of independent firms (Chiplin and Wright 1987) but are subject to qualification because of the well-known problems with this kind of study as noted already in Chapters 2 and 3 (see also Brown and Warner 1980, Hite 1986).

Spin-Offs or Demergers

There are several potential sources of gain to shareholders from a spin-off: improvements in the efficiency of productive organisation; an increase in the opportunity set of shareholders as they are able to adjust their holdings in the separated entities; a possible transfer of wealth from bondholders, where equity is distributed solely to shareholders, leaving bondholders with no claim on the assets of the new entity; and possible relaxation in regulation following spin-off (Galai and Masulis 1976, Hakansson 1983).

Announcement effect tests on voluntary spin-offs show general positive gains to shareholders, which would appear to emanate from efficiency improvements in the new structural arrangements (Boudreaux 1975, Miles and Rosenfeld 1983, Schipper and Smith 1983, Hite and Owers 1983). Rosenfeld (1984) found that gains from spin-offs were greater than those seen in sell-off announcements. Evidence in the UK, where demergers of quoted companies are much less common, indicates that for the case of Bowater, at least, similar benefits to those found in the USA are obtained (Wright 1986a).

Case studies of spin-offs of higher technology/new product subsidiaries also support the view that performance is increased as a result of greater managerial incentives and freedom from parental control (Garvin 1983).

Divestment Buy-Outs

The distinction is made between buy-outs which occur on the sale of a subsidiary and those where the management purchases the whole of a stock-exchange quoted firm. The latter do not involve a redrawing of the boundaries of a firm, even though the ownership structure changes. However, they may have important implications for the removal of agency costs (De Angelo *et al.* 1984).

Although the evidence on the performance effects of buy-outs is more limited than that for sell-offs and spin-offs, the indication is that substantial benefits are realised. In the USA, Scherer (1984) examined eight cases of sales as leveraged buy-outs and found evidence of improvements in efficiency—particularly in respect of exploiting cost-cutting opportunities, removing delays and distortions in decision making and the draining away of resources to other parts of a conglomerate organisation. Nevertheless, concern was expressed that the burden of servicing the high level of debt needed to finance the buy-out caused problems for investment, or pressure for short-run cash-flow maximisation and rapid exit via flotation or sale to a third party. UK performance has been examined in terms of the effects on industrial relations management structures, cash flow, new product development, trading relationships and profitability (Wright and Coyne 1985, Hanney 1986).

Whilst there is little evidence that buy-outs have been used to remove recalcitrant trade unions, the indication is that substantial changes in employment levels and work-place practices have occurred in the early stages. Some decoupling has been observed to occur between unions and employees which may serve to limit the power of trade unions and make the removal of recognition a non-issue (Wright, Coyne and Lockley 1984). About 35 per cent of companies, bought-out from parent groups, experienced cash flow problems, with pre-buy-out difficulties often being replaced by post-buy-out problems relating to the servicing of debt packages (Thompson and Wright 1987). More appropriate management structures and more complete and stronger management teams can also be introduced after buy-out, with available evidence suggesting that as buy-out experience develops, increasing attention is being paid to the strength of the buy-out team and to the recruitment of specialist staff (Wright, Robbie and Coyne 1988). Jones (1988), in a more detailed case study approach, found evidence of changes in accounting control systems as a result of the ownership change, but also a high level of continuation of many of the previous operational controls.

There is some indication from a study of 102 buy-outs subsequently floated on the stock market that in the longer term, post-buy-out increases in profitability begin to decline (Wright, Robbie and Coyne 1987). This is partly due to the petering out of the benefits of growing from a small base, the problems associated with assimilating acquisitions (growth in turnover and assets continued to increase) and perhaps a decline in the incentive effect of ownership (shareholdings by management declined substantially on flotation). However, further research is still required to ascertain the longer term benefits of buy-outs.

In respect of those buy-outs with trading relationships (interdependence) with their former parents, evidence indicates that both product development and customer base are enhanced by separation from the restrictions imposed by a parent (Wright 1986b). Generally speaking, the level of interdependence between buy-out and ex-parent is low; where it is significant some element of a managed market may be observed, at least in the short term, and may indeed be a condition for funds to be extended by an institution. Attempts to reduce interdependence are seen to begin, on both sides, following a buy-out. For the bought-out firm this may be especially important in order to avoid being squeezed by a former parent which has access to other suppliers/customers.

An important issue remains, however, as to the extent to which changes following buy-outs are due to a remarriage of ownership and control, or perhaps they result from the contractual requirements of financiers which produce an element of quasi-internationalisation and help resolve some of the principal–agent problems that existed in the previous group structure. The fact that financiers do require the introduction of important control systems is well known (Wright, Robbie and Thompson 1988). But the question remains as to why former parents were apparently unable to effect the same level of control.

Asset-Swaps or Strategic Trades

Industrial rationalisation has produced asset-swaps between such groups as Southam Inc. and Thomson Newspapers Ltd, in Canada, and between ICI and BP Chemicals. In 1981 trades of shares between the groups of Seagram and du Pont took place following a bidding war. However, some of the most significant examples of asset-swaps have occurred under enforced circumstances as a result of antitrust decisions or because of government prompting. These aspects are addressed in the next chapter.

10.6 Acquisition and Divestment Activity

Divestment activity may take place in isolation; alternatively, firms may engage in a dynamic programme of restructuring, whereby both divestment and acquisition take place. The intensity of divestment activity may be influenced by the number of product and geographical markets occupied by a firm, the urgency and strength of the need for corporate strategic adjustments, and the number of subsidiaries/divisions owned. Where acquisitions are being conducted simultaneously, divestment may be a convenient way of disposing of those parts of a recently purchased group which are peripheral to the main areas of interest. It is not uncommon for acquisitions of large groups to be structured in such a way that unwanted parts are already pre-sold by the time the deal is completed. In some circumstances the initial purchaser may acquire the business which is really desired for a small net cost.

In respect of UK sell-offs Chiplin and Wright (1980), examining the late 1970s, showed that 26.5 per cent of 268 divesting firms engaged in more than one parent-to-parent divestment, with 4 per cent undertaking at least four sales of subsidiaries. This process has continued in the 1980s and has been supplemented in the UK by the growth of the management buy-out as an alternative to parent-to-parent divestment. About one-fifth of firms identified as divesting by buy-out sold more than one subsidiary to its management (Wright, Coyne and Robbie 1987a). Some firms are particularly intensive divestors by buy-out, with up to eight sales of this kind being identified for some within a two-year period (Wright, Coyne, Robbie and Lloyd 1987). The special case of the privatisation of National Bus Co had produced 25 buy-outs by September 1987, with the process still not complete (Mulley and Wright 1986; Wright, Mulley and Robbie 1988).

As noted earlier, under different circumstances both managers or other groups may be the most appropriate purchasers of a divestee, so that a divestment strategy may involve sales to both sets of purchasers.

Mike Wright

For the mid-1980s a little under one-fifth of firms divesting by buy-out also made at least one sale of a subsidiary to another parental group.

Adjustment involving acquisition and divestment is of particular interest, although at an aggregate level it is difficult to distinguish between two distinct types of strategy—acquisition and simultaneous sale of unwanted parts, and acquisition accompanied by sale of subsidiaries acquired some years previously. Chiplin and Wright (1980) found that a quarter of those divesting to another parental group also made one or more acquisition in the same period. More recent evidence for the mid 1980s shows that 10 per cent of acquiring firms made at least one parent-to-parent divestment in this period (Wright, Chiplin and Coyne 1988). This level of divestment activity is greatly increased when acquiring firms which divested by a management buy-out are included (Table 10.2). Some 16 per cent of acquiring firms divested either to another group and/or to incumbent management in this period. Evidence is sparse on how long these firms had been owned by the parent before being divested. An analysis of UK divestment buy-outs for 1984 and 1985 suggests the majority of companies bought-out have been owned for a small proportion of their lives by the divesting parent (Table 10.3). However, a substantial minority of buy-outs clearly involves the sale of activities founded by the selling parent.

Table 10.2 Two-Way Frequency Distribution of Intensity of Acquisition and Divestment Activity by Companies Making Acquisitions (Jan. 1984–June 1986)

		Number of Acquisitions							*Total number*	
		1	*2*	*3*	*4*	*5*	*6*	*7+*		*%*
	0	399	98	50	13	6	9	11	586	84.0
	1	34	12	4	3	1	3	–	57	8.2
Number of	*2*	9	3	3	2	–	–	3	20	2.9
Divestments	*3*	3	1	6	1	2	–	1	14	2.0
and Buy-outs	*4*	1	5	–	1	–	–	3	10	1.4
	5	3	–	1	–	–	–	–	4	0.6
	6	–	1	–	–	–	–	–	1	0.1
	7+	3	–	1	–	1	–	1	6	0.8
									698	100.0

Table 10.3 Time-Owned by Parent Prior to Buy-Out as a Proportion of Age of Company

Proportion of life of company	Buy-outs from			
	UK parent		Non-UK parent	
	n	%	*n*	%
Less than 10%	14	15.4	4	17.4
10%–19%	11	12.1	4	17.4
20%–29%	9	9.9	3	13.1
30%–39%	12	13.2	1	4.3
40%–49%	8	8.8	1	4.3
50%–59%	6	6.6	–	–
60%–69%	1	1.1	2	8.7
70%–79%	3	3.3	–	–
80%–89%	1	1.1	–	–
90%–99%	1	1.1	1	4.3
100%	25	27.4	7	30.5
Total	91	100.0	23	100.0

A recent study by Ravenscraft and Scherer (1986) in the US shows that many divested units were previously acquired rather than having been generated internally. Also for the USA, a study by Porter (1986a) of the acquisition and divestment activity of 33 firms, from 1950 onwards, showed that of the total of 4,000 acquisitions, joint ventures and start-ups made, half took the form of diversification. Half of these diversifying acquisitions were divested by the end of the period. Some companies in the sample had divested about 10 per cent of their diversifying acquisitions, whilst others had divested three-quarters of them.

10.7 Conclusion

The theme of this chapter has been initially to appraise the arguments for the internalisation of activities, drawing on the various perspectives set out in earlier chapters, and then to examine the conditions under which internalisation may cease to be appropriate.

Since the publication of *Markets and Hierarchies* (Williamson 1975)

there has perhaps been an undue emphasis by some commentators upon the internalisation of transactions carried out by market arrangements, at the expense of both intermediate transactional relationships and governance structures, and of examination of the subsequent externalisation of activities. However, the markets-and-hierarchies approach, and subsequent work by Williamson on governance structures, has attempted to establish a framework for organisational choice. The discussion here, in reviewing this approach, has sought to extend it into a more dynamic perspective by showing why and how firms may need frequently to reassess their spread of activities and systems of control. An important part of the analysis has been to address in detail the process of divestment, an aspect of firm behaviour touched upon by Williamson but not developed by him. The implications of the discussion in this chapter for managers and shareholders concern the need to deal not only with the organisational structure of a given set of activities, but also to examine closely, and on a continuing basis, the boundaries between internal and external activities.

Notes

1. There is some evidence, however, of a positive relationship between growth and vertical integration, although studies are not unanimous in this respect. However, operationalisation of the Stigler life-cycle approach is difficult, requiring a distinction to be made between industries and firms. For a further summary of the issues involved see Wright and Thompson 1986.
2. However, see the case of Cable TV (Williamson 1976) when failure by the contractor was bailed out by the client in order to avoid a breakdown of service.

11

Policy Implications

STEVE THOMPSON AND MIKE WRIGHT

11.1 Introduction

The discussion in the previous chapter drew together several themes from earlier parts of the book in order to examine the conditions under which a firm may seek voluntarily to redraw its boundaries. The discussion here will focus upon the policy implications of the analysis in earlier chapters.

From the public policy point of view, two particular areas are of interest: first, the operation of antitrust policy; and second, government policy to privatise state-owned industries—each is examined in turn. Attention is addressed to the possible relevance for policy of where the boundaries between internal, intermediate and external provision of activities might lie. The issues covered embrace both market power and efficiency enhancing aspects.

11.2 Antitrust Policy

Two main approaches to antitrust policy may be adopted, although there are others (see Williamson 1987, Chapter 6). The traditional structure–conduct–performance approach is concerned with an examination of the detrimental effects on competition, and hence on efficiency, of the actual and potential market power implications of dominant firms, mergers and restrictive practices, including cartels and oligopolistic collusion. Mergers may involve problems relating to horizontal and vertical integration and conglomerisation. Simply stated, a causal link is held to run from the structure of an industry, which affects the conduct of firms, through to performance. Although the nature of this link is open to some doubt, the approach can provide a basis for policy analysis. The approach is, however, really concerned with industrial organisation rather than the internal organisation of firms—firms are very much viewed as production

211

functions. Hence, interest focuses upon the number and types of firms within which the activities of markets and industries are carried out, rather than how those activities are arranged and managed within firms. However, whether activities are carried out within one firm or between several is of importance. Besides market power considerations, horizontal or vertical market restrictions or integration may have efficiency implications. For example, horizontal integration may lead to economies of scale.

The second perspective is the transactions-cost approach (Williamson 1987) which emphasises efficiency over monopoly power issues as the rationale for engaging in activities which do not involve spot market transactions. The existence of transactions costs may provide an incentive for trading partners to integrate, or engage in non-standard forms of contracting, in order to obtain efficiency benefits, particularly where the relationship is long term, involving sunk costs and where it is impossible to specify and enforce complete contracts. Thus policy needs to examine the effects of both internal organisation and intermediate governance structures. The property rights and agency costs literature emphasises the efficiency rather than monopoly benefits to be derived from non-standard contracting. However, where the industry or market in question is characterised by a dominant firm or oligopolistic collusion, an examination of conventional structure and conduct relations may be warranted. Hence, there is a degree of complementarity in the structure–conduct–performance and transactions-cost analyses. In both approaches there is a need to trade off market power against efficiency.[1]

This section examines the various aspects of firm behaviour which have attracted the attention of the antitrust authorities. To the extent that the net benefits of using other than spot market transactions may be difficult to determine in advance and may change over time, an important issue becomes the means by which competition and or efficiency may be maintained or restored. Several well-known tools are available to the agents of antitrust policy. One of these tools, which is beginning to receive more attention in the UK, concerns the redrawing of the boundaries of the firm through divestment, and it is discussed in detail here.

With regard to the firm as a production function: an influential paper by Williamson (1968a) led to an important development in the argument for considering factors other than the competition effects of internalisation. He argued that there may be important welfare benefits to be had from trading off the market power increases, which arise on horizontal integration through merger, against the increasing economies of scale which may result. The gains and losses to be traded off can be seen in the simple ('naive') model shown in Figure 11.1. Pre-merger average costs are shown as AC_1, which post-acquisition are reduced to AC_2, as a result

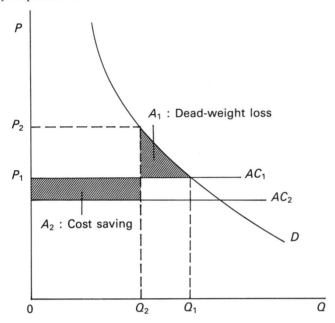

Source: Williamson (1968a)

Figure 11.1   The 'Naive' Williamson Trade-Off Model

of scale economies. However, the result of increased market power following the merger is observed to increase prices from OP_1 to OP_2, where OP_1 is assumed to represent negligible market power. The area A_1 represents the dead-weight loss of welfare due to price increases, with costs assumed to be constant. However, the reduction in costs which follows merger gives rise to a welfare gain equivalent to the area A_2. The difference between the areas A_1 and A_2 gives the net allocative effect of the merger.

In practice, this simple trade-off is complicated by several factors, (see Williamson 1968a). Of particular importance for internal organisation is the impact of merger upon managerial behaviour. Increased market power may encourage managers to relax their efforts to achieve least-cost output, so that the trade-offs need to be adjusted, especially where a divorce exists between ownership and control. The X-inefficiency which results from lower managerial effort may impose costs on the firm due to increased policing costs and higher overheads (Rowley 1973) and make cost curves difficult to identify.

Whilst the Williamson analysis was initially formulated in terms of economies of scale, it can be extended to deal with economies of scope which may occur on vertical integration and the production of more than one product. In respect of vertical integration, trade-offs would need to be made between the costs of transactions in the market prior to merger and the costs of internal arrangements afterwards, in addition to market-power considerations.

Economies of scope may relate to production, distribution and transaction costs, either independently or interactively (Baumol, Panzar and Willig 1982; Teece 1980b). Many of the transactions-cost benefits of economies of scope may arise only if a firm is suitably organised internally. From a policy point of view, where trade-offs are being attempted, it may be difficult to identify what these benefits are. This issue is returned to below.

However, it is important to bear in mind that any efficiency gains must be real rather than just pecuniary. Moreover, several other potential problems need to be considered. Vertical integration may provide scope for predatory pricing, and dominant price leadership. To the extent that it creates a barrier to entry, it may also have implications for increases in horizontal integration. From the firm's point of view, the desirability of being vertically integrated needs to be seen in a dynamic context. If, over time, new entrants do appear, it may be beneficial to switch to an outside supplier and/or divest the in-house supplier in order to obtain lower cost inputs. It is by no means clear that managers in integrated firms will voluntarily consider such divestment in the absence of shareholder or market pressure. Vertical integration may reduce the incentive to search for alternative lower cost supplies.

A related issue to integration concerns cases where trading relationships exist between firms but are subject to horizontal or vertical restraints imposed by one of the parties (see Swann 1979, for detailed discussion of the forms such restrictions might take). These restraints may be alternatives to the internalisation brought about by integration through acquisition. They may be imposed by one firm or a group of firms acting formally or informally in concert.

Franchising represents one area where a single firm places vertical restraints upon others. The rationale for franchising has been addressed in the previous chapter, from the franchisor's point of view. Franchisees are generally prevented from buying inputs from unauthorised suppliers, even though they may be cheaper. Franchise restrictions may also relate to pricing, territories and exclusive dealing.

Williamson (1985, Chapter 14), has pointed out that the franchisee in entering the franchise contract has accepted the restraints placed upon his or her behaviour. Moreover, the franchisor could presumably have chosen to expand internally by opening its own distribution outlets, but considered there to be efficiency gains such as reductions in control costs, (see Chapter 10 for further discussion). The termination of franchise contracts is also an important antitrust issue, with franchisees in the USA obtaining sympathy from the courts in such cases.

The reasons relate to an absence of 'good cause': that the franchisor can obtain the goodwill built-up by the franchisee, and that the franchisee may be a victim of unequal bargaining power with the franchisor. However Lockerby (1985) has forcefully argued for an unrestricted ability by franchisors to end agreements on the grounds that the threat of termination provides an important monitoring device and that the franchisor needs the ability to change its distribution methods if environmental conditions change. Easy termination may also help to reduce barriers to entry, whereas restricted termination moves the relationship closer to an internal one with clear implications for control and consumer welfare. A restricted termination franchise agreement effectively provides a high degree of market power for the franchisee, (Smith 1982).

Vertical restraints, however, can have serious anti-competitive effects, including bolstering horizontal cartels through such means as raising entry barriers.[2] As a result, they may help sustain inefficient firms. Vertical restraints by individual firms may have detrimental effects where they involve exclusive dealing, refusal to supply, etc., as this behaviour may also raise barriers to entry.

A further area of concern for the agents of antitrust policy concerns the conglomerate enterprise. Growth through diversification to produce a conglomerate firm may be undertaken to gain the benefits of risk pooling. Conglomerate acquisition may be the most feasible option where growth by means of horizontal or vertical merger is restricted by merger policy. The competition and efficiency effects of conglomerisation are open to some debate (e.g. Gribbin 1976, Mueller 1977b). On the one hand, conglomerisation may lead to increases in aggregate concentration and enable firms adversely to affect competition through cross-subsidisation, predatory pricing, reciprocal trading, mutual forbearance, etc. Conglomerate merger may also lead to defensive mergers by other firms. On the other hand, conglomerate mergers may be important in maintaining the market for corporate control. This form of acquisition may increase competition by placing pressure on firms in some markets which currently enjoy a quiet life.

Williamson (1975) has argued for a benign view of conglomerate mergers by the operators of antitrust policy. Where a conglomerate firm has a pure multi-divisional (M-form) structure, operation of an internal capital market may be more effective than the external capital market. Transactions-cost reduction advantages may be derived from the possession of superior information not available to outsiders, so that resources are better allocated to areas producing the highest returns.[3] However, from a more general view, conglomerate reporting practices may produce disadvantages where outside investors in the firm as a whole are not able to determine which activities contribute to its overall performance. But it may also be difficult for internal investment decision makers to obtain a reliable view, for reasons discussed throughout this book and particularly in Chapters 9 and 10. The existence of a pure M-form structure may be highly questionable.

Various behavioural problems may prevent the firm moving towards a pure M-form structure so that it becomes stuck in a transitional or corrupted phase. Moreover, as Hill and Pickering (1986b) have pointed out, even in apparent M-forms internal capital markets may not be characterised by unfettered competition between divisions. In some cases, divisional activity and resources allocation may be determined by head office plans not based on profitability, in others cash flows may simply be returned to source. Hence, where a less than pure M-form structure exists, or is able to be achieved, the implications for competition and efficiency are no longer unambiguous. The summary of the literature undertaken by Hill and Pickering (1986b), indicates that there is no consensus on the beneficial effects of conglomerisation on both increasing the level of profits and reducing their variability. The examination of conglomerate mergers by the Monopolies and Mergers Commission (MMC) in the UK has generally taken a neutral view. In a twenty-year period from 1965, when it was first possible to examine conglomerate mergers under the asset size criterion, fifteen had been examined by the MMC and five had been found to be against the public interest. This one-third rejection rate is lower than that for horizontal mergers (41 per cent against the public interest), but higher than the rarer referrals of vertical mergers (one out of five against the public interest in the period 1965–85) (Chiplin and Wright 1987). Hill and Pickering (1986b) observe that although the MMC does not appear to have addressed internal organisation in a systematic manner, there are cases where it has been an important factor in determining whether or not a particular merger is in the public interest.

The preceding discussion embraced both structure–conduct–perform- ance and transactions-cost approaches to antitrust. With both it was seen that market power and efficiency aspects need to be traded off against each other, but that this trade-off needs to be treated with care. Cost savings in the creation of dominant firms may not be realised, with technological benefits possibly being outweighed by increases in X-inefficiency. The transactions-cost benefits of vertical integration and vertical market restrictions may also involve market power enhancing problems. The benefits from internal capital markets in the conglomerate firm may not be achieved because of the problems of creating and sustaining a pure M-form structure. Additionally, the nature of any market power and efficiency trade-off may be difficult to predict *ex ante*. As the studies reviewed in Chapters 3 and 4 demonstrate, a degree of scepticism is in order, especially in respect of the longer term.

Antitrust solutions to these problems may involve a desire to redraw the boundaries of firms through enforced divestment or divestiture. Enforced divestment may occur either at the time of a merger or subsequently, when problems become apparent. US experience is considerably greater than that in the UK, where, although the power to order post-merger divestiture has been available since 1965, it has not been used.

The structure–conduct–performance approach to divestiture may proceed from a view that the structure of a market *per se* is undesirable, or that the conduct of firms is such as to require a structural solution to the problem. Where transactions cost-reducing efficiency benefits are usurped by market power enhancing intentions, structural remedies may also be sought. The structural approach encounters difficulties due to problems in defining markets, using accounting data to measure performance, and defining the structure of a market. Changing the structure of a market via divestment may preserve competitors rather than competition, and if it ignores conduct the outcome may be difficult to predict. Enforced divestiture may be justified only if significant sunk costs exist so that super-normal profits will be maintained in the long run as the market is not contestable (Baumol 1982). However, as O'Brien (1986) has pointed out, divestiture may work more quickly than waiting for new entrants to appear or technological change to occur. As such, it may be attractive for dismantling the undesirable side effects of vertical integration. Moreover, as noted in the previous chapter, the transactional cost benefits of large organisations may be outweighed by managerial diseconomies and control problems. Divestiture may also increase the potential for competition even though it does not immediately affect actual competition. A more powerful reason for enforcing divestiture may be because of undesirable conduct which can be traceable to structure.

Actually carrying out divestiture may pose severe practical problems, which relate to the incentives for offending firms to co-operate (hence the use of consent decrees), the choice of assets to be divested, the incentives for antitrust officials to ensure policy is carried out *vis-à-vis* the attractions of pursuing other cases, the difficulties in finding an appropriate buyer and the penalty to shareholders. With respect to finding an alternative purchaser, it is necessary to ensure that further competition issues are not created by selling to an unsuitable buyer. Alternatively, sale of an offending set of assets, if it could be done in the form of an independent entity, may make the management buy-out route an attractive option. Sale, as a management buy-out, creates a new independent entity and ought to minimise further competition problems. However, this may not be a permanent solution to the problem where the bought-out company is subsequently subject to a takeover-bid, which may be encouraged as financiers and management seek to realise at least part of their investment, (Wright, Robbie and Thompson 1988). Management buy-outs of this kind may also attract attention, at least in the UK, where the level of debt in the financial structure used to effect the purchase is deemed excessive and liable to make the business unstable. Until recently, there has been no provision in UK merger legislation for undertakings to be given by firms that they would divest parts, which involved the creation of excessive market power, if the rest of the acquisition of a group were allowed to proceed.

Recent proposals by the UK government, following its review of merger policy (DTI – The Department for Enterprise, *Cmnd 278*, January 1988, Chapter 2), have reaffirmed the importance of the anti-competitive effects of mergers as the main criterion of reference to the MMC. However, in an important new development, it is suggested that the Director General of Fair Trading (DGFT), will be enabled to discuss, with the parties involved, possible modifications to merger proposals, usually involving the divestment of some of the assets of the merging business. As a result mergers may escape reference to the MMC as long as the divestment which removes the competition problem is completed before the main transaction is finalised or legally binding undertakings are made to dispose of the assets within a specified period.

Failure to honour the undertakings would result in the Secretary of State ordering divestiture without an MMC investigation. The parties may also give legally binding undertakings about their post-merger conduct as a means of avoiding a referral to the MMC. This approach, if implemented, would provide important flexibility; however, agreeing identifiable problem areas *ex ante* in this way may not be easy.[4]

Empirical evidence on the effects of divestiture relates mainly to the USA. It might be expected that if a dominant firm has been enjoying its market power, its shareholders will lose from the removal of that power following divestiture. Alternatively, a possible counter effect emanating from a subsequent relaxed regulatory framework also needs to be taken into account. Studies of the effects of antitrust enforced divestitures in the USA have produced conflicting results (Table 11.1). Burns (1977, 1983) found a positive impact on shareholder wealth, but Kudla and McInish (1981) and Boudreaux (1975) recorded negative effects. Any negative effects observed may, however, be insufficient to outweigh large, positive, abnormal returns accumulated over the years prior to divestiture (Ellert 1976). Montgomery *et al.* (1984) found the consequences of enforced divestiture on shareholders to be insignificant.

The enforced break-up of AT and T, into eight separate companies, perhaps the most notable case to date, has been examined by several authors, most notably O'Brien (1986) and Chen and Merville (1986). As O'Brien (1986) shows, AT and T, under its protected and contentious regulatory regime, had shown notable signs of organisational slack and

Table 11.1 Recent Studies of the Effects of Enforced Divestiture

PRIVATISATION	
Franchising of TV	Williamson (1976)
	Domberger and Middleton (1985)
Contracting-out of health service cleaning, refuse collection, etc.	Domberger *et al.* (1987)
	Audit Commission (1984)
	Cubbin *et al.* (1987)
	Domberger *et al.* (1986)
	Hartley and Huby (1985)
	Hartley (1984)
	McDavid (1985)
	Gear (1984)
	Ganley and Grahl (1988)
	Domberger *et al.* (1988)
	National Audit Office (1987)
Privatisation sell-off or break-up	Bruce (1986)
	Mulley and Wright (1986)
Privatisation of a complete industry	Wright (1987)
	Hammond *et al.* (1985)
	Pryke (1987)
	Vickers and Yarrow (1985)
	McLachlan (1983)
ANTITRUST POLICY	
	Burns (1977, 1983)
	Kummer (1976)
	Ellert (1976)
	Boudreaux (1975)
	Kudla and McInish (1981)
	O'Brien (1986)
	Chen and Merville (1986)
	Davis (1986a, 1986b)
	Brennan (1987)
	Montgomery *et al.* (1984)

the use of cross-subsidisation of equipment as a barrier to entry, whilst at the same time being prevented from competing in other areas. The post-break-up structure is supposed to increase competition, reduce entry barriers and encourage competition in other heavily concentrated markets by allowing AT and T to compete with IBM in the computer market. However, the constituent companies remain very large and much of the impact on market efficiency and competition may derive from technical change rather than from the change in structure. Moreover, the benefits of divestiture have to be offset against the costs, particularly the burden on AT and T of bearing the expense of the transition to the new regime.

Chen and Merville (1986) use an announcements effect approach to examine the impact of deregulation, the dropping of antitrust charges and the reversal of the co-insurance benefits which stem from having an integrated set of activities. Hence, a variety of events occur during the break-up process. The authors find that positive transfers of wealth took place from consumers and the US government to AT and T shareholders and bondholders. In addition, the buffering effect which arises from the reduction in riskiness as a result of regulation was reduced as AT and T passed through the total deregulation process. The shareholders of the post-break-up operating companies also experience positive gains from customers. However, no evidence was found of wealth transfers from bondholders to shareholders.

Notable asset swaps prompted by antitrust action have been the exchange of breweries between Stroh and Pabst in the USA (Davis 1986a) and the exchange of tied public houses in certain regions of the UK between 1970 and 1979. In the case of Pabst and Stroh, Pabst became more competitive after the trade but was still not sufficient to ensure a continued independent existence, whilst Stroh shook off antitrust action and was placed in a stronger competitive position. (For fuller discussion of these cases, see Davis 1986b.)

In France, strategic trades occurred between Thomson Group and CGE, both state-owned, in 1983 in order to reduce losses, redirect the activities of the groups, and to strengthen the French presence in the telecommunications export market.

Overall, the performance effects of these strategic trades appear to have been the ability to rationalise capacity with minimum costs of closure whilst at the same time enabling low cost entry into new areas which in turn have improved longer term performance prospects. However, as Williamson (1987), has argued, given the difficulties with enforced divestiture in practice, it may be important to provide incentives to encourage firms to be more ready to undertake voluntary divestment. Such incentives could include removal of tax disincentives and imbuing divestment with a more positive image (Coyne and Wright 1986; Wright and Thompson 1987).

11.3   Privatisation

The discussion throughout the book has been implicitly related to private sector firms. The arguments may, however, be extended to state-owned firms, (Vickers and Yarrow 1988, Chs 2–4). State ownership may impose further control problems (Chiplin and Wright 1982, Kay and Thompson 1986 and Littlechild 1986). Legislation may prevent the emergence of new competition to challenge state-owned firms, and such enterprises may also be protected from the disciplines of the private capital market. Apparent natural monopolies may owe their existence to government legislation and include certain important non-natural monopoly elements, which were brought into public ownership because of a failure by government to make such a distinction. These activities may have a conglomerate-type relationship with the natural monopoly element or may provide some input to it. In the latter case, some form of contracting-out may be a more suitable transactional form. The behaviour of these non-natural monopoly elements may be adversely influenced by *ad hoc* changes forced upon the natural monopoly elements by governments and by the non-altruistic behaviour of the managers and civil servants who control enterprises under public ownership (Jackson 1981). Hence, whilst control problems may occur for the core activities, non-core subsidiaries are faced with the difficulties which stem from the existence of an extra layer of control.

These problems have led to the government considering privatisation through the splitting-off of parts of state-owned firms, either through sales to other groups (e.g. Sealink from BR) or incumbent management (Victaulic from BSC), or via the contracting-out of services following a tendering process (in refuse collection, etc.). In the unique case of the National Bus Company, it was considered more appropriate to dismantle the organisation into a large number of geographically distributed firms. Additionally, the enforced divestiture of privatisation may also involve the sale of a complete industry either on the stock market (e.g. British Telecom, British Gas), or through an employee buy-out (e.g. National Freight). Franchising is also an option and has been used in the provision of independent television services.

There are well-known issues in organising such privatisations, for example setting sale prices for stock-market flotations (see, for example, Buckland 1987; Mayer and Meadowcroft 1985), and ensuring efficient bidding and encouraging adequate investment in franchising (Williamson 1976, Domberger and Middleton 1985). However, evidence suggests that improved performance accrues from privatisation—partly from the removal of constraints imposed by governmental control and partly from the incentive effect of ownership (Domberger and Piggott 1986). Benefits may also accrue where parts are divested which have significant interdependencies with the former parent, and where the new parent is able to provide benefits from rationalisation, removal of funding constraints, and control more appropriate to the market conditions faced by the formerly nationalised entity (Bruce 1986).

As with private dominant firms, the state sell-off of complete industries with a high degree of market power raises important problems. Regulation may be difficult, as discussed below, and the protection from product market competition may mean that the incentive to improve internal efficiency may take time to work (Wright 1987).[5] Despite recent advances in takeover techniques, the size of these industries and their national strategic importance may limit the effectiveness of the discipline that might otherwise be imposed by the market for corporate control. However, there may be highly important technical efficiency benefits which need to be taken into consideration: where these trade-offs do not yield positive benefits, break-up on privatisation may be warranted (Hammond *et al.* 1985, Pryke 1987). Recent studies of the impact of privatisation are summarised in Table 11.1. In the discussion which follows, attention is focused in turn upon buy-outs, contracting-out and the privatisation of natural monopolies.

Management buy-outs, which have occurred on privatisation, appear from case study evidence to derive important benefits from the increased freedom from government interference and from the removal of constraints provoked by the difficulties experienced by the parent (McLachlan 1983; Bruce 1986; Wright, Robbie and Coyne 1987; Wright and Coyne 1985). Indeed, in respect of National Bus, the bought-out subsidiaries reported important benefits from the ending of corporate provision of certain services, which often led to inappropriate policies being forced upon them (Mulley and Wright 1986; Wright, Mulley and Robbie 1988).[6]

Recent experience in the UK in respect of the privatisation of such services as refuse collection, hospital cleaning, laundering and catering, and defence procurement also casts light on the general issue of contracting-out. Rather than continuing public provision of these services, the government has adopted a policy of allowing private contractors to bid in competition with in-house suppliers. The accumulated evidence from several studies provides a strong indication that such changes lead to substantial improvements in efficiency and cost savings.

With regard to the contracting-out of local authority and NHS services, an early study based on questionnaire data by Hartley and Huby (1985) found that the yearly cost savings from competitive tendering averaged 26 per cent, where firms were contracted to provide the same level of service as previously supplied by the in-house department. Part of the savings were found to result from contractors offering lower salaries and conditions of service, whilst other savings accrued from using fewer people and fewer hours. A more intangible reason was also given for savings which concerned the use of more efficient organisational methods.

A subsequent study by Domberger *et al.* (1987), suggests that the introduction of competition has led to cost savings of about 20 per cent (see, also, National Audit Office 1987). However, unlike refuse collection, outputs are difficult to define. Hence contracts need to be set in terms of inputs, which are more difficult to monitor. Early experience showed that projected cost savings by the winning bids had been unrealistically large, but with an adjustment, over time, to more realistic levels. Of particular importance, this study found an increasing number of contracts were being won by in-house teams who were offering improved efficiency over their previous position as salaried employees.

Estimates, by Domberger *et al.* (1986), of the cost savings to be derived from the contracting-out of refuse collection show that competitive tendering by local authorities reduced the average cost of such services by about 20 per cent. These figures have been criticised as being too optimistic, failing to take account of changes in levels of service and resulting from work-force exploitations (Ganley and Grahl 1988). However, Domberger *et al.* (1988) have strongly refuted these criticisms. A further study by some of the same authors (Cubbin *et al.* 1987) showed that the savings could be attributed mainly to improvements in technical efficiency rather than reductions in employees' remuneration packages. These changes relate to a greater ability to match manpower to fluctuations in demand, and to remove 'task and finish' payment systems which are not incentive-compatible and which do little to enhance productivity (see also Gear 1984, and Audit Commission 1984, for further UK evidence). McDavid (1985), examining Canadian experience, found that private firms used physical productivity bonuses and profit-sharing schemes.

These studies suggest that contracting-out can resolve some of the control problems inherent in internal production under public ownership. It needs to be borne in mind, though, that they relate essentially to the short-term effects, and it is not as yet clear whether such benefits are carried forward into the longer term. For example, it remains to be seen whether in-house teams who win contracts and fail to deliver will be bailed-out by authorities.

The problems of privatisation, of a natural monopoly-type industry without break-up, have been examined by Vickers and Yarrow (1985), in respect of British Telecom and electricity, and Hammond *et al.* (1985) and Wright (1987), in respect of British Gas. Key issues involve the establishment of a regulatory framework which avoids the kind of control problems inherent in public ownership but which minimises the well-known problems of regulatory capture, over-investment, price increases at the expense of efficiency improvements, information availability and strategic entry deterrence (Vickers and Yarrow 1988, Waterson 1988).

For both British Telecom and British Gas price regulation was preferred to rate-of-return regulation, in order to avoid the well-known Averch–Johnson effect whereby firms over-invest in non-optimal capacity, so as to keep their profitability below the level that would attract attention from the regulator. The RPI-X type formulae imposed on these two firms permits them to increase prices by a maximum equivalent to the rise in the Retail Price Index, less an amount aimed at encouraging increases in efficiency in order to maintain profit levels. Otherwise, such firms, essentially protected from the spur of competition, would have little incentive to improve efficiency. However, the reliable operation of the system depends upon setting a level of X high enough to have the desired effect, and it is open to the problems which derive from multi-product firms changing the balance of their tariff structures whilst keeping within the permitted average price increase. Additionally, the monitoring role of regulators may be frustrated by their inability to gain independent access to reliable information on the firm under their control.

Early experience of the regulators of British Telecom and British Gas has indicated that there have been problems with access to information, and the pricing formulae have provided the firms with scope for altering their tariff structures by subjecting certain classes of customers to larger than average price increases. Benefits to these firms have also arisen from setting a level of X below the cost improvement levels that they had actually been achieving, with consequent positive effects on profits. However, both Oftel and Ofgas, as regulators, have made great efforts to pressurise the firms into providing more reliable information, to strengthen the possibilities for increasing competition and to threaten referral to the Monopolies Commission to have the licence conditions changed.

All these moves are designed to control potential abuse of the respective monopoly positions and to demonstrate that the regulators have not been subject to regulatory capture. However, the decisions taken by the government in respect of the horizontal and vertical integration of both British Telecom and British Gas have placed a greater burden on the regulators than might otherwise have been possible. Horizontal and vertical disintegration may have had the effects of enhancing competition, providing better comparative performance information to the regulator, reducing the danger of anti-competitive behaviour, and increasing the incentives for managers to promote internal efficiency. As it is, the desire to make privatisation a success, not least by obtaining the co-operation of incumbent management, appears to have overridden the wider social and private potential for efficiency gains. (For further discussion on these points see the references cited above, especially Vickers and Yarrow 1988.)

Discussion of the proposed privatisation of the UK electricity supply industry has been influenced by the experience with telecommunications and gas, and has led to the government considering vertical disintegration as a means of increasing competition (Pryke 1987). The government proposed in February 1988 to privatise the 12 Area Boards as 12 distribution companies; to maintain the national grid in its current role but to pass ownership and control to the distribution companies from the CEGB; to end the CEGB's monopoly of electricity generation by forming a competing generating company; and to introduce a system of regulation. Additionally, further private generating companies will be encouraged. The commercial relationship between distributing and generating companies will be governed by contracts with there being no further role envisaged for the Electricity Council. This approach reflects some of the arguments seen in the USA (see, for example, Landon 1983 for a summary). Landon (1983), in reviewing the theoretical literature concerning vertical integration in the specific context of the electricity utility industry, argues that the costs of contracting versus ownership would be increased by the existence of technological interdependence and idiosyncratic capital, the requirement for long-term contracting, the informational and transactional requirements involved and the difficulties of appropriate pricing between vertical levels.

11.4 Conclusion

The discussion of policy issues in this chapter—in respect of both antitrust and privatisation—has highlighted the need to deal with trade-offs between the benefits which may result from improved technical efficiency and reductions in transactions costs occasioned by internalisation; and the detrimental effects of increased market power and the reduction in the incentive to improve efficiency brought about by an absence of competition.

Of particular importance in accepting the arguments about the efficiency benefits of moves to internalise transactions is the need to ensure that the appropriate conditions are met. It is by no means clear that a multi-divisional structure, for example, will in practice operate in the manner which leads to its claimed theoretical superiority over other forms. Similarly, the transactions cost-reducing benefits of vertical integration and vertical market restrictions may have market power implications. In respect of public sector firms, the argument for the simple transfer of ownership without structural change needs to be carefully examined.

The structure–conduct–performance and transactions-cost approaches give complementary insights for both antitrust and privatisation policy. In respect of both the agents of antitrust policy and the regulators of privatised firms, a degree of scepticism about the efficiency trade-offs from production within the boundaries of one firm or internal organisation may be in order. The UK government's Blue Paper on merger policy, issued in Spring 1988, reflected this view when it stated that claimed efficiency benefits from a merger would not be taken into account in deciding whether to make a reference to the Monopolies and Mergers

Commission, though they would be examined if a reference were made.

Whilst several tools are available to deal with the problems discussed in this chapter, structural change through divestment may warrant increasing attention, notwithstanding the difficulties involved. It may help to maintain product market competition and reduce internal control problems. Where product market competition is difficult to maintain, encouraging competition in the market for corporate control may be beneficial in putting pressure on firms to organise themselves internally in a cost-effective manner.

Notes

1. The efficiency and anti-competitive arguments have been developed in the context of the acquisition of minority shareholdings in trading partners by Shirley Meadowcroft and David Thompson in their article 'Partial integration: a loophole in competition law?' in *Fiscal Studies* (1987). They show that minority shareholdings contain elements of both efficiency and anti-competitive behaviour, enhancing strategies. They suggest a strengthening of the powers given to the DGFT under the Competition Act (1980) in respect of anti-competitive practices to include examination of the causes and consequences of minority shareholdings by individual companies.

2. The UK government's Green Paper reviewing restrictive trade practices policy, published in early 1988, commented upon franchising agreements and exclusive dealing practices. Franchise agreements were seen to be important for improving efficiency where they stimulated inter-brand competition, and enabled new entrants to establish themselves in competition with established larger outlets. Territorial restrictions may have the undesirable effect of restricting competition. Exclusive dealing arrangements may be necessary to encourage retailers to undertake investment and promotion and prevent others from free-riding. They may increase efficiency except where market power is involved in the form of creating barriers to entry. The Competition Act (1980) provides for the control of vertical restrictions by single firms with market power. The Green Paper proposed that there should be a prohibition on restrictive practices that involved price fixing, collusive tendering, market sharing, restrictions on advertising, collective refusals to supply, tie-ins and loyalty rebates.

3. The issue of the accounting treatment of merged firms has been raised in the UK government's Blue Paper on mergers (Mergers Policy—A Department of Trade and Industry Paper on the Policy and Procedures of Merger Control, London, HMSO, 1988). The Blue Paper emphasises the need for improved disclosure so that the reader of the accounts can see the impact of mergers and acquisitions more clearly, and welcomes the review by the Accounting Standards Committee of the relevant accounting standard.

4. The government has also addressed the concern of some commentators about the use of very highly leveraged takeover bids, which depend for their success on either generating sufficient post-acquisition cash flow or effecting divestment. The government appears to be taking the view that high leverage deals provide

an important stimulus to the market for corporate control by introducing real takeover threats for larger companies which may stimulate them to improve internal efficiency. Where a highly leveraged deal does take place, the debt-bonding it involves may also provide an incentive to improve efficiency. The government in the Blue Paper (ibid.) also takes the view that if break-up leads to increases in value then this is evidence of a more efficient use of resources and therefore it would only envisage referring highly leveraged deals where other public interest issues are raised.

5. Antitrust problems may also arise in the case of the privatised natural monopolies in respect of their merger activity, entry deterring behaviour, etc. There is some discussion in the literature as to the roles of industry regulators and the antitrust authorities in dealing with these issues. (Vickers and Yarrow 1988). In the UK, a two-level approach is being developed, with the regulators able to make references to the Monopolies Commission.

6. There are also important antitrust policy issues associated with the break-up of NBC. The privatisation of NBC produced a large number of independent bus operators which were often dominant in their local areas, particularly in relation to the new entrants the government was seeking to encourage through its policy of deregulation. In a test case under Section 3 of the Competition Act (1980), Southern Vectis (a buyout from NBC operating on the Isle of Wight) was found to be engaging in an anti-competitive course of conduct by refusing access by other operators to its Newport bus station. ('The Southern Vectis Omnibus Co. Ltd.: Refusal to Allow Access to Newport Bus Station Isle of Wight', OFT, 17.2.88). Southern Vectis avoided being referred to the Monopolies Commission only after giving undertakings to the DGFT that it would end the practice (OFT Press Release, 6.5.88). Further antitrust issues, following the dissolution of NBC, concern the potential anti-competitive effects which may arise from subsequent mergers between the privatised concerns, a process that was beginning to show signs of developing in early 1988.

12

Concluding Comments: Internal Organisation and Organisational Evolution

STEVE THOMPSON AND MIKE WRIGHT

12.1 Introduction

We began the preface of this book with a quote from Oliver Williamson which emphasised the need to look inside the black box which constituted the firm. The importance of so doing has become clear in the chapters which followed. However, what has also emerged is the need not only to consider the conditions which influence the way in which a given set of activities is organised, but also the changing scope of interests carried out within the boundaries of the firm. For, as Schumpeter observed over four decades ago:

> The fundamental impulse that sets and keeps the capitalist engine in motion comes from the new consumers' goods, the new methods of production or transportation, the new markets, *the new forms of industrial organisation that capitalist enterprise creates*. Joseph A. Schumpeter, *Capitalism Socialism and Democracy*, 2nd edn, 1943, p. 83 (our italics).

In this concluding chapter we summarise the discussion that has taken place throughout the book and emphasise the importance of the search for new organisational forms in enabling firms to adapt efficiently to new circumstances. This search process may be accompanied by corporate fragmentation and renewal.

12.2 The View Inside the Black Box

The contributors to this volume have examined the organisation of activities within the firm from a variety of perspectives drawn from

228

economics and accounting. Each chapter has reviewed a set of theoretical and empirical contributions. In some cases the literature covered has been narrowly defined, and in others it has been more diffuse, often intersecting with those of other chapters. In each case, however, the central issue has been the efficiency and effectiveness of the corporate form.

The pre-eminent position of the M-form in the preceding chapters was justified on two major grounds. First, for the past two to three decades it has been the major corporate form among large multi-product firms—most notably in the USA, UK and Canada. Second, following the lead of Oliver Williamson (1975, 1981, etc.), this type of structure has been the subject of particular theoretical and empirical attention from academic researchers, as seen in the foregoing chapters.

It is clear that the M-form has been an important innovation. It is also apparent that neither this structure nor any other is applicable to all sets of firm activities in all operating environments. David Otley, in Chapter 5, shows the need to design control systems contingent upon the identification of a whole set of key environmental factors for each organisation. John Cable's review of the empirical evidence on the M-form adoption, in Chapter 2, supports this approach. Cable reports that studies on US and UK firms—where companies rely relatively heavily upon well-developed stock markets—appear to be far more supportive of the M-form hypothesis than those elsewhere. Furthermore, even within the UK literature there is evidence that many divisionalised firms fail to achieve or maintain either the controls or the performance benefits attributable to the ideal type of M-form.

It has been seen that among beneficial properties attributed to the M-form is the ability to reduce managerial discretion to pursue objectives other than shareholder welfare. In particular, following Williamson (1971a), it has been considered that the separation of strategic decision making and operational responsibilities reduces any tendencies towards preferred expenditures (e.g. 'pet projects' or 'empire building') by senior managers. It is clear, however, that divisionalisation is an incomplete answer to the problems of conflicting managerial objectives.[1] Steve Thompson, in Chapter 4, considers the hierarchical firm as a multi-level, principal–agent problem. He suggests that the corollary of internalising capital supply and other transactions within the firm is a reduction in the market-based monitoring of divisional managers. This may create difficulties in designing suitable incentive structures and appears to be a cause of the trend towards divestment, to which we return below.

Dennis Mueller, in Chapter 3, presents considerable evidence from the empirical literature in support of the contention that many firms' strategic investments appear incompatible with shareholder wealth maximisation. In particular, Mueller points to the rather pessimistic evidence on the long-term performance of corporate acquirers and to empirical evaluations of the returns on corporate retentions, which tend to have shown these to be lower than their opportunity cost. Frank Stephen and Steve Thompson, in Chapter 9, suggest that the actual separation of responsibilities in internal resource allocation is less distinct than an M-form's organisation chart would imply. They cite evidence from the accounting literature which suggests that major investment decisions typically involve inputs from both headquarters staff and divisional management.

It is apparent, therefore, that whilst the M-form has been an important organisational development in facilitating the growth of large multiproduct companies in certain countries, even here it is not a panacea. Nor is it inevitable that most business activities will end up as the responsibility of divisional or subsidiary managers within a multi-divisional structure. Indeed, there is a continuing search for new organisational forms and accumulating evidence of a trend back towards decentralised ownership and control. However it is crucial to bear in mind that the novel organisational forms which are being developed mean that this movement ought to be viewed as progressive, not to say revolutionary, rather than regressive.

12.3   The Search For New Organisational Forms

It is the general case that economic activities—both within and without the firm—involve co-operative effort by the suppliers of productive inputs. The ubiquitous presence of opportunism combined with uncertainty, as discussed extensively in the preceding chapters, gives rise to non-zero sum gains of association; particular contractual or institutional arrangements are paired with particular pay-offs for different configurations of co-operative endeavour. Therefore, the search for improved institutional forms—i.e. forms offering higher joint pay-offs—is as much a part of entrepreneurial activity as the development of new products or new technological processes. Indeed, Schumpeter recognised the place of new organisational arrangements in generating 'creative destruction'—as the quotation from him at the start of this chapter indicates.

If a new and evidently superior form of organisation—the partnership, the joint-stock company, the M-form, the chain franchise, etc.—is developed, it will be adopted by imitators elsewhere. John Cable reviewed evidence, in Chapter 2, which showed that the M-form's diffusion pattern closely resembled that for product and process innovations. In particular, the spread of M-form adoption appears to have been related to those very factors—especially size and firm diversification—which would have been expected to raise the return from its introduction. This is entirely consistent with the economic literature on technical change which reports that potential profitability is the major influence in determining the rate of take-up of a new process.[2]

However, the potential of new organisational arrangements to raise the pay-offs from economic co-operation depends upon many transaction-specific factors. The slavish imitation of the institutional designs of others appears less likely to succeed than cloning rivals' products or installing similar production processes. Furthermore, in some industries rival competitors will maintain entirely different structural arrangements over long periods[3]—indicating that the specific circumstances of each require a different organisational configuration and/or that neither form has a particularly large advantage over the other. Established organisational learning systems peculiar to individual firms, may have an important role to play.

Changes in the legal framework, particularly relating to specifications of property rights, technology, consumer tastes, and the preferences and characteristics of factor suppliers must create a continuing potential for organisational evolution. For example, after the legal and institutional barriers to issuing shares in industrial companies were removed in the nineteenth century, the joint stock company rapidly succeeded the partnership as the dominant ownership form for manufacturing business.[4]

In organisation evolution—as in biological and technological change—some forms will be more enduring than others. Furthermore, since the pay-offs to a particular institutional innovation may be either inherently long term in nature or extremely difficult to isolate from the impact of external events, unsuccessful adaptations may persist for moderate periods. This probably helps to explain the abrupt changes of fashion in organisational form: for example, why conglomerate holding companies moved in and out of vogue in the late 1960s and early 1970s.

Economic logic suggests that the entrepreneurial role in initiating institutional changes is likely to be played by those who are in a position to appropriate a substantial proportion of any resulting gains. In the case of external market exchange, either buyers or sellers may have the incentive to devise superior contractual forms. Any initiative in reorganising activities within or between firms appears most likely to come from suitably motivated managers. Some other parties in the firm—e.g. employees and bondholders—may have no means of exploiting any resulting gains; whilst shareholders may face high transactions costs and free rider problems in trying to initiate change.

Of course, where managers have neither a direct interest in the residual nor a promotional incentive, inertia may result. The management buy-out—discussed by Mike Wright in Chapter 10—can be interpreted as a response to such difficulties: it allows salaried managers in wholly-owned divisions to utilise information on the profitable reorganisation of 'their' business. Less frequently, external specialists may initiate 'management buy-ins' to exploit perceived potential. It is also the case that the external capital market allows corporate raiders to acquire companies and—sometimes—effect suitable change.

12.4   Corporate Fragmentation

Despite the strength of the 1983–7 takeover wave, many of the important structural trends in the 1980s have been running towards decentralised ownership and decision making.[5] In most western economies there have been unprecedented numbers of voluntary divestment deals, including leveraged buy-outs, the securitisation or floating-off of corporate subdivisions and the privatisation of government-owned business (see Chapters 10 and 11). These changes, have had the effect of returning decision-making to enterprise management and strengthening the monitoring role of the external capital market. In addition, there has been a trend towards the hiving-off of important functions—including R & D and even manufacturing—to allow corporate managers to concentrate on the areas of their comparative advantage, which may not necessarily be their traditional areas of activity.

The trend towards decentralised ownership is related to innovations which have extended the external capital market and weakened the case for internal allocation. New financial markets—particularly for commercial bonds beneath the investment grade, i.e. so-called 'junk bonds'—have facilitated the use of debt. In the USA, this form of finance is used to cover the bulk of the purchase price in a typical buy-out deal. Similarly, corporate restructurings and management share repurchases (both frequently used to counter hostile bid approaches in the USA) involve the issue of debt to buy back equity.[6] Not only do these transactions alter the ownership claims on corporate America, they also put cash in the hands of private investors who then make investment decisions in place of corporate management.

Another result of the development of financial markets has been a recognition of the profit potential of the corporate treasury. In many countries, corporate treasurers have developed a new expertise in financial investment. This inevitably increases the competition within the internal capital market. Kensinger and Martin (1988) link this development with the widespread abandonment of the Boston Consulting Group project portfolio approach to internal allocation. This, it was suggested in Chapter 9, was a frequently used practice in which 'cash cows' businesses were used to fund 'growth stars' etc. Kensinger and Martin describe an increased role for private investors in funding individual projects, at least in the USA.

The fragmentation of the corporation may also improve information flows to the investor. For example, a firm may be considered to own a bundle of assets, each of which makes a largely disguised contribution towards reported earnings. When any asset, say the firm's premises, is sold and then leased back at an economic rental, a distortion is removed from the published profit figures. Concern has recently been expressed about the problem of lack of information to outside investors in the UK government's review of merger policy, as noted in Chapter 11.

It has long been recognised that R & D activities are difficult to incorporate within conventional business hierarchies.[7] However, it has been thought that R & D is also difficult to contract-out, not least because of the inherent uncertainty attached to research and to the problems of organising markets in technical knowledge.[8] Nonetheless, there is now substantial evidence from the USA that large firms are externalising much R & D. In some cases this takes the form of establishing joint ventures with other firms which possess expertise in the required area, as discussed in Chapter 10. Alternatively, a firm may contract with a specialist R & D problem solver (a 'wizard shop') and purchase the sole rights to the solution.

Perhaps an even more fundamental stage in dismembering the traditional corporation is the contracting-out of production itself. It has long been a characteristic of many multinational enterprises to locate basic production operations in countries where direct labour is relatively cheap, as discussed by Peter Buckley in Chapter 7. Some international 'producers' now choose to contract-out the complete manufacture of their products and to specialise in the development and marketing stages. This development appears to be related to a shortening of the product life-cycle. It has, for instance, always occurred at the high fashion end of the garment industry. Now this so-called 'dynamic networking' can be observed in consumer electronics, durable household goods and sports footwear.[9]

12.5 Conclusion

These recent developments are fundamentally changing our notion of 'the firm' as the single productive unit in the economy. In his later writings, Williamson has emphasised the importance of governance structures in moving the theory and practice of organisational choice beyond a simple markets-versus-hierarchies dichotomy. Long-term and medium-term contractual relations between independent entities display some of the characteristics of internal and external organisations.

Whilst Chapter 10 and the earlier part of this chapter have attempted

234

Steve Thompson and Mike Wright

to outline an initial framework for analysis, much work remains to be done on the movement from internalisation to other transactional forms. These arrangements now need systematic study and classification. In particular, there would appear to be a need for research effort to be focused upon the conditions for movement between different trans-actional forms and upon the comparative performance of a much wider variety of institutional arrangements than has hitherto been the case. Some of these studies are now beginning to appear, as has been seen. But the newness of many of the recent organisational phenomena means that a final verdict on their efficacy is still some way off. What is clear, however, is that the study of internal organisation is not just about the optimal decomposition of a given set of activities, but involves a dynamic perspective which places emphasis upon the conditions for change from one form to another.

Notes

1. Indeed, if the M-form was simply a device to curtail managerial discretion, it is difficult to see why managers would have introduced it at all, as Williamson (1981, p. 1565) has noted.
2. Discussed in detail in Mansfield (1968).
3. For example, Ford and General Motors, the two big American car makers, differ markedly in the extent to which they use in-house component manufacturers, but neither firm's strategy dominates (see Monteverde and Teece 1982b).
4. Described in Payne (1967).
5. In the USA leveraged buy-outs were worth $41 billion in 1986. Between 1981 and 1986, these deals amounted to well over 50 per cent of the total value of corporate takeovers. Divestments occurred to a value of $21.9 billion over the same period (see Black and Grundfest 1988, p. 6 and Thompson 1988, p. 11). In the UK, management buy-outs and divestments reached record levels over the same period (see Wright *et al.* 1987). Furthermore, Jensen (1987) has argued that the 1980s takeover wave was dominated by a desire to control the cash flow from mature low-technology products and not part of a move to extend the diversity of corporate activities.
6. Described by Stewart and Glassman (1988).
7. At some level in the hierarchy, non-technical management must approve expenditure decisions relating to technical projects. Scherer (1980, p. 414) points out that this often results in tension, leading to the exit of frustrated scientists into management or to independent rivals.
8. Much technical knowledge can, at best, be given limited protection through intellectual property rights. Unprotected secrets are difficult to sell without their contents being revealed and so given away.
9. 'Dynamic network' organisations are discussed by Miles and Snow (1986) and Kensinger and Martin (1988).

Bibliography

Abernathy, W. (1978) *The Productivity Dilemma*, Johns Hopkins University Press.

Agrawal, A. and Mandelker, G.N. (1987) 'Managerial incentives and corporate investment and financing decisions', *Journal of Finance*, 42, pp. 823–37.

Aharoni, Y. (1966) *The Foreign Investment Decision Process*, Graduate School of Business Administration, Harvard University.

Alchian, A. (1984) 'Specificity, specialization and coalitions', *Zeitschrift für de gesamte Staatswissenschaft*, 1, pp. 34–49.

Alchian, A.A. and Demsetz, H. (1972) 'Production, information costs and economic organization', *American Economic Review*, 62, pp. 777–95.

Alchian, A.A. and Woodward, S. (1988) 'The firm is dead; long live the firm', *Journal of Economic Literature*, XXVI, pp. 65–79.

Alexander, G.J., Benson, P.G. and Kampmeyer, J.M. (1984) 'Investigating valuation effects of announcements of voluntary corporate sell-off', *Journal of Finance*, 39, pp. 503–17.

Allen, G.C. (1981) *The Japanese Economy*, Weidenfeld & Nicolson.

Amigoni, F. (1978) 'Planning management control systems', *Journal of Business Finance and Accounting*, pp. 279–92.

Amihud, Y. and Lev, B. (1982) 'Risk reduction as a motive for conglomerate mergers', *Bell Journal of Economics*, 12, pp. 605–17.

Anderson, E. (1988), 'Transactions costs as determinants of opportunism in integrated and independent sales forces', *Journal of Economic Behaviour and Organisation*, 9, pp. 247–64.

Anderson, E. and Schmittlein, D.C. (1984) 'Integration of the sales force: an empirical examination', *Rand Journal of Economics*, 15, pp. 385–95.

Anthony, R.N. (1965) *Planning and Control Systems: A Framework for Analysis*, Division of Research, Harvard Graduate School of Business.

Aoki, M. (1984) *The Co-operative Game Theory of the Firm*, Clarendon Press.

Armour, H.O. and Teece, D.J. (1978) 'Organizational structure and economic performance: a test of the multidivisional hypothesis', *Bell Journal of Economics*, 9, pp. 106–12.

Arrow, K.J. (1961) 'Economic welfare and the allocation of resources for invention', in NBER *The Rate and Direction of Economic Activity*, Princeton University Press, pp. 609–25.

Arrow, K.J., (1962) 'The economic implications of learning by doing', *Review of Economic Studies*, 29, pp. 155–73.

Arrow, K.J. (1963) 'Uncertainty and the welfare economics of medical care', *American Economic Review*, 53, pp. 941–73.

Arrow, K.J. (1973) 'Higher education as a filter', *Journal of Public Economics*, 2, pp. 193–216.

235

Arrow, K.J. (1974) *The Limits of Organisation*, Norton.

Arrow, K.J. (1987) 'The economics of agency', in John W. Pratt and Richard J. Zeckhauser (eds) *Principals and Agents: The Structure of Business*, Harvard Business School Press.

Asquith, P. (1983) 'Merger bids, uncertainty, and stockholder returns', *Journal of Financial Economics*, 11, pp. 51–83.

Asquith, P., Bruner, R.F., and Mullins, D.W. Jr. (1983) 'The gains to bidding firms from merger', *Journal of Financial Economics*, 11, pp. 121–39.

Audit Commission (1984) *Securing Further Improvements in Refuse Collection*, HMSO.

Azzi, C. (1978) 'Conglomerate mergers, default risk, and homemade mutual funds', *American Economic Review*, 68, pp. 161–72.

Baddon, L., Hunter, L., Hyman, J., Leopold, J. and Ramsie, H. (1987) *Developments in Profit Sharing and Employee Share Ownership*, University of Glasgow.

Bain, J. (1956) *Barriers to New Competition*, Harvard University Press.

Barney, J.B. and Ouchi, W.G. (1986) *Organizational Economics*, Jossey-Bass.

Barzel, Y. (1987) 'The entrepreneur's reward for self-policing', *Economic Inquiry*, 25, pp. 103–16.

Baumol, W.J. (1959), *Business Behaviour, Value and Growth*, Macmillan.

Baumol, W.J. (1982) 'Contestable markets: an uprising in the theory of industrial structure', *American Economic Review*, 72, pp. 1–15.

Baumol, W.J., Heim, P., Malkiel, B.G., and Quandt, R.E. (1970) 'Earnings retention, new capital and the growth of the firm', *Review of Economics and Statistics*, 52, pp. 345–55.

Baumol, W.J., Heim, P., Malkiel, B.G., and Quandt, R.E. (1973) 'Efficiency of corporate investment: reply', *Review of Economics and Statistics*, 55, pp. 128–31.

Baumol, W.J., Panzar, J.C., Willig, R.D. (1982) *Contestable Markets and the Theory of Industrial Structure*, Harcourt Brace Jovanovich.

Beam, H., (1979) 'The new route to the top,' *Advanced Management Journal*, 44, pp. 55–62.

Beer, S. (1975) *Platform for Change*, John Wiley.

Bell, D.W. and Hanson, C.G. (1984) *Profit Sharing and Employee Shareholding Attitude Survey*, Industrial Participation Association.

Berle, A.A. and Means, G.C. (1932) *The Modern Corporation and Private Property*, Macmillan.

Berry, C.H. (1975) *Corporate Growth and Diversification*, Princeton University Press.

Bhargava, N. (1973) 'The impact of organizational form on the firm: experience of 1920–70', unpublished PhD thesis, University of Pennsylvania.

Black, B.S. and Grundfest, J.A. (1988), 'Shareholder gains from takeovers and restructurings', *Journal of Applied Corporate Finance*, 1, pp. 5–15.

Blanchflower, D.G. and Oswald, A.J. (1987) 'Profit sharing—can it work?', *Oxford Economic Papers*, 39, pp. 1–19.

Blois, K.J. (1972) 'Vertical quasi-integration', *Journal of Industrial Economics*, 20, pp.253–71.

Boland, R.J. and Pondy, L.R. (1983) 'Accounting in organizations: a union of natural and rational perspectives', *Accounting Organizations and Society*, 8, pp. 223–34.

Bonanno, and Vickers, J.S. (1988) 'Vertical separation', *Journal of Industrial Economics*, XXXVI, pp. 257–66.

Boudreaux, K.J. (1975) 'Divestiture and share price', *Journal of Financial and Quantitative Analysis*, 10, pp. 619–29.

Bower, J.L. (1970) *Managing the Resource Allocation Process: A Study of Corporate Planning and Investment*, Harvard University.

Bowles, S. (1985) 'The production process in a competitive economy: Walrasian, neo-Hobbesian and Marxian models', *American Economic Review*, 75, pp. 16–36.

Bradley, M. (1980), 'Interfirm tender offers and the market for corporate control', *Journal of Business*, 53, pp. 345–76.

Bradley, M., Desai, A. and Kim, E.H. (1983) 'The rationale behind interfirm tender offers: information or synergy?', *Journal of Financial Economics*, 11, pp. 183–206.

Brainard, W.C., Shoven, J.B., and Weiss, L. (1980) 'The financial valuation of the return on capital', *Brookings Papers on Economic Activity*, 2, pp. 453–502.

Brealey, R.A., Hodges, S.D., and Capron, D., (1976) 'The return on alternative sources of finance', *Review of Economics and Statistics*, 58, pp. 469–77.

Brennan, T.J., (1987) 'Why regulated firms should be kept out of unregulated markets: understanding the divestiture in US v AT&T', *Antitrust Bulletin*, XXXII, No. 3, pp. 741–94.

Brickley, J.A., Bhagut, S. and Lease, R.C. (1985) 'The impact of long-range managerial compensation plans on shareholder wealth', *Journal of Accounting and Economics*, 7, pp. 115–50.

Brickley, J.A. and Dark, F.H. (1987) 'The choice of organisational form: the case of franchising', *Journal of Financial Economics*, 18, pp. 401–20.

Brickley, J.A. and James, C.M. (1987) 'The takeover market, corporate board composition and ownership structure: the case of banking', *Journal of Financial Economics*, 30, pp. 161–80.

Brooke, M.Z., (1984) *Centralization and Autonomy*, Holt, Rinehard & Winston.

Brooke, M.Z. (1986) *International Management: A Review of Strategies and Operations*, Hutchinson.

Brooke, M.Z. and Remmers, H.L. (1978) *The strategy of multinational enterprise* (2nd edn) Pitman.

Brown, S.J. and Warner, J.B. (1980) 'Measuring security price performance', *Journal of Financial Economics*, 8, pp. 205–58.

Brown, W.A. (1973) *Piecework Bargaining*, Heinemann.

Brown, W.A. (ed.) (1981) *The Changing Contours of British Industrial Relations*, Blackwell.

Brown, W.A. (1983) 'Britain's unions: new pressures and shifting loyalties', *Personnel Management*, pp. 48–51.

Brown, W.B. (1984) 'Firm-like behaviour in markets—the administered channel', *International Journal of Industrial Organisation*, 2, pp. 263–76.

Brownell, P. (1983) 'Leadership style, budgeting participation and managerial behaviour', *Accounting, Organizations and Society*, 8, pp. 307–21.

Bruce, A. (1986) 'State-to-private-sector divestment: the case of Sealink', in J. Coyne and M. Wright (eds) *Divestment and Strategic Change*, Philip Allan.

Bruns, W.J. and Waterhouse, J.H. (1975) 'Budgetary control and organization structure', *Journal of Accounting Research*, 13, pp. 177–203.

Buckland, R. (1987) 'The costs and returns of the privatisation of nationalised industries', *Public Administration*, 65, pp. 241–58.

Buckley, P.J. (1983) 'New theories of international business: some unresolved problems', in M. Casson (ed.) *The Growth of International Business*, George Allen & Unwin.

Buckley, P.J. (1985) 'The economic analysis of the multinational enterprise:

Reading versus Japan?', *Hitotsubashi Journal of Economics*, 26, pp. 117–24.

Buckley, P.J. (1988) 'The limits of explanation—testing the internalisation theory of multinational enterprise', *Journal of International Business Studies*, XIX (forthcoming).

Buckley, P.J. (1987) 'An economic transactions analysis of tourism', *Tourism Management*, 87, pp. 190–4.

Buckley, P.J., Berkova, Z. and Newbould, G.D. (1983) *Direct Investment in the UK by Smaller European Firms*, Macmillan.

Buckley, P.J. and Casson, M. (1976) *The Future of the Multinational Enterprise*, Macmillan.

Buckley, P.J. and Casson, M. (1985) *The Economic Theory of the Multinational Enterprise*, Selected readings, Macmillan.

Buckley, P.J. and Casson, M. (1987) 'A theory of cooperation in international business', *Cooperative Strategies in International Business* (eds: F.J. Contractor and P. Lorange), Lexington Books, D.C. Heath & Co. Also in *Management International Review* (1987).

Buckley, P.J., Newbould, G.D. and Thurwell, J. (1987) *Foreign Direct Investment by Smaller UK Firms*, Macmillan. First edition published as *Going International—The Experiences of UK Firms Overseas* (1978) Associated Business Press.

Buckley, P.J. and Pearce, R.D. (1979) 'Overseas production and exporting by the world's largest enterprises—a study in sourcing policy', *Journal of International Business Studies*, 10, pp. 9–20.

Buckley, P.J. and Pearce, R.D. (1981) 'Market servicing by multinational manufacturing firms: exporting versus foreign production', *Managerial and Decision Economics*, 2, pp. 229–46.

Buckley, P.J. and Pearce, R.D. (1984) 'Exports in the strategy of multinational enterprises', *Journal of Business Research*, 12, pp. 209–26.

Buehner, R. (1985) 'Internal organisation and returns: an empirical analysis of large diversified German corporations', in J. Schwalback (ed.) *Industry Structure and Performance*, wzb, Edition Sigma.

Burns, A.F. (1934) *Production Trends in the United States Since 1870*, National Bureau of Economic Research (New York).

Burns, M.R. (1977) 'The competitive effects of trust-busting: portfolio analysis', *Journal of Political Economy*, 8, pp. 717–39.

Burns, M.R. (1983) 'An empirical analysis of stockholder injury under S.2 of the Sherman Act', *Journal of Industrial Economics*, 31, pp. 333–62.

Burns, T. and Stalker, G.M. (1961) *The Management of Innovation*, Tavistock Institute.

Burrell, G. and Morgan, G. (1979) *Sociological Paradigms and Organisational Analysis*, Heinemann.

Burton, R. and Obel, B. (1980) 'A computer simulation test for the M-form hypothesis', *Administration Science Quarterly*, 25, pp. 457–66.

Business Week, (1968) 'Why Litton took a slide', January 27, p. 38.

Business Week, (1982) 'What puts the whiz in Litton's fast growth?' April 16, p. 180.

Butler, R. and Carney, M.G. (1983) 'Managing markets: implications for the make–buy decision', *Journal of Management Studies*, 20, pp. 213–31.

Buzzell, R.D. and Nourse, R. (1966) *Product Innovation, the Product Life Cycle, and Competitive Behavior in Selected Food Processing Industries*, Arthus D. Little.

Cable, J. (1977) 'A search theory of diversifying merger', *Recherches Economique de Louvain*, 43, pp. 225–43.

Cable, J.R. (1980) 'Diversification via merger: some empirical evidence', in K.G. Cowling *et al. Mergers and Economic Performance*, Cambridge University Press.

Cable, J.R. (1985a) 'Capital market information and industrial performance:the role of West German banks', *Economic Journal*, 95, pp. 118–32.

Cable, J.R. (1985b) 'The bank–industry relationship in West Germany: performance and policy aspects', in J. Schwalbach (ed.) *Industry Structure and Performance*, wzb, Edition Sigma.

Cable, J. and Dirrheimer, M.F. (1983) 'Hierarchies and markets: an empirical test of the multidivisional hypothesis in West Germany', *International Journal of Industrial Organisation*, 1, pp. 43–62.

Cable, J.R. and Turner, P. (1985) 'Asymmetric information and credit rationing: another view of industrial bank lending and Britain's economic problem', in D. Currie (ed.) *Advances in Monetary Economics*, Croom Helm.

Cable, J. and Yasuki, M. (1985) 'Internal organisation, business groups and corporate performance: an empirical test of the multidivisional hypothesis in Japan', *International Journal of Industrial Organisation*, 3, pp. 401–20.

Carlson, S. (1975) *How Foreign Is Foreign Trade?* University of Uppsala.

Carter, J.R. (1977) 'In search of synergy: A structure–performance test', *Review of Economics and Statistics*, 59, pp. 279–89.

Casson, M. (1981) 'Foreword' to A.M. Rugman', *Inside the Multinationals*, Croom Helm.

Casson, M. (1985) 'Transaction costs and the theory of the multinational enterprise', in P.J. Buckley and M. Casson (1985) *The Economic Theory of the Multinational Enterprise*, Macmillan.

Casson, M. (ed.) (1986a) *Multinationals and World Trade*, George Allen & Unwin.

Casson, M. (1986b) 'Foreign divestment and international rationalisation: the sale of Chrysler (UK) to Peugeot', in J. Coyne and M. Wright (eds) *Divestment and Strategic Change*, Philip Allan.

Casson, M. (1987) 'Multinational firms', Ch. 7 in R. Clarke and T. McGuinness *The Economics of The Firm*, Basil Blackwell.

Caves, R.E. (1980) 'Corporate strategy and structure', *Journal of Economic Literature*, 18, pp. 64–92.

Caves, R.E. and Murphy, W.F. (1976) 'Franchising: firms, markets and intangible assets', *Southern Economic Journal*, 42, pp. 572–85.

Caves, R.E. and Porter, M. (1976) 'Barriers to exit', in R.J. Masson and P.W. Qualls *Essays on Industrial Organisation in Honour of J.S. Bain* Ballinger.

Caves, R.E., Porter, M.E., Spence, M. and Scott, J.T. (1980) *Competition in the Open Economy*, Harvard University Press.

Caves, R.E. and Yamey, B.S. (1971) 'Risk and corporate rates of return: comment', *Quarterly Journal of Economics*, 85, pp. 513–17.

Cavusgil, S.T. (1972) 'Some observations on the relevance of critical variables for internationalisation states', *Export Management* (eds: M.R. Czinkota and G. Tesar) Praeger.

Chamberlin, E.H. (1933) *Monopolistic Competition*, Harvard University Press.

Chandler, A.D. Jr. (1962) *Strategy and Structure: Chapters in the History of the Industrial Enterprise* MIT Press.

Chandler, A.D. Jr. (1977) *The Visible Hand: The Managerial Revolution in American Business*, Belknap Press.

Chandler, A.D. Jr. (1982) 'The M-form: industrial groups, American style', *European Economic Review*, 19, pp. 3–23.

Chandler, A.D. Jr. and H. Daems, (1980) *Managerial Hierarchies*, Harvard University Press.

Channon, D.F. (1973) *The Strategy and Structure of British Enterprise*, Graduate School of Business Administration, Harvard University.

Channon, D.F. (1978) *The Service Industries*, Macmillan.

Chen, A.H. and Merville, L.J. (1986) 'An analysis of divestiture effects resulting from deregulation', *Journal of Finance*, XLI, pp. 997–1010.

Chenhall, R.H., Harrison, G.L. and Watson, D.J.H. (1981) *The Organizational Context of Management Accounting*, Pitman.

Chenhall, R.H. and Morris, D. (1986) 'The impact of structure, environment and interdependence on the perceived usefulness of management accounting systems', *Accounting Review*, LXI, pp. 16–35.

Child, J. (1987) 'Information technology, organisation and response to strategic challenge', *California Management Review*, Fall, XXX, pp. 33–50.

Chiplin, B. (1986) 'Information technology and personal financial services', in R.L. Carter *et al.* (eds) *Personal Financial Markets*, Philip Allan.

Chiplin, B. and Wright, M. (1980) 'Divestment and structural change in UK industry', *National Westminster Bank Review*, Feb. pp. 42–51.

Chiplin, B. and Wright, M. (1982) 'Competition policy and state enterprises in the UK', *Antitrust Bulletin*, XXVII, pp. 921–56.

Chiplin, B. and Wright, M. (1987) 'The logic of mergers—the competitive market for corporate control in theory and practice', *IEA Hobart Paper*, No. 107.

Ciscel, D.H. and Carroll, T.M. (1980) 'The determinants of executive salaries: an econometric survey', *Review of Economics and Statistics*, 62, pp. 7–13.

Clarke, R. and McGuinness, A. *The Economics of the Firm*, Blackwell.

Clinch, A. (1987) 'Gillroyd Group Ltd—A management buy-in', *Acquisitions Monthly*, pp. 48–49.

Coase, R.H. (1937) 'The nature of the firm', *Economica*, (new series) 4, pp. 386–405.

Commons, J.R. (1924) *The Legal Foundations of Capitalism*, Macmillan.

Coughlan, A.T. and Schmidt, R.M. (1985) 'Executive compensation, management turnover and firm performance: an empirical investigation', *Journal of Accounting and Economics*, 7, pp. 43–66.

Cosh, A., Hughes, A. and Singh, A. (1980) 'The causes and the effects of takeovers in the United Kingdom: an empirical investigation for the late 1960s at the microeconomic level,' in Mueller (ed.) (1980) *The Determinants and Effects of Mergers: An International Comparison*, pp. 227–70, Oelgeschlager, Gunn & Hain.

Cosh, A.D. and Hughes, A. (1987) 'The anatomy of corporate control: directors, shareholders and executive remuneration in giant US and UK corporations', *Cambridge Journal of Economics*, 11.

Cowling, K., Stoneman, P., Cubbin, J., Cable, J., Hall, G., Domberger, S., and Dutton, P. (1980) *Mergers and Economic Performance*, Cambridge University Press.

Coyne, J. and Wright, M. (1986) *Divestment and Strategic Change*, Philip Allan.

Crawford, J. (1987) *Leveraged Buy-Outs*, Wiley.

Crum, W.L. (1939) *Corporate Size and Earning Power*, Harvard University Press.

Cubbin, J., Domberger, S. and Meadowcroft, S.A. (1987) 'Competitive tendering and refuse collection: identifying the sources of efficiency gains', *Fiscal Studies*, 8, pp. 49–58.

Cubbin, J. and Leech, D. (1983) 'The effect of shareholding dispersion on the degree of control in British companies: theory and measurement', *Economic Journal* 93, pp. 351–69.

Curran, S. and Stanworth, J. (1983) 'Franchising in the modern economy—towards a theoretical understanding', *International Small Business Journal* 2, pp. 8–26.

Cyert, R.M. and March, J.G. (1963) '*A Behavioural Theory of the Firm*', Prentice-Hall.

Daft, R.L. and Macintosh, N. (1978) 'A new approach to the design and use of management information', *California Management Review*, XX, pp. 82–92.

Daniel, W.W. and Millward, N., (1983) *Workplace Industrial Relations in Britain*, Heinemann.

Davies, S.W. (1979) *The Diffusion of Process Innovations*, Cambridge University Press.

Davis, G. (1986a) 'Strategic trading: rationalisation in US brewing', in J. Coyne and M. Wright (eds) *Divestment and Strategic Change*, Philip Allan.

Davis, G. (1986b) *Strategic Trading in Business Units: A Study of Strategic Aspects of Restructuring*, unpublished Ph.D. Thesis, University of Bath.

De Angelo, H., De Angelo, L. and Rice, E.M. (1984) 'Shareholder wealth and going private', *Journal of Law and Economics*, XXVII, pp. 367–402.

De Angelo, L. (1986) 'Management buy-outs of public stockholders', *Accounting Review*, LXI, pp. 400–20.

Denning, K.C. (1988) 'Spin-offs and sales of assets: an examination of security returns and divestment motivations', *Accounting and Business Research*, (forthcoming).

Dermer, J. (1977) *Management Planning and Control Systems: Advanced Topics and Cases*, Irwin.

Dodd, P. (1980) 'Merger proposals, management discretion and stockholder wealth', *Journal of Financial Economics*, 8, pp. 105–137.

Dodd, P. and Ruback, R. (1977) 'Tender offers and stockholder returns: an empirical analysis', *Journal of Financial Economics*, 5, pp. 351–74.

Domberger, S., Meadowcroft, S.A. and Thompson, D.J. (1986) 'Competitive tendering and efficiency: the case of refuse collection', *Fiscal Studies*, 7, pp. 69–87.

Domberger, S., Meadowcroft, S.A. and Thompson, D.J. (1987) 'The impact of competitive tendering on the costs of hospital domestic services', *Fiscal Studies*, 8, pp. 39–54.

Domberger, S., Meadowcroft, S.A. and Thompson, D.J. (1988) 'Competition and efficiency in refuse collection: a reply', *Fiscal Studies*, 9, pp. 86–90.

Domberger, S. and Middleton, J. (1985) 'Franchising in practice: the case of independent television in the UK', *Fiscal Studies*, 6, pp. 17–32.

Domberger, S. and Piggott, J. (1986) 'Privatisation policies and public enterprise: a survey', *Economic Record*, 62, pp. 145–62.

Downs, A. (1967) *Inside Bureaucracy*, Little, Brown & Company.

Dugger, W. (1983) 'The transactions cost analysis of Oliver E. Williamson: a new synthesis?', *Journal of Economic Issues*, XVII, pp. 95–114.

Duhaime, I.M. and Baird, I.S. (1987) 'The role of business unit size in divestment decision–making', *Journal of Management*, 13, pp. 189–98.

Duhaime, I.M. and Grant, J.H. (1984) 'Factors influencing divestment decision-making: evidence from a field study', *Strategic Management Journal*, 5, pp. 301–18.

Dunning, J.H. (1981) *International Production and The Multinational Enterprise*, George Allen & Unwin.

Dunning, J.H. and Rugman, A.M. (1985) 'The influence of Hymer's dissertation on the theory of foreign direct investment', *American Economic Review*, 7, pp. 228–33.

Dyas, G.P. and Thanheiser, H.T. (1976) *The Emerging European Enterprise: Strategy and Structure in French and German Industry*, Macmillan.

Easterbrook, F.H. (1984) 'Two agency–cost explanations of dividends' *American Economic Review*, 74, pp. 650–9.

Easterbrook, F.H. (1987) 'Insider trading as an agency problem', in J. Pratt and R.J. Zeckhauser (eds) *Principals and Agents: The Structure of Business*, Harvard Business School Press.

Edwards, J. (1987) 'Recent developments in the theory of corporate finance', *Oxford Review of Economic Policy*, 3, pp. 1–15.

Edwards, R. (1979) *Contested Terrain*, Heinemann.

Edwards, R.C. (1975) 'The social relations of production in the firm and labor market structure', in R.C. Edwards (ed.) *Labor Market Segmentation*, D.C. Heath.

Eis, C. (1969) 'The 1919–1930 merger movement in American industry', *Journal of Law and Economics*, 12, pp. 267–96.

Ellert, J.C. (1976) 'Mergers, antitrust law enforcement and shareholder returns', *Journal of Finance*, 31, pp. 715–32.

Emmanuel, C.R. and Otley, D.T. (1985) *Accounting for Management Control*, Van Nostrand Reinhold.

Enderwick, P. (1984) 'The labour utilisation practices of multinationals and obstacles to multinational collective bargaining', *Journal of Industrial Relations*, 26, pp. 345–64.

Estrin, S., Grout, P. and Wadhwani, S. (1987) 'Profit-sharing and employee share ownership', *Economic Policy*, 2, pp. 13–62.

Ezzamel, M.A. (1980) 'Estimating the cost of capital for a division of a firm and the allocation problem in accounting: a comment', *Journal of Business Finance and Accounting*, 7, pp. 65–9.

Ezzamel, M.A. (1985) 'On the assessment of the performance effects of multidivisional structures—a synthesis', *Accounting and Business Research*, 61, pp. 23–34.

Falus-Szikra, K. (1985) 'Small enterprises in private ownership in Hungary', *Acta Oeconomica*, 34, pp. 13–26.

Fama, E. (1980) 'Agency problems and the theory of the firm', *Journal of Political Economy*, 88, pp. 288–307.

Fama, E. and Jensen, M. (1983a) 'Separation of ownership and control', *Journal of Law and Economics*, XXVI, pp. 301–26.

Fama, E. and Jensen, M. (1983b) 'Agency problems and residual claims', *Journal of Law and Economics*, XXVI, pp. 327–52.

Fama, E.F. and Miller, M.H. (1972) *The Theory of Finance*, Holt, Rinehard.

Firth, M. (1979) 'The profitability of takeovers and mergers', *Economic Journal*, 89, pp. 316–28.

Firth, M. (1980) 'Takeovers, shareholder returns, and the theory of the firm', *Quarterly Journal of Economics*, 94, pp. 315–47.

Fisher, L. and Lorie, J.H. (1964) 'Rates of Return on Investments in Common Stocks', *Journal of Business*, 37, pp. 1–21.

Fitzroy, F.R. and Kraft, K. (1985) 'Unionization, wages and efficiency', *Kyklos*, 38, pp. 537–54.

Fitzroy, F.R. and Kraft, K. (1987) 'Efficiency and internal organisation: works councils in West German firms', *Economica*, 54, pp. 493–504.

Fitzroy, F.R. and Mueller, D.C. (1979) 'Contract and the economics of organisation, *Acton Society Occasional Paper*.

Flamholtz, E.G. (1983) 'Accounting, budgeting and control systems in their organizational context: theoretical and empirical perspectives', *Accounting, Organizations and Society*, 8, pp. 153–69.

Forbes (1965) 'Xerox Corporation', 15 October, pp. 32–6.

Forbes (1968) 'Litton's troubles,' 15 February, pp. 46–9.

Forbes (1969) 'Litton's Shattered Image,' 1 December, p. 26 ff.

Francis, A., Turk, J. and Willman, P. (eds) (1983), *Power, Efficiency and Institutions*, Heinemann.

Frank, R.H. (1984) 'Are workers paid their marginal products?', *American Economic Review*, 74, pp. 549–71.

Franko, L.G. (1976) *The European Multinationals*, Harper and Row.

Franks, J.R., Broyles, J.E. and Hecht, M.J. (1977) 'An industry study of the profitability of mergers in the United Kingdom', *Journal of Finance*, 32, pp. 1513–25.

Furubotn, E. and Pejovich, S. (1972) 'Property rights and economic theory: a survey of recent literature', *Journal of Economic Literature*, X, p. 1137.

Galai, D. and Masulis, R.W. (1976) 'The option pricing model and the risk factor of stock', *Journal of Financial Economics*, 3, pp. 53–81.

Galbraith, J. (1977) *Organizational Design*, Addison Wesley.

Galbraith, J.K. (1967) *The New Industrial State*, Penguin.

Gale, B.J. (1972) 'Market share and rate of return', *Review of Economics and Statistics*, 54, pp. 412–23.

Gale, B.J. and Branch, B.S. (1982) 'Concentration versus market share: which determines performance and why does it matter?', *Antitrust Bulletin*, 27, pp. 83–106.

Ganley, J. and Grahl, J. (1988) 'Competition and efficiency in refuse collection: a reply', *Fiscal Studies*, 8, November, pp. 42–56.

Garvin, D.A. (1983) 'Spin-offs and the new firm formation process', *California Management Review*, XXV, pp. 3–20.

Gear, M. (1984) 'Efficient refuse collection—an approach to the problem of efficient collection of household waste', *Contract Services*, November/December.

Geroski, P.A., (1985) 'Do dominant firms decline?', University of Southampton, mimeo.

Ghertman, M. (1988) 'Foreign subsidiary and parents' roles during strategic investment and divestment decisions', *Journal of International Business Studies*, 19, pp. 47–68.

Giddy, I.H. (1978) 'The demise of the product cycle in international business theory', *Columbia Journal of World Business* 13, pp. 90–7.

Gilbert, D. (1971) *Mergers and Diversification and the Theories of the Firm*, Doctoral Dissertation, Harvard University.

Gilmour, S.C. (1973) *The Divestment Decision Process*, unpublished PhD thesis, Harvard Business School.

Gold, B. (1964) 'Industry growth patterns: theory and empirical results', *Journal of Industrial Economics*, 13, pp. 53–73.

Goldberg, L.G. (1973) 'The effect of conglomerate mergers on competition', *Journal of Law and Economics*, 16, pp. 137–58.

Gordon, L.A. and Miller, D. (1976) 'A contingency framework for the design of accounting information systems', *Accounting, Organizations and Society*, 1, pp. 59–70.

Gordon, L.A. and Narayanan, V.K. (1984) 'Management accounting systems, perceived environmental uncertainty and organization structure: an empirical investigation', *Accounting, Organizations and Society*, 9, pp. 33–47.

Gorecki, P.K. (1975) 'An inter-industry analysis of diversification in the UK manufacturing sector', *Journal of Industrial Economics*, 24, pp. 131–46.

Gort, M. (1962) *Diversification and Integration in American Industry*, National Bureau of Economic Research (Princeton).

Gort, M. and Klepper, S. (1982) 'Time paths in the diffusion of product innovations', *Economic Journal*, 92, pp. 630–53.

Govindarajan, V. (1984) 'Appropriateness of accounting data in performance evaluation: an empirical examination of environmental uncertainty as an intervening variable', *Accounting, Organizations and Society*, 9, pp. 125–35.

Govindarajan, V. and Gupta, A.K. (1985) 'Linking control systems to business unit strategy: impact on performance', *Accounting Organizations and Society*, 10, pp. 51–66.

Grabowski, H.G. and Mueller, D.C. (1975) 'Life-cycle effects on corporate returns on retentions', *Review of Economics and Statistics*, 57, pp. 400–9.

Gribbin, J.D. (1976) 'The conglomerate merger', *Applied Economics*, 8, 19–36.

Grinyer, P.H., Yasai-Ardekani, M. and Al-Bazzaz, S. (1980) 'Strategy, structure, the environment and financial performance in 48 United Kingdom companies', *Academy of Management Journal*, 23, pp. 193–220.

Grossman, S. and Hart, O. (1982) 'Corporate financial structure and managerial incentives', in J.J. McCall (ed.) *The Economics of Information and Uncertainty*, University of Chicago Press.

Grosvenor, W.M. (1929) 'The seeds of progress', *Chemical Markets*, p. 23 ff.

Hakansson, N.H. (1983) 'Changes in the financial market: welfare and price effects and the basic theorems of value conservation', *Journal of Finance*, XXXVII, pp. 977–1004.

Hall, M. and Weiss, L. (1967) 'Firm size and profitability', *Review of Economics and Statistics*, 49, pp. 319–31.

Halpern, P.J. (1973) 'Empirical estimates of the amount and distribution of gains to companies in mergers', *Journal of Business*, 46, pp. 554–75.

Hamberg, D. (1963) 'Invention in the industrial research laboratory', *Journal of Political Economy*, 71, pp. 95–115.

Hamberg, D. (1966) *R & D. Essays on the Economics of Research and Development*, Random House.

Hammond, E., Helm, D. and Thompson, D.J. (1985) 'British Gas: options for privatisation', *Fiscal Studies*, 6, pp. 1–20.

Hannah, L. (1976) *The Rise of the Corporate Economy*, Johns Hopkins University Press.

Hannah, L. (1983) *The Rise of the Corporate Economy* (2nd edn), Methuen.

Hanney, J. (1986) 'Management buy-outs—an offer you can't refuse', *Omega*, 14, pp. 119–34.

Harrigan, K.R. (1980) *Strategies For Declining Businesses*, Lexington Books.

Harris, B.C. (1983) *Organisation: The Effect On Large Corporations*, University of Michigan Press.

Harris, W.B. (1958) 'Litton shoots for the moon', *Fortune*, 57, pp. 210–11.

Harris, M. and Raviv, A. (1978) 'Some results on incentive contracts with application to education, employment, health insurance and law enforcement', *American Economic Review*, 68, pp. 20–30.

Hartley, K. (1984) 'Policy towards contracting-out: the lessons of experience', *Fiscal Studies*, 5, pp. 98–105.

Hartley, K. and Huby, M. (1985) 'Contracting-out in health and local authorities:

prospects, progress and pitfalls', *Public Money*, pp. 23–6.

Harvey, E. (1968) 'Technology and the structure of organizations', *American Sociological Review*, 3, pp. 247–59.

Hassid, J. (1975) 'Recent evidence on conglomerate diversification in UK manufacturing industry', *Manchester School of Economic and Social Studies*, 43, pp. 372–95.

Hassid, J. (1977) 'Diversification and the firm's rate of growth', *Manchester School of Economic and Social Studies* 45, pp. 16–28.

Hayes, D. (1977) 'The contingency theory of management accounting', *Accounting Review*, pp. 22–39.

Heal, G.M. (1973) *The Theory of Economic Planning*, North-Holland.

Healy, P.M. (1985) 'The effect of bonus schemes on accounting decisions', *Journal of Accounting and Economics*, 7, pp. 85–108.

Hearth, D.P. and Zaima, J.K. (1986) 'Divestiture uncertainty and shareholder wealth: evidence from the USA', *Journal of Business Finance and Accounting*, 13, pp. 71–86.

Heckerman, D.G. (1975) 'Motivating managers to make decisions', *Journal of Financial Economics*, 2, pp. 273–92.

Hemenway, D. (1985) *Monitoring and Compliance: The Political Economy of Inspection*, JAI Press.

Hennart, J.F. (1986) 'What is internalisation?' *Weltwirtschaftliches Archiv*, 122, pp. 791–804.

Hicks, J.R. (1946) *Value and Capital* (2nd edn) Clarendon Press.

Hill, C.W.L. (1984) 'Organisational structure, the development of the firm and business behaviour', in J.F. Pickering and T.A.J. Cockerill (eds) *The Economic Management of the Firm*, Philip Allan.

Hill, C.W.L. (1985a) 'Internal organization and enterprise performance: some UK evidence', *Managerial and Decision Economics*, 6, pp. 210–16.

Hill, C.W.L. (1985b) 'Oliver Williamson and the M-form firm: a critical review', *Journal of Economic Issues* XIX, pp. 731–51.

Hill, C.W.L. and Hoskisson, R.E. (1987) 'Strategy and structure in the multiproduct firm', *Academy of Management Review*, 12, pp. 331–41.

Hill, C.W.L. and Pickering, J.F. (1986a) 'Divisionalization, decentralization and performance of large UK companies', *Journal of Management Studies*, 23, pp. 26–50.

Hill, C.W.L. and Pickering, J.F. (1986b) 'Conglomerate mergers, internal organization and competition policy', *International Review of Law and Economics* 6, pp. 59–75.

Hiller, J.R. (1977) 'The life cycle theory of the firm: an empirical test', Discussion Paper 77–7, International Institute of Management (Berlin).

Hiller, J.R. (1978) 'Long-run profit maximization: an empirical test', *Kyklos*, 31, pp. 475–90.

Hirsch, S. (1972) 'The United States electronics industry in international trade', in Louis T. Wells, Jr. (ed.) *The Produce Life Cycle and International Trade*, Harvard University Press, pp. 39–52.

Hirschey, M. (1986) 'Mergers, buyouts and fakeouts', *American Economic Review*, Papers and proceedings issue, 76, pp. 317–22.

Hirschleifer, J. (1956) 'On the economics of transfer pricing', *The Journal of Business*, 29, pp. 172–84.

Hirschman, A.O. (1970) *Exit, Voice and Loyalty*, Harvard University Press.

Hirst, M. (1981) 'Accounting information and the evaluation of subordinate performance: a situational approach', *Accounting Review*, pp. 771–84.

Hite, G.L. (1986) 'Discussion on Klein', *Journal of Finance*, XLI.

Hite, G.L. and Owers, J.E. (1983) 'Security price reactions around corporate spin-off announcements', *Journal of Financial Economics*, 12, pp. 409–36.

Hite, G.L., Owers, J.E. and Rogers, R.C. (1987) 'The market for interfirm asset sales: partial sell-offs and total liquidations', *Journal of Financial Economics*, 18, pp. 229–52.

Hogarty, T.F. (1970a) 'Profits from mergers: The evidence of fifty years', *St. John's Law Review*, special edition 44, pp. 378–91.

Hogarty, T.F. (1970b) 'The profitability of corporate mergers', *Journal of Business*, 43, pp. 317–27.

Holmstrom, B. (1979) 'Moral hazard and observability', *Bell Journal of Economics*, 10, pp. 74–91.

Holthausen, R.W. (1981) 'Evidence on the effect of bond covenants and management compensation contrasts', *Journal of Accounting and Economics*, 3, pp. 73–109.

Hopper, T. and Berry, A.J. (1983) 'Organizational design and management control' in T. Lowe, and J.L.J. Machin (eds), *New Perspectives in Management Control*, Macmillan.

Hopwood, A.G. (1972) 'An empirical study of the role of accounting data in performance evaluation', *Empirical Research in Accounting: Special Supplement to Journal of Accounting Research*, pp. 156–93.

Horngren, C.T. (1962) *Cost Accounting: A Managerial Emphasis*, Prentice-Hall.

Hoskisson, R.E. and Galbraith, C.S. (1985) 'The effects of quantum versus incremental M-form reorganisation on performance: a time-series exploration of intervention dynamics', *Journal of Management*, 11, pp. 55–70.

Hughes, A. and Singh, A. (1980) 'Mergers, concentration and competition in advanced capitalist economies: an international comparison', in Mueller (ed.) (1980), *The Determinants and Effects of Mergers: An International Comparison*, Oelgeschlager, Gunn & Hain, pp. 1–26.

Hunt, J. (1988) 'A survey of UK acquisitions', *London Business School*, mimeo.

Hyman, R. (1975) *Industrial Relations: A Marxist Introduction*, Macmillan.

Hymer, S.H. (1976) *The International Operations of National Firms*, Lexington Books.

Imai, K. and Itami, H. (1984) 'Interpenetration of organisation and market', *International Journal of Industrial Organization*, 161, pp. 185–310.

Imel, B. and Helmberger, P. (1971) 'Estimation of structure–profit relationships with application to the food processing sector', *American Economic Review*, 61, pp. 514–27.

Incomes Data Services (1986) 'Profit Sharing and Share Options', Study 357.

Jackson, P. (1981) *The Political Economy of Bureaucracy*, Philip Allan.

Jacquemin, A.P. and de Jong H.W. (1977) *European Industrial Organization*, Macmillan.

Jacquemin, A.P. and Lichtbuer, M.C. de (1973) 'Size structure, stability and performance of the largest British and EEC firms', *European Economic Review*, 4, pp. 393–408.

Jacquemin, A.P. and Saez W. (1976) 'A comparison of the performancé of largest European and Japanese industrial firms', *Oxford Economic Papers*. 28, pp. 271–83.

Jain, P.C. (1985) 'The effect of voluntary sell-off announcements on shareholder wealth', *Journal of Finance*, 40, pp. 209–24.

Jarrett, J.E. (1980) 'Estimating the cost of capital for a division of a firm and the allocation problem in accounting: a reply', *Journal of Business Finance on Accounting*, 7, pp. 71–3.

Jenny, F. and Weber, A.P. (1976) 'Profit rates and structural variables in French manufacturing industries', *European Economic Review*, 7, pp. 187–206.

Jenny, F. and Weber, A.P. (1980) 'France, 1962–72', in Mueller (ed.) (1980) *The Determinants and Effects of Mergers: An International Comparison*, pp. 133–62.

Jensen, M.C., (1983) 'Organisation theory and methodology', *Accounting Review*, 58, pp. 319–39.

Jensen, M.C. (1986) 'Agency costs of free cash flow, corporate finance and takeovers', *American Economic Review Papers and Proceedings*, 76, pp. 323–29.

Jensen, M.C. (1987) 'The takeover controversy: analysis and evidence', in J. Coffee, L. Lowenstein and S. Rose-Ackerman (eds) *Takeovers and Contests for Corporate Control*, Oxford University Press.

Jensen, M.C. and Meckling, W.H. (1976) 'The theory of the firm: managerial behaviour, agency costs and ownership structure', *Journal of Financial Economics*, 3, pp. 305–60.

Jensen, M.C. and Meckling, W.H. (1979) 'Rights and production functions: an application to labor-managed firms and codetermination', *Journal of Business*, 52, pp. 469–506.

Jensen, M.C. and Ruback, R.S. (1983) 'The market for corporate control', *Journal of Financial Economics*, 11, pp. 5–50.

Jensen, M.C. and Smith, C.W. Jr. (1985) 'Stockholder, manager and creditor interests: applications of agency theory', in E.I. Altman and M.G. Subrahmanyan *Recent Advances in Corporate Finance*, Richard Irwin.

Jewkes, J. *et al.* (1969) *The Sources of Invention*, Norton.

Johanson, J. and Vahlne, J.E. (1977) 'The internationalisation process of the firm—a model of knowledge development and increasing foreign market commitments', *Journal of International Business Studies*, 8, pp. 23–32.

Johnson, W.B., Magee, R.P., Nagarajan, N.J. and Newman, H.A. (1985) 'An analysis of the stock price reaction to sudden executive death: implications for the managerial labour market', *Journal of Accounting and Economics*, 7, pp. 151–74.

Jones, C.S. (1985) 'An empirical study of the role of management accounting systems following takeover or merger', *Accounting, Organisations and Society*, 10, pp. 177–200.

Jones, C.S. (1988) 'Management buy-outs and accounting control systems', British Accounting Association Annual Conference, Nottingham.

Jones, G.R. and Hill, C.W.L. (1988) 'Transactions cost analysis of strategy–structure choice', *Strategic Management Journal*, 9, 2, March/April, pp. 159–72.

Juul, M. and Walters, P.G.P. (1987) 'The internationalisation of Norwegian firms—a study of the UK experience', *Management International Review*, 27, pp. 58–66.

Kamien, M.I. and Schwartz, N.L. (1982) *Market Structure and Innovation*, Cambridge University Press.

Katz, D. and Kahn, R.L. (1966) *The Social Psychology of Organizations*, John Wiley.

Kay, J.A. and Thompson, D. (1986) 'Privatisation: a policy in search of a rationale', *Economic Journal*, 96, pp. 18–32.

Kensinger, J.W. and Martin, J.D. (1988) 'The quiet restructuring', *Journal of Applied Corporate Finance*, 1, pp. 16–25.

Khandwalla, P.N. (1972) 'The effects of different types of competition on the use of management controls', *Journal of Accounting Research*, pp. 275–85.

Kilman, P. (1983) 'The costs of organisation structure: dispelling the myths of independent divisions and organisation-wide decision-making', *Accounting, Organisations and Society*, 8, pp. 341–60.

Kim, W.S. and Sorensen, E.H. (1986) 'Evidence of the impact of the agency costs of debt on corporate debt policy', *Journal of Financial and Quantitative Analysis*, 21, pp. 131–44.

King, P. (1974) 'Strategic control of capital investment', *Journal of General Management* 2, pp. 17–28.

Klein, A. (1986) 'The timing and substance of divestiture announcements: individual, simultaneous and cumulative effects', *Journal of Finance*, XLI, pp. 685–95.

Klein, B. (1983) 'Contracting costs and residual claims', *Journal of Law and Economics*, XXVI pp. 367–74.

Klein, B. and Saff, L.F. (1985) 'The law and economics of franchise tying contracts', *Journal of Law and Economics*, 28, pp. 345–61.

Klein, B., Crawford, R. and Alchian, A. (1978) 'Vertical integration, appropriable rents and the competitive contracting process', *Journal of Law and Economics*, 21, pp. 297–326.

Klein, B.H. (1977) *Dynamic Economics*, Harvard University Press.

Klepper, S. and Graddy, E. (1984) 'Industry evolution and the determinants of market structure', mimeo, Carnegie-Mellon.

Knight, F. (1921) *Risk, Uncertainty and Profit*, Houghton Mifflin.

Knight, P.J. (1984) 'Financial discipline and structural adjustment in Yugoslavia', *World Bank Staff Working Papers*, No. 705.

Kochan, T.A., Katz, H. and McKersie, R.B. (1986) *The Transformation of American Industrial Relations*, Basic Books.

Kocka, J. (1980) 'The rise of the modern industrial enterprise in Germany', in A.D. Chandler and H. Daems *Managerial Hierarchies*, Harvard University Press.

Kogut, B. (1988) 'Joint ventures: theoretical and empirical perspectives', *Strategic Management Journal*, 9, pp. 319–32.

Kojima, K. (1973) 'A macroeconomic approach to foreign direct investment', *Hitotsubashi Journal of Economics*, 23, pp. 1–19.

Kojima, K. (1978) *Direct Foreign Investment*, Croom Helm.

Kojima, K. (1982) 'Macroeconomic versus international business approach to direct foreign investment', *Hitotsubashi Journal of Economics*, 25, pp. 1–20.

Kojima, and Ozawa, T. (1984a) 'Micro and macro economic models of direct foreign investment', *Hitotsubashi Journal of Economics*, 25, pp. 1–20.

Kojima, K. and Ozawa, T. (1984b) *Japan's General Trading Companies: Merchants of Economics Development*, OECD.

Kojima, K. and Ozawa, T. (1985) 'Towards a theory of industrial restructuring and dynamic comparative advantage', *Hitotsubashi Journal of Economics*, 26, pp. 135–45.

Kornai, J. (1985) *Contradictions and Dilemmas*, Corvine.

Kornai, J. (1986) 'The soft budget constraint', *Kyklos*, 39, pp. 3–30.

Kudla, R.J. and McInish, R.S. (1981) 'The microeconomic consequences of an involuntary corporate spin-off', *Sloan Management Review*, 22, pp. 41–6.

Kummer, D.R. (1976) 'Valuation consequences of forced divestiture', *Journal of Business and Economics*, pp. 130–36.

Kummer, D.R. and Hoffmeister J.R. (1978) 'Valuation consequences of cash tender offers', *Journal of Finance*, 33, pp. 505–16.

Kumps, A.M. and Wtterwulghe, R. (1980) 'Belgium, 1962–74', in Mueller (ed.)

(1980), *The Determinants and Effects of Mergers: An International Comparison*, pp. 67–97.

Lall, S. (1973) 'Transfer pricing by multinational manufacturing firms', *Oxford Bulletin of Economics and Statistics*, 35, pp. 173–95.

Lall, S. (1978) 'The pattern of intra-firm exports by US multinationals, *Oxford Bulletin of Economics and Statistics*, 40, pp. 20–34.

Lambert, R. and Larcker, D. (1985a) 'Executive compensation, corporate decision-making, and shareholder wealth: a review of the evidence', *Midland Corporate Finance Journal*, 2, pp. 6–22.

Lambert, R. and Larcker, D. (1985b) 'Golden parachutes, executive decision making and shareholder wealth', *Journal of Accounting and Economics*, 7, pp. 179–204.

Landon, J.H. (1983) 'Theories of vertical integration and their application to the electric utility industry', *Anti-Trust Bulletin*, 28, pp. 101–30.

Langetieg, T.C. (1978) 'An application of a three-factor performance index to measure stockholder gains from merger', *Journal of Financial Economics*, 6, pp. 365–84.

Larcker, D. (1983) 'The association between performance plan adoption and corporate capital investment', *Journal of Accounting and Economics* 5, pp. 3–30.

Lawrence, P.R. and Lorsch, J.W. (1967) *Organization and Environment: Managing Differentiation and Integration*, Harvard Graduate School of Business Administration.

Lawrimsky, M.L. (1984) 'A critical view of studies examining the performance effects on the separation of ownership from control', *Revista Internazionale di Scienze Economiche e Commerciali*, 31, pp. 312–28.

Lawton, P. (1984) 'Demergers: an assessment', *The Company Lawyer*, V, pp. 17–26.

Lazonick, W. (1979) 'Industrial relations and technical change: the case of the self-acting mule', *Cambridge Journal of Economics*, 3, pp. 231–62.

Lecraw, D.J. (1984) 'Diversification strategy and performance', *Journal of Industrial Economics*, 33, pp. 179–98.

Leech, D. (1987) 'The separation of corporate ownership and control: a new look at the evidence of Berle and Means', *Oxford Economic Papers*, 39, pp. 534–51.

Leibenstein, H. (1966) 'Allocative efficiency versus X-efficiency', *American Economic Review*, 56, pp. 392–415.

Leontiades, M. (1980) *Strategies for Diversification and Change* Little, Brown & Company.

Lerner, S.W. and Bescoby, J. (1966) 'Shop steward combine committees in the British engineering industry', *British Journal of Industrial Relations*, IV, pp. 154–64.

Lerner, S.W. and Marquand, J. (1963) 'Regional variations in earnings demand for labour and shop stewards' combine committees in the British engineering industry', *Manchester School of Economics and Social Studies*, XXI, 3, pp. 261–96.

Lev, B. (1983) 'Observations on the merger phenomenon and a review of the evidence' *Midland Corporate Finance Journal*, 1, pp. 6–16.

Lev, B. and Mandelker, G. (1972) 'The microeconomic consequences of corporate mergers', *Journal of Business*, 45, pp. 85–104.

Levine, P. and Aaronvitch, S. (1981) 'The financial characteristics of firms and theories of merger activity', *Journal of Industrial Economics* 30, pp. 149–73.

Levy, H. (1983) 'The capital asset pricing model: theory and empiricism', *Economic Journal*, 93, pp. 145–65.

Levy, H. and Sarnat, M. (1970) 'Diversification, portfolio analysis and the uneasy case for conglomerate mergers', *Journal of Finance*, 25, pp. 795–802.

Lewellen, W.G. and Huntsman, B. (1970) 'Managerial pay and corporate performance', *American Economic Review* 60, pp. 710–20.

Lillis, C.M., Narayama, C.L. and Gilman, J.L. (1976) 'Competitive advantage variation over the life cycle of a franchise', *Journal of Marketing*, pp. 77–80.

Lintner, J. (1965) 'The valuation of risk assets and the selection of risky investments in stock portfolios and capital budgets', *Review of Economics and Statistics*, 48, pp. 13–37.

Littlechild, S.C. (1986) *The Fallacy of the Mixed Economy*, IEA Hobart Paper, (2nd edn).

Lloyd, P.J. (1983) 'Why do firms produce multiple outputs?' *Journal of Economic Behaviour and Organisation* 4, pp. 41–52.

Lockerby, M.J., (1985) 'Franchise termination restrictions: a guide for practitioners and policy makers', *Anti-Trust Bulletin*, 30, pp. 791–871.

Lowe, T. and Machin, J.L.J. (eds) (1983) *New Perspectives in Management Control*, Macmillan.

Luostarinen, R. (1978) 'Internationalization process of the firm', *Working Papers in International Business 1978/1*, Helsinki School of Economics.

Luostarinen, R. (1980) *Internationalization of the Firm*, Helsinki School of Economics.

McDavid, J.C. (1985) 'The Canadian experience with privatising residential solid waste collection services', *Public Administration Review*, 45, pp. 602–8.

McFetridge, D.G. (1978) 'The efficiency implications of earnings retentions', *Review of Economics and Statistics*, 60, pp. 218–24.

Macintosh, N.B. (1981) 'A contextual model of information systems', *Accounting, Organisations and Society*, 6, pp. 39–53.

McLachlan, S. (1983) *The NFC Buy-out—The Inside Story*, Macmillan.

McManus, J.C. (1972) 'The theory of the international firm', in G. Paquet (ed.) *The Multinational Firm and the Nation State*, Macmillan.

McNally, G.M. (1980) 'Responsibility accounting and organizational control: some perspectives and prospects', *Journal of Business Finance and Accounting*, pp. 165–82.

Magenheim, E.B. and Mueller, D.C. (1987) 'On measuring the effect of acquisitions on acquiring firm shareholders, or are acquiring firm shareholders better off after an acquisitions than they were before?' in John C. Coffee, Jr., Louis Lowenstein, and Susan Rose-Ackerman (eds) *Takeovers and Contests for Corporate Control*, Oxford University Press.

Malatesta, P.H. (1983) 'The wealth effect of merger activity and the objective functions of merging firms,' *Journal of Financial Economics*, 11, pp. 155–81.

Mandelker, G. (1974) 'Risk and return: the case of merging firms' *Journal of Financial Economics*, 1, pp. 303–35.

Manne, H.M. (1965) 'Mergers and the market for corporate control', *Journal of Political Economy*, 73, pp. 110–20.

Mansfield, E. (1968) *The Economics of Technological Change*, Norton.

Mansfield, E., Rapoport, J., Schnee, J., Wagner, S. and Hamburger, M. (1971) *Research and Innovation in the Modern Corporation*, W.W. Norton.

Marcus, M. (1969) 'Profitability and size of firm: some further evidence', *Review of Economics and Statistics*, 51, pp. 104–7.

Marginson, P. (1985) 'The multidivisional firm and control over the work process'. *International Journal of Industrial Organisation*, 3, pp. 37–56.

Marginson, P. (1986) 'Labour and the Modern Corporation: Mutual Interest or Control', Warwick Papers in Industrial Relations, No. 9.

Marginson, P., Edwards, P.K., Purcell, J., Martin, R. and Sisson, K. (1988) *Beyond the Workplace: Managing Industrial Relations in Large Enterprises*,' Blackwell.

Marglin, S.A. (1963) 'The social rate of discount and the optimum rate of interest', *Quarterly Journal of Economics*, 77, pp. 95–111.

Marglin, S.A. (1974) 'What do bosses do?', *Review of Radical Political Economics*, 6, pp. 60–112.

Markham, J.W. (1955) 'Survey of the evidence and findings on mergers, business concentration and price policy', *National Bureau of Economic Research*, pp. 141–82.

Markham, J.W. (1973) *Conglomerate Enterprise and Public Policy*, Harvard Business School.

Markus, M.L. and Pfeffer, J. (1983) 'Power and the design and implementation of accounting and control systems', *Accounting, Organizations and Society*, 8, pp. 205–18.

Marris, R.L. (1964) *The Economic Theory of Managerial Capitalism*, Macmillan.

Marris, R.L. and Mueller, D.C. (1980) 'The corporation, competition, and the invisible hand', *Journal of Economic Literature*, 8, pp. 32–63.

Marshall, A. (1920) *Principles of Economics*, (1st edn, London 1890; 8th edn, New York) Macmillan.

Mason, E.S. (1939) 'Price and production policies of large scale enterprise', *American Economic Review*, Supplement, 29, 61–74.

Mathewson, G.F. and Winter, R.A. (1985) 'The economics of franchise contracts', *Journal of Law and Economics*, 28, pp. 503–26.

Mayer, C. and Meadowcroft, S., (1985) 'Selling public assets: techniques and financial implications', *Fiscal Studies*, 6, pp. 42–56.

Meeks, G. (1977) *Disappointing Marriage: A Study of the Gains from Merger*, Cambridge University Press.

Merchant, K.A. (1981) 'The design of the corporate budgeting system: influences on managerial behaviour and performance', *Accounting Review*, LVI, pp. 813–29.

Merchant, K.A. (1984) 'Influences on departmental budgeting: an empirical examination of a contingency model', *Accounting, Organizations and Society*, 9, pp. 291–307.

Merchant, K.A. (1985a) 'Organizational controls and discretionary program decision making: a field study', *Accounting, Organizations and Society*, 10, pp. 67–85.

Merchant, K.A. (1985b) 'Budgeting and the propensity to create budgetary slack', *Accounting, Organizations and Society*, 10, pp. 201–10.

Merchant, K.A. (1986) *Control in Organizations*, Pitman.

Miles, J.A. and Rosenfeld, J.D. (1983) 'The effect of voluntary spin-off announcements on shareholder wealth', *Journal of Finance*, XXXVIII, pp. 1597–606.

Miles, R.E. and Snow, C. (1986), 'Network organisations: new concepts for new forms', *California Management Review*.

Miller, D. (1982) 'Evolution and revolution: a quantum view of structural change in organisations', *Journal of Management Studies*, 19, pp. 131–52.

Miller, R.A. (1969) 'Market structure and industrial performance: relation of profit rates to concentration, advertising intensity and diversity', *Journal of Industrial Economics*, 17, pp. 104–18.

Mills, A. (1987) 'The neglected spin-out', *Acquisitions Monthly*, pp. 36–8.

Mintzberg, H. (1979) *The Structuring of Organizations*, Prentice-Hall.

Mirlees, J.A. (1976) 'The optimal structure of incentives and authority within an organisation', *Bell Journal of Economics*, 7, pp. 105–31.

Modigliani, F. and Miller, M.H. (1958) 'The cost of capital, corporation finance and the theory of investment', *American Economic Review*, 48, pp. 261–97.

Monsen, R.J. Jr. and Downs, A. (1965) 'A theory of large managerial firms', *Journal of Political Economy*, 73, pp. 221–36.

Monteverde, K. and Teece, D.J. (1982a) 'Appropriable rents and quasi-vertical integration', *Journal of Law and Economics*, 25, pp. 321–8.

Monteverde, K. and Teece, D.J. (1982b) 'Supplier switching costs and vertical integration in the automobile industry', *Bell Journal of Economics*, 13, pp. 207–13.

Montgomery, C.A., Thomas, A.R. and Kamath, R. (1984) 'Divestiture, market valuation and strategy', *Academy of Management Journal*, 27, pp. 830–40.

Montgomery, D. (1979) *Workers' Control in America*, Cambridge University Press.

Morvan, Y. (1972) *La Concentration de L'Industrie en France*, Colin.

Mueller, D.C. (1972) 'A life cycle theory of the firm', *Journal of Industrial Economics* 20, pp. 199–219.

Mueller, D.C. (1976) 'Information, mobility and profit', *Kyklos*, 29, pp. 419–48.

Mueller, D.C. (1977a) 'The persistence of profits above the norm,' *Economica*, 44, pp. 369–80.

Mueller, D.C. (1977b) 'The effects of conglomerate merger: a survey of the empirical evidence', IIM Berlin, mimeo.

Mueller, D.C. (ed.) (1980) *The Determinants and Effects of Mergers: An International Comparison*, Oelgeschlager, Gunn & Hain.

Mueller, D.C. (1984) 'Further reflections on the invisible-hand theorem', in P. Wiles and G. Rourk, (eds) *Economics in Disarray*, Blackwell.

Mueller, D.C. (1985) 'Mergers and market share,' *Review of Economics and Statistics*, 67, pp. 259–67.

Mueller, D.C. (1986) *Profits in the Long Run*, Cambridge University Press.

Mueller, D.C. (1987) *The Corporation: Growth, Diversification and Mergers* (Harwood Academic Publishers.)

Mueller, D.C. and Tilton, J.E. (1969) 'Research and development costs as a barrier to entry', *Canadian Journal of Economics*, 2, pp. 570–79.

Mulley, C. and Wright, M. (1986) 'Buy-outs and the privatisation of National Bus', *Fiscal Studies*, 7, pp. 1–24.

Murphy, K.J. (1985) 'Corporate performance and managerial remuneration: an empirical analysis, *Journal of Accounting and Economics*, 7, pp. 11–42.

National Audit Office (1987) 'Competitive tendering for support services in the NHS', *HC318*, HMSO.

Nees, D. (1981) 'Increase your divestment effectiveness', *Strategic Management Journal*, 2, pp. 119–30.

Nelson, R.L. (1959) '*Merger Movements in American Industry, 1895–1956*', Princeton University Press.

Nelson, R.R. and Winter, S.G. (1982) *An Evolutionary Theory of Economic Change*, Harvard University Press.

Nicholas, S.J. (1986) 'Multinationals, transaction costs and choice of institutional form', *University of Reading Discussion Papers in International Investment and Business Studies*, No. 97.

Nickell, S. and Wadhwani, S.B. (1987) 'Myopia, the "dividend puzzle", and share prices', *Discussion Paper No. 272*, Centre for Labour Economics, London School of Economics, February.

Norton, S.W. (1988) 'An empirical look at franchising as an organisational form', *Journal of Business*, 61, pp. 197–218.

O'Brien, D.P. (1978) 'Mergers—time to turn the tide', *Lloyds Bank Review*, October, pp. 32–44.

O'Brien, D.P. (1984) 'The evolution of the firm', in F. Stephen (ed.) *Firms, Organization and Labour*, Macmillan.

O'Brien, D.P. (1986) 'Divestiture—the case of AT & T' in J. Coyne and M. Wright (eds) *Divestment and Strategic Change*, Philip Allan.

Otley, D.T. (1978) 'Budget use and managerial performance', *Journal of Accounting Research*, 16, pp. 122–49.

Otley, D.T. (1980) 'The contingency theory of management accounting: achievement and prognosis', *Accounting, Organizations and Society*, 5, pp. 413–28.

Otley, D.T. (1984) 'Management accounting and organization theory: a review of their interrelationship' in R.W. Scapens, D.T. Otley and R.J. Lister, *Management Accounting, Organizational Theory and Capital Budgeting: Three Surveys*, Macmillan/ESRC.

Ouchi, W.G. (1980) 'Markets bureaucracies and clans', *Administrative Science Quarterly*, 25, pp. 129–41.

Ouchi, W.G. (1984) *The M-Form Society*, Addison-Wesley.

Ozanne, R. (1967) *A Century of Labor-Management Relations*, University of Wisconsin Press.

Panzar, J.C. and Willig, R.D. (1981) 'Economies of scope', *American Economic Review* (Papers and Proceedings), 71, pp. 268–72.

Parry, T.G. (1985) 'Internalisation as a general theory of foreign direct investment', *Weltwirtschaftliches, Archiv.*, Vol. 121, pp. 564–69.

Pavan, J. (1972) *The Strategy and Structure of Italian Enterprise*, unpublished DBA thesis, Graduate School of Business Administration, Harvard University.

Payne, P. (1967), 'Emergence of the large scale company in Great Britain, 1870–1914', *Economic History Review*, 20, pp. 519–42.

Penrose, E.T. (1959) *The Theory of the Growth of the Firm*, Basil Blackwell.

Perrow, C. (1967) 'A framework for the comparative analysis of organizations', *American Sociological Review*, pp. 194–208.

Pfeffer, J. (1981) *Power in Organizations*, Pitman.

Pfeffer, J. (1982) *Organizations and Organization Theory*, Pitman.

Pfeffer, J., and Salancik, G.R. (1978) *The External Control of Organisations: A Resource Dependence Perspective*, Harper and Row.

Pienkos, A. (1986) 'Organizational contradiction and policy inertia in Yugoslav institutional evolution', *Journal of Economic Issues*, 20, pp. 583–92.

Pike, R.H. (1983a) 'A review of recent trends in formal capital budgeting process', *Accounting and Business Research*, 51, pp. 201–8.

Pike, R.H. (1983b) *A Major Survey of the Investment Practices in large Companies*, Institute of Cost and Management Accountants Occasional paper.

Piper, J. (1978) 'Determinants of financial control systems for multiple retailers: some case study evidence', unpublished working paper, University of Loughborough.

Plasschaert, S.R.F. (1981) 'The multiple motivations for transfer pricing modulations in multinational enterprises and governmental counter measures: an attempt at clarification', *Management International Review*, 21, pp. 49–63.

Poensgen, O.H. (1974) 'Organisational structure, context and performance', Working Paper 74–49, European Institute for Advanced Studies in Management.

Poensgen, O.H. (1980) 'Between market and hierarchy', *Zeitschrift für der Gesamte Staatswissenschaft*, 136, pp. 209–25.

Polli, R. and Cook, V., (1969) 'Validity of the product life cycle', *Journal of Business*, 42, pp. 385–400.

Porter, M.E. (1976) 'Please note location of nearest exit', *California Management Review*, XIX, pp. 21–33.

Porter, M.E. (1980) *Competitive Strategy*, The Free Press.

Porter, M.E. (1986a) 'The trouble with takeovers', *Financial Times*, 8 December, p. 14.

Porter, M.E. (ed.) (1986b) *Competition in Global Industries*, Harvard Business School Press.

Prais, S.J. (1976) *The Evolution of Giant Firms in Britain: A Study of the Growth and Concentration in British Manufacturing 1909–1970*, Cambridge University Press (for the National Institute of Economic and Social Research).

Prais, S.J. (1981) *The Evolution of Giant Firms in Britain*, Cambridge University Press.

Pratt, J. and Zeckhauser, R.J. (eds) (1987) *Principals and Agents: The Structure of Business*, Harvard Business School Press.

Price, R. and Bain, G.S. (1983) 'Union growth in Britain: retrospect and prospect', *British Journal of Industrial Relations*, XXI, pp. 46–68.

Pryke, R. (1987) 'Privatising electricity supply', *Fiscal Studies*, 8, 75–88.

Pugh, D.S. (1984) *Organization Theory: Selected Readings* (2nd edn), Penguin.

Pugh, D.S. and Hickson, D.J. (1976) *Organizational Structure and Its Context*, Saxon House.

Pugh, D.S. and Hinings, C.R. (1976) *Organizational Structure: Extensions and Replications*, Saxon House.

Pugh, D.S. and Payne, R.L. (1977) *Organizational Behaviour in Its Context*, Saxon House.

Putterman, L. (1986) *The Economic Nature of the Firm: A Reader*, Cambridge University Press.

Qualls, D. (1974) 'Stability and persistence of economic profit margins in highly concentrated industries', *Southern Economic Journal*, 40, pp. 604–12.

Radner, R. (1986) 'The internal economy of large firms', *Economic Journal*, 96, (supplement), pp. 1–22.

Ravenscraft, D.J. (1983) 'Structure–profit relationships at the line of business and industry level', *Review of Economics and Statistics*, 65, pp. 22–31.

Ravenscraft, D.J. and Scherer, F.M., (1986), *Mergers, Sell-Offs and Economic Efficiency*, Brookings Institute.

Reid, S.R. (1968) *Mergers, Managers and the Economy*, McGraw-Hill.

Reinganum, J.F. (1985) 'Innovation and industry evolution', *Quarterly Journal of Economics*, 100, pp. 81–99.

Révész, G. (1984) 'Enterprise business partnerships (VGMK) in Hungary—a case study', *Acta Oeconomica*, 33, pp. 337–59.

Rhoades, S.A. (1973) 'The effect of diversification on industry profit performance in 241 manufacturing industries,' *Review of Economics and Statistics*, 55, pp. 146–55.

Rhoades, S.A. (1974) 'A further evaluation of the effect of diversification on industry profit performance', *Review of Economics and Statistics*, 56, pp. 557–9.

Rice, A.K. (1958) *The Enterprise and Its Environment*, Tavistock Institute.

Richardson, G.B. (1972) 'The organisation of industry', *Economic Journal*, 82, pp. 883–96.

Ricketts, M. (1987) *The Economics of Business Enterprises: New Approaches to the Firm*, Wheatsheaf.

Rieser, C. (1963) 'When the crowd goes one way Litton goes the other', *Fortune*, May, 67, pp. 224–5.

Roberts, G.S. and Viscione, J.A. (1981) 'Captive finance subsidiaries and the M-form hypothesis', *Bell Journal of Economics*, 12, pp. 285–95.

Robinson, J. (1933) *The Economics of Imperfect Competition*, Macmillan.

Roll, R. (1977) 'A critique of the asset pricing theory's tests', *Journal of Financial Economics*, 4, pp. 129–76.

Rosen, S. (1972) 'Learning by experience as joint production', *Quarterly Journal of Economics*, 86, pp. 366–82.

Rosenfeld, J. (1984) 'Additional evidence on the relation between divestiture announcements and shareholder wealth', *Journal of Finance*, 39, pp. 1437–48.

Ross, S. (1973) 'The economic theory of agency: the principal's problem', *American Economic Review*, 62, pp. 134–9.

Rowley, C.K. (1973) *Antitrust and Economic Efficiency*, Macmillan Studies in Economics.

Rowley, C.K. and Peacock, A. (1974) *Welfare Economics: A Liberal Restatement*, Martin Robertson.

Royal Commission on Trade Unions and Employers' Associations (1968) *Report*, Cmnd. 3623, HMSO.

Rubin, P.H. (1978) 'The theory of the firm and the structure of the franchise contract', *Journal of Law and Economics*, 21, pp. 223–33.

Rugman, A.M. (1980) 'Internationalisation as a general theory of foreign direct investment: a reappraisal of the literature', *Weltwirtschaftliches Archiv.*, VR116, pp. 365–79.

Rugman, A.M. (1981) *Inside the Multinationals*, Croom Helm.

Rugman, A.M. (1985) 'Internalisation is still a general theory of foreign direct investment', *Weltwirtschaftliches Archiv.*, VR 121, pp. 570–5.

Rugman, A.M. and Eden, L. (1985) *Multinational Enterprises and Transfer Pricing*, Croom Helm.

Rukeyser, W.S. (1968) 'Litton down to earth', *Fortune*, 77, p. 138ff.

Rumelt, R.P. (1974) *Strategy, Structure and Economic Performance*, Division of Research, Graduate School of Business Administration, Harvard University.

Rumelt, R.P. (1982) 'Diversification strategy and profitability', *Strategic Management Journal*, 3, pp. 359–70.

Russell, R. (1985) 'Employee ownership and internal governance', *Journal of Economic Behaviour and Organization*, 6, pp. 217–41.

Ryden, B. and Edberg, J.O. (1980) 'Large mergers in Sweden, 1962–1976', in Mueller (ed.) (1980), pp. 193–226.

Sacks, S.R. (1983) *Self-Management and Efficiency: The Large Corporation in Yugoslavia*, George Allen & Unwin.

Samuels, J.M. and Smyth, D.J. (1968) 'Profit, variability of profits and firm size', *Economica*, 35, pp. 127–39.

Scapens, R.W. and Sale, J.T. (1981) 'Performance measurement and formal capital expenditure controls in divisionalised companies', *Journal of Business Finance and Accounting*, 8, pp. 389–419.

Schall, L.D., Sundem, G.L. and Geijsbeek, W.R. (1978) 'Survey and analysis of capital budgeting methods', *Journal of Finance*, 33, pp. 281–287.

Scherer, F.M. (1980) *Industrial Market Structure and Economic Performance*, (second edn), Rand McNally.

Scherer, F.M. (1984) 'Mergers, sell-offs and managerial behaviour', paper presented to the 11th EARIE Conference, Fontainebleau, August 1984.

Scherer, F.M. and Ravenscraft, D.J. (1984) 'Growth by diversification: entrepreneurial behavior in large-scale United States enterprises', *Zeitschrift für Nationalekonomie*, pp. 119–218.

Schipper, K. and Smith, A. (1983) 'Effects of recontracting on shareholder wealth: the case of voluntary spin-offs', *Journal of Financial Economics*, 12, pp. 437–67.

Schmalensee, R. (1982) 'Product differentiation advantages of pioneering brands,' *American Economic Review*, 72, pp. 349–66.

Schonberger, R.J. and Gilbert, J.P. (1983) 'Just-in-time purchasing: a challenge for US industry', *California Management Review*, XXVI, pp. 54–68.

Schumpeter, J.A. (1934) *The Theory of Economic Development*, Harvard University Press.

Schwarz, M. and Thompson, E.A. (1986) 'Divisonalization and entry deterrence', *Quarterly Journal of Economics*, 101, pp. 307–21.

Scott, W.R. (1981) 'Developments in organization theory 1960–1980', *American Behavioural Scientist*, pp. 407–22.

Seligman, D. and Wise, T.A. (1966) 'How Litton keeps it up—the view from the inside', *Fortune*, September, 74, p. 152.

Shaban, R.A. (1987) 'Testing between competing models of sharecropping', *Journal of Political Economy*, 95, pp. 893–920.

Sharpe, W.F. (1964) 'Capital asset prices: a theory of market equilibrium under conditions of risk', *Journal of Finance*, 19, pp. 425–42.

Shaw, R.W., (1973) 'Investment and competition from boom to recession: a case study in the process of competition—the dry cleaning industry', *Journal of Industrial Economics*, 21, pp. 308–24.

Shepherd, W.G. (1972) 'The elements of market structure', *Review of Economics and Statistics*, 54, pp. 25–37.

Shepherd, W.G. (1975) *The Treatment of Market Power*, Columbia University Press.

Shiller, R.J. (1981) 'Do stock prices move too much to be justified by subsequent changes in dividends?', *American Economic Review*, 71, pp. 421–36.

Sicherman, N.W. and Pettway, R.H. (1987) 'Acquisition of divested assets and shareholders wealth', *Journal of Finance*, 42, pp. 1261–74.

Silverman, D. (1970) *The Theory of Organisations*, Heinemann.

Simon, H.A. (1955) 'A behavioural model of rational choice', *Quarterly Journal of Economics*, 69, pp. 99–118.

Singh, A. (1971) *Takeovers*, Cambridge University Press.

Singh, A. and Whittington, G. (1968) *Growth, Profitability and Valuation*, Cambridge University Press.

Sirc, L. (1979) *The Yugoslav Economy Under Self-Management*, Macmillan.

Sisson, K. (1987) *The Management of Collective Bargaining: An International Comparison*, Blackwell.

Smiley, R.H. and Ravid, A.S. (1983) 'The importance of being first: learning price and strategy', *Quarterly Journal of Economics*, 98, pp. 353–62.

Smirlock, M., Gilligan, T. and Marshall, W. (1984) 'Tobin's q and the structure–performance relationship', *American Economic Review*, 74, pp. 1051–60.

Smith, A. (1937) *The Wealth of Nations*, Random House.

Smith, C. and Warner, J.B. (1979) 'On financial contracting: an analysis of bond covenants', *Journal of Financial Economics* 7, pp. 117–61.

Smith, R.L. (1982) 'Franchise regulation: an economic analysis of state restrictions on automobile distribution', *Journal of Law and Economics*, 25, pp. 125–54.

Smith, V.L. (1970) 'Corporate financial theory under uncertainty', *Quarterly Journal of Economics*, 84G, pp. 451–71.

Smyth, D.J., Boyes, W.J. and Peseau, D.E. (1975) *Size, Growth, Profits and Executive Compensation in the Large Corporation*, Holmes & Meier.

Solomons, D. (1965) *Divisional Performance: Measurement and Control*, Richard D. Irwin.

Spence, A.M. (1974) *Market Signalling; Information Transfer in Hiring and Related Screening Processes*, Harvard University Press.

Spence, A.M. (1981) 'The learning curve and competition', *Bell Journal of Economics*, 12, pp. 49–70.

Spence, M. and Zeckhauser, R. (1971) 'Insurance, information and individual action', *American Economic Review*, 61, pp. 119–32.

Spicer, B.H. and Ballew, V. (1983) 'Management accounting systems and the economics of internal organisation', *Accounting, Organisations and Society*, 8, pp. 73–96.

Srivastava, P. (1983) 'A typology of organisational learning systems', *Journal of Management Studies* 20, pp. 1–35.

Stark, D. (1985) 'The micro politics of the firm and the macro politics of reform: new forms of workplace bargaining in Hungarian enterprises', in P. Evans, D. Rueschemeyer and E.H. Stephens, (eds) *States vs. Markets in the Work-System*, Sage Publications.

Steer, P.S. (1973) 'An investigation into the managerial organisation of firms', unpublished M.A. dissertation, University of Warwick.

Steer, P. and Cable, J. (1978) 'Internal organization and profit: an empirical analysis of large UK companies', *Journal of Industrial Economics*, XXVII, pp. 13–30.

Steiner, P.O. (1975) *Mergers: Motives, Effects, Policies*, University of Michigan Press.

Stekler, H.O. (1963) *Profitability and Size of Firm*, University of California.

Stephen, F. (1984) *The Economic Analysis of Producers' Cooperatives* Macmillan.

Stewart, G.B. and Glassman, D. (1988), 'The motives of corporate restructuring', *Journal of Applied Corporate Finance*, 1, pp. 85–99.

Stigler, G. (1951) 'The division of labour is limited by the extent of market', *Journal of Political Economy*, 59, pp. 189–200.

Stigler, G. (1950) 'Monopoly and oligopoly by merger', *American Economic Review*, 40, pp. 23–34.

Stigler, G.J. (1963) *Capital and Rates of Return in Manufacturing*, Princeton University Press.

Stiglitz, J.E. (1985) 'Credit markets and the control of capital', *Journal of Money, Credit and Banking*, 17, pp. 133–52.

Stopford, M. and Wells, T. Jr. (1972) *Managing the Multinational Enterprise: Organization of the Firm and Ownership of the Subsidiaries*, Longman.

Strong, N. and Walker, M. (1987) *Information and Capital Markets*, Blackwell.

Strong, N. and Waterson, M. (1987) 'Principals, agents and information', in R. Clarke and T. McGuinness (eds), *The Economics of the Firm*, pp. 18–41, Blackwell.

Sussman, J.A. (1979) 'Making it to the top: a career profile of the senior executive', *Management Review*, 68, pp. 14–21.

Swann, D. (1979) *Competition and Consumer Protection*, Penguin.

Teece, D.J. (1980a) 'The diffusion of an administrative innovation', *Management Science*, 26, pp. 464–70.

Teece, D.J. (1980b) 'Economies of scope and the scope of the enterprise', *Journal of Economic Behavior and Organisation*, pp. 223–4.

Teece, D.J. (1981) 'Internal organization and economic performance: an empirical analysis of the profitability of principal firms', *Journal of Industrial Economics*, 30, pp. 173–200.

Teece, D.J. (1983) 'Technological and organisational factors in the theory of the multinational enterprise', in Mark Casson (ed.) *The Growth of International Business*, George Allen & Unwin.

Teece, D.J. (1986) 'Transaction cost economics and the multinational enterprise: an assessment', *Journal of Economic Behaviour and Organisation*, 7, pp. 21–45.

Teece, D.J. (1988) *Theory of the Firm and Internal Organization*, Harwood Academic Publishers.

Tehranian, H. and Waegelein, J.F. (1985) 'Market reaction to short-term executive compensation plan adoption', *Journal of Accounting and Economics*, 7, pp. 131–44.

Thanheiser, H.T. (1976) 'Strategy and structure in Germany', in G.P. Dyas and H.T. Thanheiser *The Emerging European Enterprise*, Macmillan.

Thomas, H. and Logan, C. (1982) *Mondragon: An Economic Analysis*, George Allen & Unwin.

Thompson, J.D. (1967) *Organisations in Action*, McGraw-Hill.

Thompson, R.S. (1980) 'Quality control under regulation: a comment on the prior report', *Applied Economics*, 12, pp. 357–62.

Thompson, R.S. (1981) 'Internal organisation and profit: a note' *Journal of Industrial Economics*, 30, pp. 201–11.

Thompson, R.S. (1983a) 'Diffusion of the M-form structure in the UK: rate of imitation, inter-firm and inter-industry differences' *International Journal of Industrial Organisation,* 1, pp. 297–315.

Thompson, R.S. (1983b) 'M-form adoption and M-form performance: an empirical investigation,' *Recherches Economiques de Louvain*, 49, pp. 3–24.

Thompson, R.S. (1988) 'Management buyouts: a review of trends', in B. de Caires and M. Wright (eds) *Management Buyouts*, Euromoney Publications.

Thompson, R.S. and Wright, M. (1986) 'Management buy-outs, debt finance and bonding', *Centre for Management Buy-Out Research*, Occ. Paper No. 2.

Thompson, R.S. and Wright, M. (1987) 'Markets to hierarchies and back again: the implications of management buy-outs for factor supply', *Journal of Economic Studies*, 14, pp. 5–22.

Thompson, R.S. and Wright, M. (1988) 'Bonding, agency costs and management buyouts: a note' *Bulletin of Economic Research* (forthcoming).

Thorelli, H.B. (1986) 'Networks: between markets and hierarchies', *Strategic Management Journal*, 7, pp. 37–51.

Tiessen, P. and Waterhouse, J.H. (1978) 'The contingency theory of management accounting: a comment', *Accounting Review*, 53, pp. 523–9.

Tilton, J.E. (1971) *International diffusion of technology: the case of semiconductors*, Brookings Institution.

Tinbergen, J. (1967) 'Some suggestions on a modern theory of the optimum regime', in C.H. Feinstein (ed.) *Socialism and Economic Growth*, Cambridge University Press.

Trist, E.A. and Bamforth, K.W. (1951) 'Some social and psychological consequences of the Longwall method of coal-getting', *Human Relations*, 4, pp. 6–38, reprinted in D.S. Pugh (1984).

Tullock, G. (1965) *The Politics of Bureaucracy*, Public Affairs Press.

Utterback, J.M., (1979) 'The dynamics of product and process innovation in industry', in Christopher T. Hill and James M. Utterback (eds) *Technological Innovation for a Dynamic Economy*, Pergamon Press.

Utton, M.A. (1974) 'On measuring the effects of industrial mergers', *Scottish Journal of Political Economy*, 21, pp. 13–28.

Vernon, R. (1966) 'International Investment and International Trade in the Product Cycle', *Quarterly Journal of Economics*, 80, pp. 190–207.

Vickers, J. and Yarrow, G. (1985) *Privatisation and the Natural Monopolies*, Public Policy Centre.

Vickers, J. and Yarrow, G. (1988) *Privatization: An Economic Analysis*, MIT Press.

Wainwright, H. and Elliot, D. (1982) *The Lucas Plan: A New Trade Unionism in the Making?* Allison and Busby.

Waterhouse, J.H. and Tiessen, P. (1978) 'A contingency theory framework for management accounting systems research', *Accounting, Organizations and Society*, 3, pp. 65–76.

Waterson, M. (1983) 'Economies of scope within market frameworks', *International Journal of Industrial Organization*, 1, pp. 223–37.

Waterson, M. (1984) *The Theory of the Industry*, Cambridge University Press.

Waterson, M. (1988) *Regulation of the Firm and Natural Monopoly*, Basil Blackwell.

Watts, R.L. and Zimmerman, J.L. (1983) 'Agency problems, auditing, and the theory of the firm: some evidence', *Journal of Law and Economics*, 26, pp. 613–33.

Weiss, L.W. and Pascoe, G. (1983) 'The extent and permanence of market dominance', paper presented at EARIE meeting, August, 1983.

Welch, L. and Wiedersheim-Paul, F. (1980a) 'Domestic expansion—internationalization at home' *South Carolina Essays in International Business*, 2.

Welch, L. and Wiedersheim-Paul, F. (1980b) 'Initial exports—a marketing failure' *Journal of Management Studies*, 17, pp. 333–44.

Weston, J.F. (1970) 'The nature and significance of conglomerate firms', *St. John's Law Review*, special edition 44, pp. 66–80.

Weston, J.F. and Mansinghka, S.K. (1971) 'Tests of the efficiency performance of conglomerate firms', *Journal of Finance*, 26, pp. 919–36.

White, R.G. and Poynter, T.A. (1984) 'Strategies for foreign-owned subsidiaries in Canada', *Business Quarterly*.

Whittington, G. (1971) *The Prediction of Profitability and Other Studies of Company Behavior*, Cambridge University Press.

Whittington, G. (1972) 'The profitability of retained earnings', *Review of Economics and Statistics*, 54, pp. 152–60.

Whittington, G. (1978) 'The profitability of alternative sources of finance—some further evidence', *Review of Economics and Statistics*, 60, pp. 632–4.

Wiedersheim-Paul, F. (1972) *Uncertainty and Economic Distance*, Uppsala Studies in International Business, Uppsala University.

Wilkins, M. (1970) *The Emergence of Multinational Enterprise: American Business Abroad from the Colonial Era to 1914*, Harvard University Press.

Wilkins, M. (1974) *The Maturing of Multinational Enterprise: American Business Abroad from 1914 to 1970*, Harvard University Press.

Williamson, O.E. (1964) *The Economics of Discretionary Behaviour: Managerial Objectives in a Theory of the Firm*, Prentice-Hall.

Williamson, O.E. (1967) 'Hierarchical control and optimum firm size', *Journal of Political Economy*, 75, pp. 123–38.

Williamson, O.E., (1968a) 'Economies as an antitrust defense: the welfare trade-offs', *American Economic Review*, 58, pp. 18–36.

Williamson, O.E., (1968b) 'Economies as an antitrust defense: correction and reply', *American Economic Review*, 58, pp. 1372–6.

Williamson, O.E. (1970) *Corporate Control and Business Behaviour: An Inquiry into the Effects of Organization Form on Enterprise Behaviour*, Prentice-Hall.

Williamson, O.E. (1971a) 'Managerial discretion, organisation form and the multi-division hypothesis', in R. Marris and A. Wood (eds) *The Corporate Economy*, pp. 343–88, Harvard University Press.

Williamson, O.E. (1971b) 'The vertical integration of production: market failure considerations', *American Economic Review: Papers and Proceedings*, 27, pp. 112–23.

Williamson, O.E. (1972) 'Antitrust enforcement and the modern corporation' in Fuchs, V.R. (ed.) *Policy Issues and Essays on Research Opportunities in Industrial Organisation*, N.B.E.R.

Williamson, O.E. (1975) *Markets and Hierarchies: Analysis and Antitrust Implications*, Free Press.

Williamson, O.E. (1976) 'Franchise bidding for natural monopolies in general and with respect to CATV', *Bell Journal of Economics*, 7, pp. 73–104.

Williamson, O.E. (1979) 'Transaction cost economics: the governance of contractual relations', *Journal of Law and Economics*, 22, pp. 233–62.

Williamson, O.E. (1980) 'The organisation of work: a comparative institutional assessment', *Journal of Economic Behaviour and Organisation*, 1, pp. 5–38.

Williamson, O.E. (1981) 'The modern corporation: origins, evolution, and attributes', *Journal of Economic Literature*, 19, pp. 1537–68.

Williamson, O.E. (1984) 'Efficient labour organization', in F. Stephen (ed.). *Firms, Organization and Labour: Approaches to the Economics of Work Organization*, Macmillan.

Williamson, O.E. (1985) *The Economic Institutions of Capitalism: Firms, Markets and Relational Contracting*, Free Press.

Williamson, O.E. (1986) *Economic Organisation: Firms, Markets and Policy Control*, Wheatsheaf Books.

Williamson, O.E. (1987) *Antitrust Economics: Mergers, Contracting and Strategic Behavior*, Basil Blackwell.

Williamson, O.E. and Bhargava, N. (1972) 'Assessing and classifying the internal structure and control apparatus of the modern corporation', in K.G. Cowling (ed.) *Market Structure and Corporate Behaviour*, Gray-Mills.

Williamson, O.E. and Ouchi, W.G. (1983) 'The markets and hierarchies programme of research: origins, implications, prospects', in Arthur Francis, Jeremy Turk and Paul Willman (eds) (1983) *Power, Efficiency and Institutions*, Heinemann.

Williamson, O.E., Wachter, M.L. and Harris, J.E. (1975) 'Understanding the employment relations: the analysis of idiosyncratic change', *Bell Journal of Economics*, 6, pp. 250–78.

Willman, P. (1982) 'Opportunism in labour contracting: an application of the organisational failures framework', *Journal of Economic Behaviour and Organisation*, 3, pp. 83–98.

Willman, P. (1983) 'The Organisational Failures Framework and Industrial Sociology', in A. Francis, J. Turk and P. Willman (eds) *Power, Efficiency and Institutions*, Heinemann.

Winn, D.N. (1977) 'On the relations between rates of return, risk, and market structure', *Quarterly Journal of Economics*, 91, pp. 157–64.

Woodward, J. (1958) *Management and Technology*, HMSO.

Woodward, J. (1965) *Industrial Organisation: Theory and Practice*, Oxford University Press.

Worcester, D.A. (1957) 'Why do dominant firms decline?', *Journal of Political Economy*, 65, pp. 338–47.

Wright, M. (1985) 'Divestment and organisational adaptation', *European Management Journal*, 3, pp. 85–93.

Wright, M. (1986a) 'Demergers', in J. Coyne and M. Wright (eds) *Divestment and Strategic Change*, Philip Allan.

Wright, M. (1986b) 'The make–buy decision and managing markets: the case of management buy-outs', *Journal of Management Studies*, 23, pp. 443–64.

Wright, M. (1986c) 'Housing finance and consumer credit', in R.L. Carter *et al.* (eds) *Personal Financial Markets*, Philip Allan.

Wright, M. (1987) 'Government divestments and the control of natural monopolies in the UK: the case of British Gas', *Energy Policy*, 15, pp. 193–216.

Wright, M., Chiplin, B. and Coyne, J. (1988) 'The market for corporate control: the divestment option', in J.A. Kay and J. Fairburn (eds) *Mergers and Merger Policy*, IFS/Oxford University Press.

Wright, M. and Coyne, J. (1985) *Management Buy-Outs in British Industry*, Croom Helm.

Wright, M., Coyne, J. and Lockley, H. (1984) 'Management buy-outs and trade unions: dispelling the myths', *Industrial Relations Journal*, 15, pp. 45–52.

Wright, M., Coyne, J. and Mills, A. (1987) *Spicer and Pegler's Management Buy-Outs*, Woodhead-Faulkner.

Wright, M., Coyne, J. and Robbie, K. (1987a) 'Management buy-outs in Britain', *Long Range Planning*, 20, pp. 38–49.

Wright, M., Coyne, J. and Robbie, K. (1987b) 'Trends in management buy-outs', in L. Blackstone (ed.) *Guide to Management Buy-Outs* (4th edn), EIU.

Wright, M., Coyne, J., Robbie, K. and Lloyd, S. (1987) *Trends in UK Buy-Outs*, CMBOR/Venture Economics, July.

Wright, M., Mulley, C. and Robbie, K. (1988) 'The initial impact of buying-out—the case of National Bus', mimeo.

Wright, M., Rhodes, D.J. and Jarrett, M. (1983) 'Growth, survival and control in small manufacturing systems', *European Journal of Operational Research*, 14, pp. 40–52.

Wright, M., Robbie, K. and Coyne, J. (1987) *Flotations of Management Buy-Outs*, CMBOR/Spicer and Pegler Associates, May.

Wright, M., Robbie, K., Coyne, J. (1988) 'Managing management buy-outs', *Management Decision* (Forthcoming).

Wright, M., Robbie, K., and Thompson, S. (1988) 'On the financial, accounting and organisational implications of management buyouts', mimeo.

Wright, M. and Thompson, R.S. (1986) 'Vertical disintegration and the life cycle of industries and firms', *Managerial and Decision Economics*, 7, pp. 141–44.

Wright, M. and Thompson, R.S. (1987) 'Divestment and the control of divisionalised firms', *Accounting and Business Research*, 67, pp. 259–67.

Wrigley, L. (1970) 'Divisional autonomy and diversification', unpublished D.B.A. thesis, Harvard Business School.

Wrigley, L. (1976) 'Conglomerate growth in Canada', School of Business Administration, University of Western Ontario, mimeo.

Yannopoulos, G.N. (1983) 'The growth of transnational banking', in M. Casson (ed.) *The Growth of International Business*, George Allen & Unwin.

Yasuki, H. (1982) 'Internal organisation and corporate groupings in Japan', *Kansai University Review of Economics and Business*, 11, pp. 29–48.

Yoshihara, H., Sakuma, A., Itami, H. and Kagono, T. (1981) *Nihon Kigyo no Takakuka Senryaka: Keiei Shigen Approach*, (*The Strategy of Diversification in Japanese Companies: A Managerial Resource Approach*).

Young, S. (1987) 'Business strategy and the internationalization of business: recent approaches', *Managerial and Decision Economics*, 8, pp. 31–40.

Index

263